The Athlete in the Ancient Greek World

Oklahoma Series in Classical Culture

OKLAHOMA SERIES IN CLASSICAL CULTURE

SERIES EDITOR
Ellen Greene, *University of Oklahoma*

ADVISORY BOARD
Ronnie Ancona, *Hunter College and CUNY Graduate Center*
Carolyn J. Dewald, *Bard College*
Nancy Felson, *University of Georgia*
Helene P. Foley, *Barnard College*
Thomas R. Martin, *College of the Holy Cross*
John F. Miller, *University of Virginia*
Richard F. Thomas, *Harvard University*

The Athlete in the Ancient Greek World

Reyes Bertolín Cebrián

UNIVERSITY OF OKLAHOMA PRESS : NORMAN

An earlier version of chapter 2 was published as "Change of Athlete Development Methods in Hellenistic and Roman Imperial Sport?" *Nikephoros* 26 (2013): 139–60; and an earlier version of chapter 5 was published as "Psychological Characteristics of Ancient Greek Athletes," *Nikephoros* 27 (2014): 9–35.

Library of Congress Cataloging-in-Publication Data

Names: Bertolín Cebrián, Reyes, author.
Title: The athlete in the ancient Greek world / Reyes Bertolín Cebrián.
Description: Norman: University of Oklahoma Press, 2020. | Series: Oklahoma series in classical culture; volume 61 | Includes bibliographical references and index. | Summary: "Explores the development of athletes in ancient Greece from archaic to Roman Imperial times"—Provided by publisher.
Identifiers: LCCN 2019057956 | ISBN 978-0-8061-6626-1 (paperback)
Subjects: LCSH: Athletics—Greece—History—To 1500. | Athletes—Greece—History—To 1500. | Physical education—Greece—History—To 1500. | Education, Greek. | Sports—Greece—History—To 1500. | Greece—History—To 146 B.C.
Classification: LCC GV21 .B46 2020 | DDC 796.48093/88—dc23
LC record available at https://lccn.loc.gov/2019057956

The Athlete in the Ancient Greek World is Volume 61 in the Oklahoma Series in Classical Culture.

The paper in this book meets the guidelines for permanence and durability of the Committee on Production Guidelines for Book Longevity of the Council on Library Resources, Inc. ∞

Copyright © 2020 by the University of Oklahoma Press, Norman, Publishing Division of the University. Manufactured in the U.S.A.

All rights reserved. No part of this publication may be reproduced, stored in a retrieval system, or transmitted, in any form or by any means, electronic, mechanical, photocopying, recording, or otherwise—except as permitted under Section 107 or 108 of the United States Copyright Act—without the prior written permission of the University of Oklahoma Press. To request permission to reproduce selections from this book, write to Permissions, University of Oklahoma Press, 2800 Venture Drive, Norman, OK 73069, or email rights.oupress@ou.edu.

To Denis,
my husband, my friend, my coach

Contents

List of Abbreviations   ix

Introduction   1

Part I. The Competitive Athlete

1 The Athlete as Young Man   11

2 High-Performance Training   34

3 The Role of Genetics   61

4 Nature versus Training   81

5 Psychological Characteristics of Athletes   96

Part II. The Athlete during the Formative Years

6 Sport and Education   123

7 Sport and War   159

8 Initiation Aspects of Historical Sport Practices   177

Part III. The Recreational Athlete

9 The Rise of Recreational Sport   187

   Final Words   208

   Appendix: List of Authors and Their Works   211

   Bibliography   215

   Index   227

Abbreviations

Collections of Inscriptions

Alabanda   McCabe, Donald F., ed. *Alabanda Inscriptions. Texts and List*. The Princeton Project on the Inscriptions of Anatolia, The Institute for Advanced Study. Princeton, 1991.
ArchEph   *Archaiologike Ephemeris*. Athens, 1837–.
Inscr. Métr   Bernand, Étienne. *Inscriptions métriques de l'Égypte gréco-romaine: Recherches sur la poésie épigrammatique des Grecs en Égypte*. Annales littéraires de l'Université de Besançon, vol. 98. Paris, 1969.
CIRB   Struve, Vasilii, ed. *Corpus inscriptionum regni Bosporani*. Moscow, 1965.
ID   *Inscriptions de Délos*. 7 vols. Paris, 1926–1972.
Ephesos   McCabe, Donald F., ed. *Ephesos Inscriptions. Texts and List*. The Princeton Project on the Inscriptions of Anatolia, The Institute for Advanced Study. Princeton, 1991.
FD   *Fouilles de Delphes, III, Épigraphie, 1–6 & Chron. delph*. Paris, 1929.
Halikarnassos   McCabe, Donald F., ed. *Halikarnassos Inscriptions. Texts and List*. The Princeton Project on the Inscriptions of Anatolia, The Institute for Advanced Study. Princeton, 1991.
IG   *Inscriptiones Graecae*. 15 vols. Berlin, 1877–.

IGUR	Moretti, Luigi, ed. *Inscriptiones graecae urbis Romae*. 4 vols. Rome, 1968–1990.
ISestos	Krauss, Johannes. *Die Inschriften von Sestos und der thrakischen Chersones*. Inschriften griechischer Städte aus Kleinasien, vol. 19. Bonn, 1980.
IMyl	Blümel, Wolfgang, ed. *Die Inschriften von Mylasa*. 2 vols. Inschriften griechischer Städte aus Kleinasien, vols. 34–35. Bonn, 1987–1988.
IPriene	McCabe, Donald F., ed. *Priene Inscriptions. Texts and List*. The Princeton Project on the Inscriptions of Anatolia, The Institute for Advanced Study. Princeton, 1987.
Iscr. di Cos	Segre, Mario. *Iscrizioni di Cos*, eds. Maria Letizia Lazzarini and Giulio Vallarino. Monografie della Scuola Archeologica di Atene e delle Missioni Italiane in Oriente, vol. 6, no. 2. Rome, 2007.
IvO	Dittenberger, Wilhelm, and Karl Purgold, eds. *Die Inschriften von Olympia*. Olympia, vol. 5. Berlin, 1896.
Magnesia	McCabe, Donald F., ed. *Magnesia Inscriptions. Texts and List*. The Princeton Project on the Inscriptions of Anatolia, The Institute for Advanced Study. Princeton, 1991.
MDAI(A)	*Mitteilungen des deutschen archäologischen Instituts. Athenische Abteilung*. Berlin, 1876.
Miletus	McCabe, Donald F., ed. *Miletos Inscriptions. Texts and List*. The Princeton Project on the Inscriptions of Anatolia, The Institute for Advanced Study. Princeton, 1984.
Et. Anat.	Robert, Louis. *Études anatoliennes. Recherches sur les inscriptions grecques de l'Asie Mineure*. Paris, 1937.
PPAphr	Roueché, Charlotte. *Performers and Partisans at Aphrodisias in the Roman and Late Roman Period: A Study Based on Inscriptions from the Current Excavations at Aphrodisias in Caria*. Journal of Roman Studies Monographs, vol. 6. London, 1993.
Samos	McCabe, Donald F., ed. *Samos Inscriptions. Texts and List*. The Princeton Project on the Inscriptions of Anatolia, The Institute for Advanced Study. Princeton, 1986.
SEG	*Supplementum epigraphicum graecum*. Leiden, 1923–.
SIG	Dittenberger, Wilhelm, ed. *Sylloge inscriptionum graecarum*. 2 vols. Leipzig, 1883.

Smyrna   McCabe, Donald F., ed. *Smyrna Inscriptions. Texts and List.* The Princeton Project on the Inscriptions of Anatolia, The Institute for Advanced Study. Princeton, 1988.

Teos   McCabe, Donald F., ed. *Teos Inscriptions. Texts and List.* The Princeton Project on the Inscriptions of Anatolia, The Institute for Advanced Study. Princeton, 1985.

Tralles   McCabe, Donald F., ed. *Tralles Inscriptions. Texts and List.* The Princeton Project on the Inscriptions of Anatolia, The Institute for Advanced Study. Princeton, 1991.

Collections of Papyri

P.Lond.   Kenyon, F. G., ed. *Greek Papyri in the British Museum.* London, 1893.

P.Mich.Zen.   Edgar, C. C., ed. *Zenon Papyri in the University of Michigan Collection.* Ann Arbor, 1931.

Introduction

My interest in studying sport in ancient Greece dates back to when I was a doctoral student in the early nineties. At the time, I was studying Homeric epic, and sport was a neat side interest but not the focal point of my career. When I came to Canada shortly after I finished my degree, I was pleasantly surprised to see that sport in ancient Greece was a vibrant area of study for a group of internationally recognized Canadian scholars working both in Canada and the United States. This realization made me desire to deepen my knowledge of ancient sport. It took a few years until I could teach my own class. Many points of my discussion in this book have developed as a result of my teaching.

In addition to that, I have always practiced some kind of sport. Although I have never done very well in any, I have always been enthusiastic about sport. I am married to a coach, and I have become a coach myself and helped run and administer several sport clubs. The current book stems from both aspects of my life. On the one hand, there is the academic aspect, and on the other, there are very practical skills that I have developed to explain to children and youth how to perform and enjoy sport.

In recent scholarship, there is a call for the study of sport to become widely accepted within Greek social history, and my project wants to make a contribution to it.[1] My project presupposes that ancient sport was anchored in society and that sport advancements and declines had a cause within society.

1. Christesen 2013.

Conversely, sport had also the ability to influence society. Athletic development depends not only on the value and goals that a society ascribes to sport itself but also on the value ascribed to the people practicing the sport. In my book, I aim to unite the history of sport in ancient Greece to the understanding of youth and educational concerns, keeping sport in the forefront.

The main argument of my book is that, after the fifth century B.C. and with the introduction of a new educational model, sport diminished in its general educating role to become, on the one hand, a pastime for those with an elite liberal arts education and, on the other hand, a highly specialized and highly paid pursuit for a few. In addition, there was recreational sport for those men, perhaps a bit older, who kept practicing sport as a way to mingle with friends and maintain health. Consequently, the book is divided into three parts corresponding to the different types of athletic involvement. Needless to say, transitions between these three categories were fluid, and there was certainly overlap between them.[2] Most athletes would have participated in sport as part of their schooling and in a recreational manner; only the few would have competed at the highest levels.

Part I of this book is dedicated to the competitive athlete. I have opted to dedicate the first part to the high-performance athlete, because this is the most common association in our minds. The first chapter starts by stating the fact that athletes were young men and, therefore, in need of training. It also explores how youth were perceived by their society and calculates how many athletes there might have been in a city. The second chapter deals with the career lengths of athletes in view of what could be a change of training systems from the classical to the Hellenistic times. Chapter 3 discusses the not-always-easy relation between a perceived superiority by nature and the actual need to train. Chapter 4 discusses genetic superiority in opposition to the need for training. The last chapter of this part, chapter 5, is dedicated to the study of the mind of competitive athletes. I will delve into their psychological characteristics as far as we can see them represented in ancient texts.

Part II focuses on the student athlete or, better expressed, the athlete during the school years. This second part stems from the hypothesis that the intellectualization of education during the fifth century B.C. and the change in the political system during Hellenistic times coalesced to produce a change in the understanding of sport, which eventually led to the three-tier system

---

2. König 2017: 155 distinguishes two classes of athletes, the high performance and the athletes during the educational years. I will add the recreational athlete to my discussion.

described above. Chapter 6 addresses the fact that, because the Greeks conceived of human beings as a combination of the body and the mind, training was deemed necessary for each of these two components. The relationship between body and mind changed over time, and this division had consequences for the perception and practice of sport. The chapter also deals with the places, times, and manners in which sport was taught during the school year. A short excursus about the role of coaches follows. This is in order to ascertain the difference that some ancient authors propose between the high-performance coach and the school coach. Chapter 7 describes the use of sport as training for war, especially for children and ephebes. Chapter 8 places sport as part of cultic initiations for younger men. Part III of the book has only one chapter (chapter 9), and it deals with the recreational athlete, specifically how the recreational athlete became the new model for the gentleman.

Besides the analysis of sport itself, I will work from the hypothesis that (nonrecreational) athletes, at least during classical times, were young, mostly single men. This assumption centers the study of athletics within the studies of youth and education, offering in this regard a unique perspective. The three areas that are part of my investigation (sport, education, and youth) have not been studied jointly, although they were closely connected in antiquity. Studies in the physical education of the young have concentrated exclusively on the ephebate or *ephebeia*, a one-to-three-year period of education in the life of a late teenager in which he would have learned military techniques and social practices coupled with physical education.[3] In contrast to the early monumental works on education,[4] newer scholarship concentrates mostly on a specific period or a specific region.[5] Although physical education is acknowledged in most of these works, the focus remains academic education.

Similarly, although athletes were young men and scholarship on ancient youth (children and young men) increased since the 1970s in the background of the study of the conflict of generations,[6] there is no study that unites the scholarship of youth with the scholarship of sport. The age of the youth involved in sport varied according to the purpose of the participation. When sport was practiced at school, children would have been around seven years old when they started their training and young teenagers when they completed the first cycle of education. This would have been the time also for some boys

---

3. Hin 2007.
4. Jaeger 1945; Marrou 1956.
5. See for instance the works by Cribiore 2001; Kah and Scholz 2004; Kennell 1995; Too 2001.
6. Golden 1990; Reinhold 1976; Strauss 1993.

to start competing in organized festivals, whether local or Panhellenic. Those who could afford a second period of education would have been in school until they were about twenty. The later part of this "secondary" education would have coincided with the ephebate, when sport was a common subject. After the ephebate, the high-performance track was open for those talented, dedicated, and probably wealthy individuals who wished to follow such an inclination. Obviously, some boys opted for high-performance careers already at the young age of fourteen. The length of competitive careers varied, with some athletes competing only in their younger years and some others going all the way into their thirties. The third division of sport came when sport was practiced for itself as recreation, without it being associated to the school or competition system. Although the practice of this type of sport was not new, I will argue that it came to the foreground during the Hellenistic times as a pastime of the liberal education of the elites. Participants in recreational sport may have been over thirty, which was certainly not considered a young age.

My book also concerns the question of how technical changes in athletics can be explained within the framework of the socialization and education of the young in ancient Greece. I will argue that in ancient Greece during the Hellenistic period,[7] one can observe the introduction of changes in the methods for developing athletes by training athletes in a specialized manner before puberty instead of after puberty. This change consisted in applying what is nowadays called an early specialization model instead of a late specialization model.

Sports are divided physiologically into those for which it is necessary to learn the skills before puberty, like gymnastics or figure skating (early specialization), and most other sports, for which one can master the skills after puberty (late specialization). All sports practiced by the ancient Greeks fall physiologically into the late specialization category. I will make the case from the known results and by comparison with the modern world that athletes in Hellenistic times applied early specialization when it was not physiologically necessary, thereby increasing remarkably the number of early victories achieved by athletes. This shift had consequences for the perception of sport and athletes.

---

7. Greek history is traditionally divided into three periods: (1) the archaic period, from the eighth century B.C. to the democratic constitution of Athens (510/509 B.C.); (2) the classical period, 510/509 B.C. to the death of Alexander the Great (323 B.C.); and (3) the Hellenistic period, from 323 to 31 B.C., when Octavian (later Augustus) defeated the combined troops of Mark Antony and Cleopatra at the Battle of Actium and the Hellenistic world was integrated into the larger Roman world. In this project, I will discuss evidence from the three periods of Greek history, but also evidence from the Roman imperial times.

Throughout the book, I will be mentioning several sport competitions. The Greeks had two main types of organized competitions: those of a Panhellenic character, which were celebrated at sanctuaries where Greeks from all over the Mediterranean and Black Sea basins came to compete, and those of a local character, which were associated with local cults and festivals to the gods. Before the Hellenistic period, there were four Panhellenic games: the Olympic, Isthmian, Nemean, and Pythian. These games were also called *stephanitic*, or crown, games, because the only prize given to the victor at the games was a crown of perishable material: olive for the Olympics, pine for the Isthmian, celery for the Nemean, and laurel for the Pythian. Some of the local festivals were very famous, like the Panathenaean games, which also included participants from all over the Greek world. Other local games were very small and probably featured a lower caliber of participant. Victory at local games was rewarded with material prizes, some of them enough for a participant to make several times more money at a single competition than the average annual earnings of a skilled worker.

The frequency of the games varied. Some local games were annual, but the most important games tended to be every second or fourth year. The Olympic and Pythian Games were celebrated every fourth year, whereas the Isthmian and Nemean occurred every second year. They formed a circuit called the *periodos* (cycle) and were thus called "periodic" games. Nemean and Isthmian Games were celebrated on the years before and after the Olympics. The Pythian Games were held on the third year of the cycle.

The evaluation of and search for the athlete will concentrate exclusively on those athletes' participation in gymnic events (the different disciplines of running,[8] the pentathlon,[9] and the heavy or combat sports of wrestling, boxing, and the pancratium). The other set of sport, namely, the equestrian, is left out of the examination since the victor was the owner of the horses and not the jockey or the driver. Consequently, equestrian sports did not involve special physical or mental abilities on the part of the owner, who could be a woman (like Cynisca) or an old, sick man (like Hieron of Syracuse). Charioteers were athletes in full fashion.[10]

---

8. The disciplines of running were the stadium race, *diaulos* (or double stadium), *dolichos* (or long distance), and the *hoplitodromos* (or race in armor). There were also other races depending on the type of festivals, such as torch races, the *apobatēs*, which involved the jumping of a chariot and running beside it, and others.

9. The pentathlon comprised five events: stadium race, long jump, javelin throw, discus throw, and wrestling.

10. For the "absence of the charioteer," see Nicholson 2003 and 2006.

This book is intended primarily for classicists, who may or may not have knowledge of ancient sport. It is also meant for scholars and students of sport history. With them in mind, I have added some explanations of Greek history, literature, and geography at the risk of stating the obvious to classicists. All dates are B.C. unless otherwise stated.

My methodology combines different approaches. Besides the analysis in detail of ancient texts, both literary and epigraphic, and historical context, I use my experience with athletes and athletics, both as coach and as administrator at the club and provincial levels. My personal experience has allowed me to witness the development of young athletes from beginners to international performance and has exposed me to the politics of sport. In addition, I will include as a valid method of study comparisons with current sport literature, which provides a natural theoretical framework for the study of ancient athletics. Current studies on sport will provide a set of questions to be identified in ancient authors. Ancient authors did not use the same categories as we do now, but they describe similar matters. Furthermore, interviews with modern successful athletes, whether in books or media, can be used as parallels to illustrate a point where ancient sources are silent. Of course, one ought to use prudence when making comparisons between modern and ancient athletes. Nevertheless, this is still a legitimate tool.

There are mainly three types of ancient sources in this book: literary (which include poetry, history, and philosophy), epigraphical, and artistic. Most professional classicists are familiar with them. However, for those readers who are not yet proficient in our discipline, I would like to contextualize the sources. The very first factor that needs to be taken into account is that, just as athletics themselves, the sources also span many centuries and reflect the ideology of their time periods. I have accepted the traditional dates for them. So, for instance, I place Homer and Hesiod at the end of the eight century B.C. and accept the dates of the inscriptions given by the editors. I also accept the traditional dates of the performances of athletes.

I have translated the written sources, but I have not included the texts in their original languages. These can be found in the standard editions, whether in print or on line. I have used the online edition of inscriptions provided by the Packard Humanities Project.[11] The literary sources come from the Perseus Project,[12] the Loeb Collection,[13] and several printed editions. All literary texts

---

11. Packard Humanities Institute 2007.
12. Crane 2019.
13. Loeb and Henderson 1999.

appearing here have been translated into major languages numerous times. The inscriptions have not always been translated, and as far as I know, some of the inscriptions in the book have been translated here for the first time. Because of that and because the inscriptions are lesser known texts in general, I tend to leave the text of the inscriptions as complete as possible even if it can sometimes become a bit tedious. Most of the inscriptions appearing in this book come from the Hellenistic period. This is neither by choice nor coincidence; it is simply a fact that we possess more inscriptions from the Hellenistic and Roman imperial times than from classical and certainly archaic ones. This is due to the fact that literacy was more widespread, and so was Greek culture. Probably, also more money was available to private individuals to display their achievements, whether inscribed while they were still alive or dedicated by family members after they had died.

I have tried to shorten and summarize the literary texts whenever possible. Obviously, the scope of the authors is very different. Some of them are poets singing the virtues and decrying the vices of their times, some could be considered to be cultural critics, moral philosophers, historians, or all of the above. The texts come from three distinct time frames. Some of the sources belong to authors of the archaic period. Among these are authors like Homer and Hesiod, the first literary testimonies in Greek and the common base of Greek culture. Also, lyric poets like Mimnermus, Solon, Theognis, Tyrtaeus, and Xenophanes belong to the archaic period, from the seventh and sixth centuries, although some of the dates are impossible to know with certainty. The next group of authors belong to the classical period of the fifth and fourth centuries. These are mainly Aristophanes, Aristotle, Isocrates, Plato, Pindar, and Xenophon.

The rest of the authors come from Roman times; most of them are culturally Greek and write in Greek. Only the technical writer Vitruvius, a Roman of the first century B.C., and the medical writer Celsus, a Roman perhaps contemporary to Augustus or Tiberius, wrote in Latin. Except for the apostle Paul, the rest of the authors can be dated to the so-called Second Sophistic.[14] This was an intellectual movement of the second and third centuries A.D. Writers belonging to this movement considered the authors mentioned above to be already classical, and they tried by and large to imitate them. They saw the classical past as a model, yet because they were inhabitants of the Roman Empire, they had a complex relation with the previous authors. Authors associated without doubt to the Second Sophistic are Galen, Lucian, and Philostratus.

---

14. See Richter and Johnson 2017.

Plutarch is a contemporary, but his ascription to the movement is debated. Pausanias is a contemporary to the movement as well. Although his work is more of a "travel guide," it shares certain features with the Second Sophistic, such as the imitation of the masters and admiration for the classical times. Athenaeus was an antiquarian who gathered many of the fragments of lyric poetry preserved until now. Finally, the *Greek Lyric Anthology* contains poems, mostly epigrams, from the classical period to the Byzantine period. In many cases, dating these works is difficult.

Traditional Timeline for the Major Games
776 Alleged origin of the Olympic Games
586 Origin of the Pythian Games
582 Origin of the Isthmian Games
573 Origin of the Nemean Games
566 Origin of the Panathenaean Games
391 A.D. Prohibition of Pagan Cults
393 A.D. Alleged Abolition of the Olympic Games

Sample of a Cycle for the Periodic Games
First year of Cycle: for example, the 524 Olympics
Second year of Cycle: 523 Nemean and Isthmian
Third year of Cycle: 522 Pythian
Fourth year of Cycle: 521 Nemean and Isthmian
First year of Cycle: 520 Olympics

The Nemean Games may have taken place in the spring or even winter (Pausanias 2.15.3). This would make sense because all other periodic games were celebrated in the summer, and the Nemean were the last that were created. Athletically, it would also make sense to have several months in between major games.

Part I

The Competitive Athlete

1

The Athlete as Young Man

1.1 🖋 Athletes' Age

On August 7, 2012, the British journal *The Guardian* published in its digital sport section an article with the title "Could You Be an Athlete? Olympics 2012 by Age, Weight and Height." The article has a series of interactive graphs where one can see how old, heavy, or tall the athletes were, both in general and by specific sports or by country. Out of the 10,578 athletes that participated in the London Olympics, 4,847 were women and 5,731 men. Since the ancient Greek athletes were all men, I will not discuss the women. The average age of the men in the 2012 Olympics was twenty-six years. There were only 91 participants forty years old or older, and they participated either in shooting or equestrian events. Most of the five thousand athletes were either in the range from twenty-five to thirty years old (2,040) or twenty to twenty-five (2,010); the next largest group was comprised by those in their thirties, namely, 963 athletes. With regard to individual sports, wrestlers were twenty-six years old in average, with the majority of them being twenty-five. Boxers' ages ranged from eighteen to thirty-two and averaged to twenty-four. Track-and-field athletes were twenty-six years old on average, and their ages ranged from eighteen to thirty-eight. The older athletes were not involved in speed-based disciplines but rather in strength-based ones, like shot put.

Although one has to be always careful when making parallels between the ancient and modern worlds, it should come as no surprise to find out that the vast majority of athletes were and are young. It is a simple biological fact.

Physical strength, speed, and recovery time are at their highest in men when they are in their twenties. It should be a commonsense statement that ancient Greek athletes were young. On the other hand, the social concomitants to the fact that ancient Greek athletes were young have not been explained sufficiently. It is important not to consider the athletes as living in a vacuum but to place them within their societies. The aim of this consideration is to develop a clearer understanding not just about how societies shaped athletes' lives and the practice of athletics, but also about how athletes and athletics in turn contributed to the development of society. I will suggest that the continuous practice of athletics beyond the school years may have created the perception of athletes' inability to step into adult roles, which left them open to criticism. Athletes were prototypical Greek males: youthful, strong, and independent. On the other hand, youth was also associated with rambunctiousness, which was often not welcomed by the cities. First, I will establish the age of Greek high-level athletes. I will then present evidence for the ambiguous perception of all youth. Finally, I will calculate the number of potential athletes in a city in order to ascertain whether they would have constituted a group substantial enough to be taken into account by the city policies and politics.

1.1.1. Biological Age

Anthropologists distinguish between three types of ages: chronological, physiological, and structural. Whereas both chronological and physiological ages are biological facts, determined by the number of years since birth and bodily developments, respectively, structural age is "determined by an individual's chronological relationship to ceremonies or rituals marking the passage from one life stage to another."[1] First, I will establish the chronological age of the athletes. Even if we do not possess direct evidence about the athletes' age, we can estimate it very well from the length of careers and the age of entry at competition. It is a known fact that the Greeks divided the competitors in the gymnic events into at least two separate groups: the boys (*paides*) and the men (*andres*).[2] Boys were those individuals under eighteen. At Olympia, children younger than twelve were probably not allowed to participate, and those older than seventeen were considered adults already.[3] Even festivals

---

1. Kennell 2013: 2.
2. For the age of boys, see Crowther 2004: 87–92. For other divisions based on age, see Golden 1998: 104–7.
3. Golden 1998: 105.

that accounted for more age divisions among those who were not men (e.g., *ageneioi* or beardless youth) set a limit at age twenty.[4] So when athletes are said to have won several Olympics as an adult, we can deduce that they were at least eighteen years old for their first one. Those who had victories as children started competing probably at the age of fourteen, the (traditional) onset of puberty.[5] Thus, from the length of the careers we can calculate the age of the athletes.

The youngest athlete to win at the boys' competition at Olympia was Damiscus of Messene, who was proclaimed victor at twelve in the stadium race in 368 (Pausanias 6.2.9). Also, Pherias of Aegina was considered too young at the Olympics of 468 and was not allowed to wrestle. When he entered and won the next Olympics four years later, he was still a boy under eighteen (Pausanias 6. 14.1).[6] We do not have information about his age when he first attempted to compete. He might have been also about twelve, but since wrestlers were physically bigger and heavier than runners, he was not allowed to compete, perhaps for fear of injury. Most child athletes, however, would have been pubescent boys.

Although we have news of some victors having competed in several Olympics (up to four or five of them), they still remained an exception. For instance, the wrestler Milo of Croton is said to have participated in seven Olympics, the first one as a boy in 536. The seventh time he competed was in 512, when he was defeated not by his younger countryman's technical superiority but by his better fitness. This gives Milo twenty-four years of active competition from presumably the age of fourteen to thirty-eight. But Milo is an exception in Greek athletics.[7] Most athletes that participated in several Olympics did not compete in more than four.

The list of the Panhellenic circuits' victors (the *periodonikēs*, that is, the athlete who won at least once in each periodic game, but not necessarily in a row) is illustrative for observing the age and length of the careers of vic-

---

4. The *ageneioi* or "beardless youth" known from Nemea, Isthmia, and Athens comprised a group apparently between the start of puberty and twenty. See Golden 1998: 106. Modern sports in which age divisions are current also place the division between youth and adults at around twenty (e.g., fencing) or twenty-one (e.g., soccer).

5. Although there was one winner in the stadion event as young as twelve, most probably the majority would have been pubescent boys. Traditional age to set the start of puberty was fourteen; see Golden 1990: 28.

6. Age was also largely calculated by looks. Pausanias (6.14.2) contrasts Pherias with another wrestler. In this case Nicasylus of Rhodes looked too old, namely, 18, and was not allowed to compete with the boys and won with the men. He also won Isthmian and Nemean Games, but when he was on his way home to Rhodes he died at age 20.

7. See Roubineau 2016: 40–42.

torious athletes. Heavy athletes (those who competed in boxing, wrestling, and the pancratium) could compete up to twenty years, as we shall see later. The boxer Glaucus competed successfully from 520 to 502. He entered as an adult in his first Olympics; this means that he probably retired when he was about thirty-six years old. Theagenes, also a boxer, competed from 490 to 470. His first victory was as a boy, which brings his retirement to the age between thirty-four and thirty-eight. Other heavy athletes had a career of about twelve years. For instance, Pausanias (6.4.1) mentions that Sostratus, a pancratiast, earned twelve victories at the Nemean and Isthmian Games together, two victories at Delphi, and three at Olympia. The length of the career of these athletes is truly remarkable and puts the average competition age of the heavy athletes between twenty and the late thirties. They must have been very lucky to avoid injuries despite the brutality of some of the sports. Perhaps it is right to assume that less successful athletes had shorter careers and were quickly forgotten.

A possible exception to the youth of athletes might have been Diagoras, who managed to become a *periodonikēs* in only six years, namely from 470 to 464, and retired after his Olympic victory. He had a total of eighteen victories, ten within the periodic games[8] and eight in local games. He might have started competing before his years at the crown games. Unfortunately, we do not have information about his age. Since Diagoras did not have a victory as a boy or beardless youth at the Isthmian Games, this means that his first victory at those games must have occurred after he was twenty, but most likely he was older than that. On the other hand, his children and grandchildren might have started to compete rather early in their lives. They all won Olympic victories and were renowned throughout the Greek world as one of the most famous athletic clans (Pausanias 6.7.1–7). His son Dorieus won the pancratium in three successive Olympiads from 432 to 424. He also won eight victories at the Isthmian, seven at the Nemean, and four at the Pythian Games (Pausanias 6.7.1–2), which probably brings the first victory at these games to 438.[9] This would bring his career to a minimum of twelve years of active competition as an adult, perhaps sixteen years, placing his retirement in his early to mid-thirties. Diagoras's elder sons, Damagetus and Acusilaus, won the pancratium and boxing, respectively, in the Olympics of 448. We

---

8. Diagoras is credited with four Isthmian victories, two Nemean, one Pythian, and one Olympic victory, a very busy schedule for such a short time.

9. Knab 1980 [1934]: 29.

know that Diagoras may have been still alive in 448 from a late anecdote[10] that says that Diagoras died, elated in happiness, when he was carried through the stadium on the shoulders of his two elder sons after their victories. The last attested victory of Diagoras was at the Olympics of 464. This is only sixteen years before his sons' victories, twelve if we consider Damagetus's previous solo victory in 452. Obviously, Diagoras must have married while still an active athlete since Damagetus was born at the latest in 470. Whether Diagoras was an exception or not, it is hard to say, since we do not have evidence for the age at which he completed the Panhellenic circuit. Whether he married early or he competed late, or both, is impossible to ascertain. There are at least twelve years in age difference between Diagoras's older son Damagetus and the younger Dorieus. This perhaps would indicate that he competed rather late in his life, and that, just sixteen years after his victory, his grown-up sons were in their athletic prime.

Runners generally had shorter careers than heavy athletes, but still we have news of them competing for two or three Olympics. This means a career of at least eight years. Dromeus, a *dolichos* runner, had a highly successful career of eight years from 487 to 479. Dandis competed in the stadium race from 479 to 471, and Dicon had a twelve-year career as an adult runner from 392 to 380. Pausanias (6. 3.11) mentions that Dicon won five victories in running at Delphi (obviously in more than one event), three at the Isthmus, and four at Nemea. At Olympia he won one victory among the boys and two others among the men. This means that by the time he was in his late twenties, he had retired from active competition. Ergoteles was perhaps one of the longest-standing runners with ten years of competition as an adult, from 474 to 464. Astylus won three successive times at Olympia both in the stadium race and the double race (488–480). Although we do not know the precise age of these runners, it is improbable that they ran successfully past their thirties. Runners seem to have had an adult career between eight to twelve years, which brings them to an average retirement age of under thirty, considerably shorter than the career of heavy athletes. In modern days, competitive sprinters over thirty are scarce. Some disciplines, especially long-distance running, allow for some older competitors, but sprinters peak in their late twenties or early thirties and then retire.[11] Literary and epigraphic sources as well as modern

10. Gellius, *Attic Nights* 3.15. Pausanias (6.7.3) only mentions Diagoras being pelted with flowers by the spectators.
11. Two of the most emblematic athletes of the twentieth century, Jesse Owens and Carl Lewis, did not extend their careers beyond their thirties. Jesse Owens achieved three world records and tied a fourth

parallels indicate that the majority of athletes in Greece must have been in their twenties. Especially in a culture that emphasized winning, there was no room for athletes who were past their peak without risking their reputation.[12]

1.1.2. Structural Age

In this section, I contend that athletes constituted a separate group within their cities, not just because of their youth but especially because the activities that they practiced were mostly typical of a certain age. Being an athlete was not only connected to biological age but also to structural or social age, which is not always equivalent to its biological counterpart. Structural age is a term used by anthropologists to describe institutionalized age divisions within a society that aim at distributing the power in society with the focus of creating a smooth transition.[13]

Athletes practiced what we could call "youthful" activities. The first "youthful" activity that comes to mind is obviously education, which was not universal in Greek society but was nevertheless desired by many. Children and sometimes young men up to their early twenties received school education in order to become useful citizens. Often we tend to forget that sport was first of all a part of that education; thus, sport constituted also primarily an

---

one in 1935 at the age of twenty-two. After the Olympics in 1936 he stopped competing owing to the difficult economic situation of his family. It is impossible to know for how long he would have competed under different circumstances. Carl Lewis matched Owens's record in long jump at the age of eighteen. He established a world record in 1991 at the age of thirty but had started to lose to rivals in the previous three years. He retired from active sport at thirty-five. In the 1988 Seoul Olympics, Lewis's rival, Ben Johnson, was twenty-seven years old. In the Beijing Olympics of 2008, Usain Bolt celebrated his twenty-second birthday on the same day he broke the record in the 200-meter race and after having broken the record of the 100m two days before. He retired in 2017 at the age of thirty-one after competing in the World Championships. He won only the bronze medal in the 100-meter dash and had a very dramatic ending in his final relay when he pulled a muscle and had to be helped by his teammates across the finish line.

12. Milo, whose last attested competition was a loss, had already established a reputation that could withstand the loss, but he might have been an exception in this regard as well. He did not compete subsequently, especially since his much younger opponent did not win because of his superior technique but basically wore him out by not allowing himself to be caught.

13. Structural age can be built on an age-class system in which individuals passed collectively through a series of age grades usually marked by communal ceremonies. Although there have been attempts to characterize Greece as a society based on an age-class system, Kennell 2013 denies that such was the case. According to this scholar, the closest examples that ancient Greece presents for an age-class system are the Athenian ephebate and the Spartan training system, called *agōgē*. He argues that neither could be considered an age-class system. The ephebate would not include all eligible male youths, some of whom may not have taken part in it because of disability, absence from the city, poverty, and even disinclination. In the case of Sparta, according to Kennell, the age-class system could work only by excluding the majority of the people living in the city and focusing in a small minority of people.

activity of the young not just in schools but even at competitions. It is true that by the time of retirement, many athletes had long ceased to be young men according to Greek standards and that recreational sport may have included the not-so-young. However, biological and cultural considerations placed sport in the realm of the young, especially because delayed marriage would have prolonged the perceived "adolescence" of athletes.[14]

According to social age, athletes would have been considered to not yet be adults since the majority of men in their twenties would have been single. Young, single men were not always well perceived in their cities and were associated with excesses in political, social, and other areas. Hence, the cities may have had an interest in keeping them occupied in practicing sports. In ancient Greece, the norm was to marry, but marriage for men was by and large delayed until around thirty. This seems to have been the case since the beginning of Greek culture for most cities.[15] We read something to this effect already in the eighth century in Hesiod: "At the right time bring a wife to your house, neither much short of thirty years old, nor much older. This is the proper time for marriage. Let your wife be four years past her puberty, then in the fifth marry her" (*Works and Days* 695–98).

In this manner, traditional social-age divisions situate the age of physical athletic prime before the age for marriage, which is often also associated with the abandonment of competitive sport. For instance, concerning the ideal age to beget children, Plato mentions that it is at the time when both parents are in their prime, which is described in the following terms:

> "Does it also seem to you that the proper time of the prime is at twenty years for a woman and thirty for a man?" "Why so?" he said. "The women," I said, "beginning at the age of twenty until the age of forty shall bear children for the city, and the man, whenever the fastest prime for running may be, after that, he shall beget for the city until the age of fifty-five." (*Republic* 460e)

The passage opposes the ideal age for being a runner to that for having children and being in full maturity of mind and body. Whereas ideally men would beget from thirty to fifty-five, they would have gone past their prime

---

14. Golden 2003: 25: "What is beyond doubt is that Archaic and Classical Greek adolescence, defined as the period between puberty and social maturity, was prolonged."

15. Although we are not entirely sure of Greek facts, in the Roman world, where marriage generally took place for men in their early twenties, in the conservative Augustan legislation men were not fully considered adults until then. See Harlow and Laurence 2010: 59–61.

in running by the age of thirty. This age division is not exclusive to Plato's *Republic*. Aristotle mentions that the bodily condition of athletes is not beneficial for begetting children because their bodies are excessively exercised (*Politics* 1335b). Consequently, the age division of the contests themselves and the traditional age for marriage established a period of about ten to fifteen years, in which the male athlete was at the peak of his competing phase, namely, roughly between the age of eighteen and thirty.[16] This same period coincides with the period of not fully integrating into society's structures, such as marriage or being eligible for political office.

The age for athletics and marriage are just two among the social ages of men in the Greek cities. Traditionally accepted and idealized social-age divisions were set every seven years. For instance, Aristotle divides the ages for the appropriate education into groups of seven years, since this seemed to him the most natural: from birth to seven years old, to puberty, to twenty-one. Each of these stages required different methods, from playing games and listening to stories to more formalized education (*Politics* 1336b–37a). After the education of the mind was completed, then the young men would go into the next phase of their lives, when it was appropriate to train hard for competition. Aristotle describes the role of athletics in his *Politics*, where he states,

> It has been agreed that one ought to use gymnastic training, and how it should be used. For until puberty lighter exercises should be added, forbidding harsh diet and obligatory exertions, in order that nothing may be an impediment for growth; there is no small sign that they can provide these results in the fact that among the Olympic victors one would find two or three persons who have won both as men and as boys,[17] because the strength (*dynamis*) is robbed from

---

16. Children were athletes in full right, and their victories were highly valued. For instance, *Olympic Ode* 8 by Pindar (518–438?) is dedicated to Alcimedon of Aegina, victor in the boys' wrestling; *Olympic Ode* 10 is dedicated to Hagesidamos from Epizephyrian Locri, victor in the boys' boxing. Nevertheless, participation of boys at major competitions was not as numerous as that of adults. Crowther (2004: 109–13) calculates that out of the 4,449 overall possible victors at Olympia, we know by name and city 956. Out of these only 124 are boys (of 920 possible ones), 28 from Elis alone and 57.5 percent from the Peloponnese. There is no evidence of multiple victories, perhaps because of the age limit. This would again indicate that the majority of boys would be fourteen years old and up.

17. Crowther (2004: 113) comments on this passage. He mentions that Aristotle was trying to support his educational theory. Aristotle might have been exaggerating his numbers, but the numbers Crowther presents do not invalidate his theory, either. Crowther mentions that by the time of Aristotle there were six or seven known victors successful both as boys and men, and after Aristotle's death another five. He extrapolates that to mean that out of the over nine hundred boy victors, about twenty were also successful victors as adults. That is only slightly above 2 percent.

those who train in youth through the obligatory exercises. But when they have spent already three years after puberty upon their other studies, then it is fit to occupy the following age with exercises and strict eating diet; for we must not work hard with the mind and the body at the same time; for each one of the efforts works in opposite directions, bodily toil impeding the development of the mind and mental toil that of the body. (1338b–39a)

Aristotle divides sport into two separate categories: sport practiced as part of a general education and as high performance. For the latter, Aristotle suggests training the young boys toward athletic success three years after their puberty. That would be approximately at the age of seventeen.[18] After the age of seventeen, the next period of the life of the athlete would start. This is a period in which formal academic education would have been finished and the young men would concentrate on training for high performance, being subjected to strict diets and competition. It is from assertions like this and the fact that many athletes competed for several Olympics that we calculated the average age of ancient athletes. The starting age in high performance would indicate a competitive career throughout one's twenties and perhaps early thirties.

The division of age into periods of seven years is not a new idea in Aristotle. A well-known poem by the sixth-century Athenian lawgiver Solon (fragment 27) also divides the ages of men into ten groups of seven-year periods, from childhood to the old age of seventy, when it is supposedly a good time to die. The poem is a response to the traditional Ionian lyric, which praises youth as the age of love and fears old age. Solon uses a mix of chronological age and the social activities associated with a certain age.[19] After childhood, puberty, and young adulthood, the young man in his fourth hebdomad (i.e., from twenty-one to twenty-eight years old) is described as being "the very best in strength (*ischys*) through which men show signs of manly virtue (*aretē*)." Although the poem does not mention the practice of sport explicitly, the reference to physical strength and virtue may imply it. Also, the fact that this virtue needs to be proved implies a type of contest. It seems very probable

---

18. Starting hard training after puberty seems to be a widespread opinion among many athletes and sports experts. See Bannister (2004: 43) about an eighteen-year-old who ran a mile in 4 minutes, 12.8 seconds in 1954: "The improvement seems fantastic, but I am not so sure that the training of the intensity required to produce such a remarkable time is wise at that age."

19. Falkner (1990: 5–12) explains that the reasons are that this allows Solon to reappropriate the ages according to his own political ideas.

that Solon also considered the prime age of the athletes to be during their twenties,[20] which corresponds to the pattern we have calculated from the biological age at which athletes entered competition. The next division that Solon introduces, from twenty-eight to thirty-five, is the time to marry and beget children. The next implication would be that athletes were for the most part young single men. We have also seen this in Aristotle, who delayed the ideal marriage age for men to about thirty-seven.[21]

After their athletic careers were over, athletes had to come back to their cities and start the normal life of a citizen, which included political participation, marriage, and some kind of way to make a living. As literary sources repeatedly attest, this took place for runners when the young men were in their late twenties, but most likely for everyone else in their early to midthirties. The group of people that Plato and Aristotle had in mind must be mostly aristocratic youth, as would have been most of their students. Lower-class individuals would have perhaps married earlier, although we do not have much data about it.[22] They would have also entered the work force much earlier.[23]

Let us, however, express the caveat that traditional social age is an ideal that may not have always corresponded with reality. Social historians calculate that the average life expectancy of ancient Greeks and Romans would not have exceeded thirty years.[24] Even scholars that argue for a longer life expectancy

---

20. This division into seven-year periods is found as well in Galen in the second century A.D. He attributes it directly to Asclepius. Obviously, it is a very traditional way of dividing the age of men. In *De sanitate tuenda* (6.60.5–6.61.10), Galen asserts that until the children are fourteen years old, the exercise they should practice is not much and not very violent. Fourteen to twenty-one, when the young men are on the top of their growth, is the time for them to become accomplished, whether as soldiers, wrestlers, or in any other sport. This is the time when the young men are to be trained less in the virtues of the soul (wisdom and knowledge), but rather more in the development of character. From twenty-one to twenty-eight is the time for young men to pick a trade, whether physical or not. Considering that Galen despised professional athletes, the division into seven-year periods must have been really very ingrained in the society for him to accept that the adolescent boys be trained first in the physical realm, then the mind.

21. "It is fitting for women to marry at eighteen, for men at thirty-seven or a bit earlier" (Aristotle, *Politics* 1335a). The aim of this age regulation was, according to Aristotle, a double one: to produce healthy children when both parents were considered to be at their reproductive vigor, and also to establish the succession of generations at an age when the children are beginning their prime and the fathers are losing their vigor. Aristotle delays the marriage age past the most common thirty to thirty-five, which would be part of the seven-year division.

22. Delayed marriage after retirement from active sport would imply an aristocratic background of athletes since elites would have most likely tried to keep the size of the family smaller in order to preserve their estates, especially when all living male heirs received an equal portion of it. See Caldwell 2004.

23. Beaumont 2012: 121.

24. Caldwell 2004; Scheidel 2006.

do not go much past the late thirties.²⁵ Hansen calculates that life expectancy was no more than twenty-five years by the fourth century, but he still sets the generations at thirty years, so three generations for a century.²⁶ In order to keep the population stable or even growing at a rate of 0.5 percent, each woman would have given live birth to five or six children, only two or three of which would have made it into adulthood and reproduced.²⁷ Despite this average life expectancy, the length of the careers of many of the known athletes places them in active competition in their mid-thirties. Perhaps athletes were exceptionally healthy individuals. On the other hand, if life expectancy was as low as social historians calculate, it should come as no surprise that many athletes were willing to risk their health and sometimes their lives in the pursuit of glory.

In conclusion, it is safe to assume that the majority of high-performance athletes were young men, about eighteen to thirty or perhaps thirty-five years of age, that is, from their eligibility for citizenship²⁸ to their marriage.²⁹ Individuals belonging to this age group were usually referred to by the name of ephebes (from eighteen to twenty years old) and later *neoi* (young men).³⁰ These young men were in an ambiguous situation. On the one hand, they were considered adults because of their military and civic duties. On the other

---

25. Morris (2005: 10) argues that in order for the urban population of the first millennium to increase, considering the high mortality rate at birth, we need to hypothesize a life expectancy of thirty-seven and seven live births per woman.

26. Hansen 2006: 59. This means he sets the general age of marriage for men at thirty, for women at eighteen.

27. Ibid., 55.

28. As with everything else in relation to the archaic and classical periods, most of our data come from Athens. The age when an Athenian youth was eligible for citizenship was called *ephebeia* or ephebate (coming of age). This term refers as well to an institution of military training and civic education. It is still debated whether the institution of the ephebate was in existence before the 330s, perhaps since the sixth century, and it was then formalized into an institution sponsored by the state, or whether it was a new creation. See Friend 2009. The age to enter the ephebate in classical Athens was eighteen, and it lasted for two years (Aristotle, *Athenian Constitution* 42), but in other cities and at other times the age of entry and duration varied. Hin (2007: 151–53) argues that participation in the ephebate was not just for the upper classes and that boys of middle-class families whose work was not needed to support the family could have been part of this institution. Aristocratic boys would have been expected to act as benefactors toward their peers and were assigned honorary tasks. In this way, Greeks would have maintained social distinctions within the ephebate. See also Hin 2007: 141–47; Chankowski 2010.

29. Whereas it seems assured that Athenian men married in their thirties, Spartans married at a much younger age, probably in their early twenties. Plato argues that men should be married between the ages of twenty-five and thirty-five, combining perhaps the Dorian practices of his interlocutors with the Athenian ones (*Laws* 772d).

30. Generally speaking, the *neos* refers to the young man after the ephebate and until age thirty or marriage.

hand, as long as they were single and had no household of their own, they were still dependent on their fathers' household and were barred from some of the political offices.[31] These young adults without a clear position in society may have been a problem not only for their families but also for their cities, which often might have been glad to see these young men involved in sports and away from politics.[32] Sport constituted for some individuals a stage in the difficult socialization of young adult males in the polis.[33]

1.2 ⚔ Perceptions of Ancient Youth

By examining the duration of athletes' careers, two things I hope have become a little clearer. First, just as today and as a biological fact, athletes were at the height of their physical strength during their twenties up to their thirties. Second, this time coincides with the social period when Greek men during archaic and classical times would have been for the most part single. Young single men were thought of as in need of mental and social development and not always perceived in a positive light; sometimes they were even perceived as problematic.

1.2.1. Ancient Perceptions of Ancient Youth

We see this for instance in Aristotle's *Rhetoric*, which delineates the characteristics of the young, the old, and the man at his prime.[34] For him, young men possess a combination of good and bad traits.

> 12.3. Young men with respect to their characters have strong desires, and they do whatever they desire.... While they love honor (*philotimoi*), they love victory (*philonikoi*) still more; for youth desires prominence, and victory is one form of prominence.... They are more courageous for they are passionate and hopeful. Of these, the first makes them not to fear, the second to dare.... They are modest,

---

31. Strauss 1993: 67–71.
32. Kleijwegt (1991: 64) explains that for Roman times ways to reduce tension between fathers and adult sons may have been to send the sons to manage property outside of the city or send them to be part of the army. I would like to suggest that Greeks used sport for the same purpose.
33. Müller 1996.
34. Wisse (1989: 42) argues that "the practice of dividing people into classes, according to age, strength, etc., was an old one." It was a way of bringing forth arguments according to probability, for instance, by asserting that since young men are more prone to excess, a particular young man standing accused must be guilty.

for they do not conceive anything but what is beautiful but they have been educated only by law. They are high-minded because they have not yet been humbled by life or experienced its necessities; it is high-mindness to think oneself worthy of great things and also being hopeful. They prefer to do beautiful deeds rather than useful ones: they live more according to character than reasoning; for reasoning deals with what is useful, virtue with what is beautiful. (*Rhetoric* 2.12.3–12)

The character of the young man is diametrically opposed to that of the old man (*Rhetoric* 2.13.1) because old men have been disappointed by others and made mistakes of their own, and thus they are rather not enthusiastic or energetic about things. Aristotle idealizes the man at his prime (2.14.1–3). The philosopher describes him as being not overconfident but judging the facts accurately and acting accordingly. Men at their prime are also courageous and possess self-control and moderation. The man at his prime is a combination of the positive aspects of both old and young, making him the image of the Greek ideal removed from all excesses. Despite young men possessing many good characteristics, Aristotle also states that they are still far from being moderate and temperate individuals. The most negative aspects of the youth are impulsiveness and hot-temperedness, but those can be mitigated because the young men accept the rule of society. For our purposes, it is important to note that, besides their impetuous character, young men are characterized for being eager for honor (*philotimoi*) and victory (*philonikoi*) as a sign of superiority over others. Although there is no direct mention of athletics, it is certainly very easy to assume that the adjectives may refer to it.[35] We shall see later on that competitiveness is one of the psychological characteristics of successful athletes.[36]

Interesting as well is the mention that men are at the physical prime from thirty to thirty-five, whereas one's mental prime comes at forty-nine (*Rhetoric* 2.14). Furthermore, the age of forty-nine coincides with Solon's divisions as being at the highest in mental ability with the end of the seventh hebdomad. This assertion underlines, on one hand, the traditionality of the ages of man and, on the other, the consideration of athletes as young men in need of development. Furthermore, it sustains the disparity between physical and

---

35. For a study of the word *philotimia*, see Whitehead 1983.
36. Other psychological characteristics of youth applicable to athletes are their courage, hopeful disposition, and desire to do noble things.

mental maturity, which in turn presents the athlete as a young, immature person and opens up the possibility of later criticisms of athletes as having developed the body in excess but not the mind.

Aristotle's views about youth, which show perhaps a deeper understanding than his views on old men and a less idealized one than his views on men at their prime, present youth as a combination of good and bad. On the other hand, other authors focus only on one aspect. For instance, archaic elegy idealizes youth itself more than young men. Nevertheless, young men as possessors of youth become a source of envy since youth and its concomitants are valued as one of the fleeting good things of life. As much as Aristotle criticized the intemperate behavior of the young man with respect to sex, the archaic poets praised it.

In the generally pessimistic worldview of the archaic poets, they considered that there were no more pleasures, especially sexual ones, after youth was gone.

> But what is life, what is pleasure, without golden Aphrodite? Let me die when to me no longer these things matter: secret love, gentle gifts, and the bed. Such things are the blooms of youth, to be taken by men and women. And when painful old age comes, which makes man to all reproachful and evil, bad worries always tear apart his heart, he does not delight in looking at the rays of the sun, but he is hateful, dishonoured by women, so painful has god made old age.
> (Mimnermus 1)

Besides the physical advantages of being young, Mimnermus also emphasizes the careless, free spirit of youth. It is common in archaic Greek thought to oppose pairs of concepts, in this case youth and old age, with nothing in between them. The characteristics presented in Mimnermus are not so different from Aristotle's description, except there is no "golden mean."

Contrary to this idealization of youth, there is a general perception of the young man as the rowdy disturber of social order. For instance, in one of Aristophanes's comedies, a slave complains about his master's behavior at a banquet using the word *neanikōs*—in the manner of a young man[37]: "He started moving, jumped, farted, laughed, just as a little donkey which has had

---

37. The use of a word related to *neoi* to indicate a rebellious youth goes all the way back to Rome. The young poets in the first century like Catullus called themselves *neoterici* as a manner to distinguish themselves from epic production. See Christes (1998: 153), who argues that there is a change in youth's perception of itself at the time of the transition from republic to principate.

a banquet of barley, and he hit me savagely in the manner of a young man (*neanikōs*), calling out 'boy, boy' (*The Wasps* 1305–7)."

The sausage seller in another comedy is also addressed as being most *neanikos*, which cannot refer to his youth, since he is an elderly man, but to his daring and outrageous nature, ready to challenge the establishment (Aristophanes, *Knights* 611). Demosthenes's speeches offer as well testimonies that the word *neanikos* shifted meanings from young to arrogant or something similar. For instance, in the *Third Olynthiac* speech, he opposes a magnanimous spirit to a "youngish" one (32.2). In his speech *Against Midias*, *neanikon* is juxtaposed to shameful (*aischron*) (201.3). Literature abounds in instances where the adjective *neanikos* has negative connotations, not only connoting rowdiness or impropriety, but also something contrary to freedom. This is seen in Aristotle's assertion in his *Politics* that *out of the most "young-ish" (neanikē) democracy comes tyranny* (1296a). This is not the place to develop a whole study of the word, but the examples suffice to show that the adjective that in its original meaning did not mean more than "typical of the young" underwent a change in meaning since something "typical of the young" became equated with something considered arrogant, shameful, and outrageous.

Another aspect related to this one is the perception that youth were immature. Athenian boys were considered to come of age at 18 (Aristotle, *Athenian Constitution* 42.10). At this age, they could participate in the assembly (*ekklēsia*), but they could not be elected to the council (*boulē*) until 30. In his *Memorabilia*, Xenophon relates how Socrates is forbidden to maintain any contact with the youth. When Socrates asks for clarification about the meaning of youth, his angry interlocutor Charicles responds: "As long as it is not possible for them to sit in the council, for they are not yet prudent. You shall not speak to those younger than thirty" (1.2.35). This passage manifests not only the common view that members of this age group were susceptible to being corrupted, but also the political limitations to which this group was subjected based on a perceived lack of maturity of the mind and excessive development of the body.[38]

And yet despite a lack of political participation, young men were expected to fulfill their military duties. On the other hand, because the young men had not yet acquired all political and citizenship rights, their cities could easily dispose of them. In this respect the young men appear as a separate group

---

38. Aristotle (*Politics* 1335b) mentions explicitly how the bodily condition of the athlete is not fit for civic well-being, health, or procreation.

in the elegies of Tyrtaeus.[39] A fragment of his poetry specifically addresses the young men in respect to their duties toward the city. Part of these duties was to defend not only the children but also the married men who fought in their ranks. The young men were considered more dispensable than the married, older men: "Young men (*neoi*), fight remaining side by side each other. . . . Do not flee abandoning the older ones. This is shameful, when an older man lies having fallen among the front ranks in front of the young" (Tyrtaeus, 10.15, 20–22).

Not only did they fight in the first ranks, but they were the ones sent to establish colonies when there was an excess of young men.[40] In the case of Sparta's colony Taras, the young men were accused of threatening to destabilize the current society. In order to avoid generational and other conflicts, cities took harsh measures, even at the price of the lives of the young men. Although the *poleis* were not always at war and had different needs to establish colonies, the promotion of sport among the young men would be a good alternative to keep them away from politics and occupied in some worthy trade that could bring glory to the city.

1.2.2. Modern Perceptions of Ancient Youth

The study of ancient youth from a modern perspective is a relatively new academic subfield. There are basically two schools of thought regarding the status of ancient youth: one considers youth in antiquity as a separate subculture,[41] and one argues for an "absence of adolescence," that is, children were integrated into the adult structures of society without a transitional period.[42] The debate has not been settled[43] in part because those scholars in favor of youth as a separate stage tend to base their studies on literary evidence (mostly in reference to the elite), whereas those who argue for the lack of a transitional period build their arguments on epigraphic evidence, which often includes nonelite classes.[44]

Studies on ancient youth have focused either on academic education or mostly on the integration of young men in the adult world, whether in the

---

39. Steinrück 2000: 98–106.
40. For an analysis of the analogy between the victor at the games and the founder of a colony, see Dougherty 1993: 103–19, 120–35.
41. Bertolín 2008; Eyben 1993; Steinrück 2000.
42. Kleijwegt 1991; Pleket 1979.
43. See Laes-Strubbe 2014: 17.
44. Christes 1998: 143.

working, political, social, or religious spheres, but to my knowledge no one has focused on sport. Concerning sport, the same facts can be interpreted from different perspectives. If we start from the premise that youth was not a separate stage in the lives of the Greeks, obviously, sport cannot be a youthful activity. Consequently, even children's events at competitions (the events for the *paides*) can be considered as the children imitating the men and therefore part of the adult world already. The argument given for this is that high-performance children's sport is never conceived as a game, but as a true competition.[45] On the other hand, if the starting premise is that there was a separate youth-oriented stage in the lives of the Greeks, one can argue that children's sport at the crown games differed somewhat from that of the adults. For instance, the pancratium event for adults was incorporated into the Olympic program relatively early in 648, but the children's event was not included until the year 200, when training conditions had changed profoundly, as we shall later see. Other competitions included events exclusive to children—ephebes and those at the age of physical and mental development—but not open to adults, such as torch races, fitness, coordination, or the handling of weapons. Even if children's high-performance sport was taken very seriously, it was not totally equivalent to adult sport. Certainly, educational sport was a youthful activity since only the young attended school.

One of the most important proponents of the absence of adolescence is Kleijwegt, whose research deals mostly with Roman standards. He argues that introducing the young men early into the economic and political life strengthened the family position, despite the fact that the older generation was reluctant to yield its place and allow the new generation to take over.[46] This tension resulted in the ambiguous position of young men, who were considered at the same time "young adults"—that is, adults even if chronologically young and "subordinate youngsters."[47] Thus, even proponents of the lack of adolescence recognize that sometimes the transition between child and adult roles was not entirely smooth. Kleijwegt states that the dominant ideology was that the older generation wanted the younger to become like them and that the younger wanted to be like their elders. On the other hand, Kleijwegt also points out that the dominant ideology was built on personal excellence and on the idea of surpassing others and always being the best, as expressed already

---

45. Young 1985: 171.
46. Kleijwegt 1991: 72–73. See also Pratt 2007: 29.
47. Kleijwegt 1991: 57–58.

in *The Iliad* (6.208). Imitation of the older generation was not a goal in itself but a way to enter in competition with one's peers and preceding generations. According to him, a reason for the survival of this ideology was that "there were no areas specifically reserved for youthful activities.... There was no youth-oriented culture centered around sport for instance."[48] He argues that every age group was present in the gymnasia, all the way from children to mature and older adults.

I profoundly disagree with Kleijwegt's generalization of the nature of sport. Whereas it is true that in most gymnasia groups of different ages were present, there is no evidence that they trained together in one group. On the contrary, evidence points to the fact that the different age groups would have been divided mostly according to an appropriate use of schedule, as we shall see shortly.[49] We shall further discuss evidence that points to the existence of several palestras that were used primarily by one age group more than another. Even if members of different age groups shared the use of gymnasia, I believe it is crucial to distinguish between the specific goals that participants in sport had for their activity. The younger generation would have had the pressure to perform its utmost best in sport, whereas for biological reasons the older generation would no longer have that pressure. Thus, we can say that it is not the activity in itself that defines whether or not it is exclusive to one group, but the goals behind it. The presence of persons of mixed ages does not per se invalidate the claim that sport (at least some type of it) did represent an aspect of youth-oriented culture. Though not all sport would have been youth-oriented, certainly some aspects of it were. The same applies to hunting, which is also an activity that scholars qualify as an elite youth activity, because Xenophon's treatise *On Hunting* (which will be discussed later) specifically points to this activity as appropriate to the twenty-year-old man and links it to the old education.

Some scholars who argue that there was a separate youth culture claim that the development of a specific *paideia* by the Greeks and its adoption by the Romans created a "free space" (*Freiraum*) for the youth-oriented lifestyle.[50] This means that the youth-oriented lifestyle appeared only after the change in the education system after the fifth century because education was prolonged until the age of around twenty for those who could afford it. Elite

---

48. Ibid., 68–69.
49. See the gymnasiarchal law of Beroia (*SEG* 27: 261).
50. Christes 1998: 153–57.

young men became, then, controversial figures in a double sense: first for being young and then for continuing to be athletes after the days of schooling,[51] which placed them in a prolonged adolescence. Because athletes were young men, they were perceived as being in need of civic training and education, but they also belonged to an age-group that did not have a clearly defined role in the society.[52] This would be more acute in the case of the young men of well-to-do families who had to wait for their fathers' decline to take over the role of head of the family.

Besides the age group, class factors as well play an important role in the perception of youth. During archaic and classical times, athletes were mostly aristocratic.[53] It is precisely this group of young men who would be more difficult to socialize.[54] Individuals from lower classes would have followed their fathers into their occupations, probably at a rather young age. From this point of view, it is probably not inappropriate to speak about a lack of adolescence among lower classes. Conversely, young aristocrats would have also followed their fathers into their occupations, except their fathers' occupations were mostly political and civic duties, which were barred to the sons until their thirtieth birthday.[55] For those talented and dedicated individuals, sport would have seemed a good choice until they were able to take over their fathers' business. Whereas a certain number of young (aristocratic) men may have entered into a public career or private administration of their affairs at an early age, as Kleijwegt suggests, there might have still been a certain group of them waiting to take over responsibilities.[56] Although we are not sure how this played out for every individual athlete, the perception of their inability to function in adult life was not unknown.

---

51. Pritchard 2013 argues that athletics did not receive criticism by lower classes because of its perceived role as a training for war. On the other hand, intellectual elites started criticizing athletes and athletics already by the sixth century, the time of the creation of athletic culture.

52. Steinrück 2000:1-4, 44-52; Bertolín 2008: 70-79.

53. There is a long debate about the social class of athletes. Most scholars agree now that only relatively wealthy families could afford for their boys and young men not to work. For the contrary argument, see Young 1985. For an overview of the debate, see Pritchard 2013: 35-46 and Kyle 2014: 159-75.

54. See, for instance, Aristophanes's *Clouds* as a parody of the socialization of the young in view of the old and new model of education.

55. Elite activities, such as the symposium with its excessive drinking and *hetairai*, pederastic relations, and horsemanship, were often subject to criticism in literature and otherwise. Athletics was an elite activity that escaped this sort of criticism for a while. According to Pritchard 2013:138, this was due to the fact that Athenians considered that athletics had a close relation to war. We shall explore that relation further on.

56. Christes 1998: 164.

1.3 Athletes as an Influential Group

In terms of social class, currently, there are three different opinions about the provenance of athletes.[57] The first position maintains that even in democratic Athens athletes were aristocratic, mostly because of the expense of training.[58] The second position acknowledges some social changes but doubts extensive democratization (i.e., a general extension of aristocratic practices to nonaristocrats) and admits nonaristocratic athletes only after the classical times.[59] The third position argues for a wide democratization of sport already during archaic and especially classical times.[60] The debate is still not closed, and since evidence is limited, it might never be totally resolved. Evidence suggests a shift in the social classes of athletes from mostly aristocrats during the archaic times to a wide spectrum of social classes, ranging from aristocrats all the way to perhaps even freedmen and slaves during the Hellenistic and especially during Roman times. Whether the democratization of sport started already during classical times, owing in part to the state sponsored gymnasium,[61] or did not occur until the Hellenistic period is harder to prove.

The controversy about the social status of athletes started at the beginning of the twentieth century when the first scholars of Greek sport saw in the idealized image of the Greek athlete the Oxbridge gentleman, someone who did not need to train excessively and most importantly was not a paid, professional athlete.[62] The fact that the Olympic and other crown games were undertaken for glory but not prizes was, according to these scholars, indicative that athletics were at the beginning only for aristocrats who played sports for the glory of it without seeking any material rewards. They argued for a system of decline after the Hellenistic times when professional

---

57. The Greeks divided themselves into two classes: the rich and the poor. According to Pritchard, 2003: 301 the rich were privileged elite families, whereas the poor ranged from the homeless to those people just some drachmas short of the elite. Pritchard argues that acting as an elite citizen was not always advantageous, because the person would be responsible for further taxes and liturgies. Since belonging to the elite was self-declared, many would have opted not to do so. Contrary to Pritchard, Christesen 2012a argues for further subdivisions of classes, which would consist of those people, such as rich farmers, who had to work but only for parts of the year. This would allow them to dispose of leisure time for sport during other parts of the year. He argues also for a progressive democratization of sport. See also Kyle 2014: 166–67.

58. See Pritchard 2013.

59. Within this school of thought we can count scholars such as Pleket (2001 and 2005), Golden (2008), and Kyle (1987), who accepts a shift from birth aristocracy to wealth aristocracy in the practice of sport.

60. Miller 2004a and Christesen 2012a would be representative of this position.

61. Pleket 1974: 79.

62. Gardiner 1930.

athletes made their appearance at the games, and with them, corruption came into athletics.⁶³

In 1984 David Young questioned the view of sport being the exclusive domain of aristocrats. He argued that "professionalism" and "decline" were not concurrent terms and that many of the earlier athletes were not aristocrats but middle- or lower-class citizens.⁶⁴ He argued that the concept of amateurism in Greek athletics was a projection of the debate that was taking place at the time about the role of professional sports in Europe and North America and that earlier scholars forgot that the same athletes that participated for the glory at the Olympic and other periodic games participated for the prizes at the many other games.⁶⁵ Thus, Young hypothesized that a naturally talented child or even beardless athlete would have been able to win some prizes at some local games and with that could have launched an athletic career and moved up in social class.⁶⁶ It is certainly not an implausible scenario, but perhaps more the exception than the norm. Young's ideas have been revised since he first proposed them, resulting in the above-mentioned positions. I believe that we need to look at other avenues in order to further the current debate on athletes' social status, which was determined not only by class but by age, both social and biological. The debate about the athlete should be viewed, consequently, within a larger anthropological frame.

Athletes may have been a group representative and influential enough not only in terms of class but also in terms of numbers. The number of potential athletes within a given city (whether high performance, educational, or recreational) depends on the number of the total population. Hansen calculates the total population of the Greek world in the fourth century to be around 7.5 million. This is the population in the Greek mainland, Epirus, Macedonia, and in the colonies.⁶⁷ About 10 percent of all *poleis* known to us, this is about one hundred *poleis*, would have accommodated 40 percent of the total population.⁶⁸ Hansen further estimates the number of family members per household to be between five and seven, and the number of slaves to be one every two households.⁶⁹ He also calculates the population of Boeotia to be

63. Gardiner 1910.
64. Young 1985.
65. See Pleket 1976: 59. Some prizes were worth several times the average annual wage of a skilled worker. See Young 1985: 128–33.
66. Young 1985: 158–60.
67. Hansen 2006: 27.
68. Ibid., 30.
69. Ibid., 58–60.

around 150,000 people and that of Attica as about 100,000.⁷⁰ Following these numbers, we can roughly calculate the number of potential athletes. Within a population of 100,000 divided into households of five persons we obtain 20,000 households. If each of them had half a slave, that leaves 90,000 nonslaves, citizens, and foreigners. Since sport was open to all Greek males, there is no reason to distinguish further among them, especially since there might be epigraphic evidence that children of metics participated at local festivals.⁷¹ Out of the 90,000, about half would have been male, or 45,000. Let us assume conservatively that between a fourth and a third of them would have been of athletic age beyond the first schooling, that is, between fourteen and thirty years of age. This gives 11,250 to 15,000 young men. About half of them would have belonged to hoplite status or above.⁷² Perhaps it is best to assume that only about 5 percent belonged to the upper class⁷³ and, thus, were most likely athletes. This would give as a minimum number of potential athletes 560 to 750, and up to ten times that many.⁷⁴ Obviously, not all of them would have been equally talented or inclined or had the same opportunities, but the number is significant enough in the city, especially when dealing with elite citizens.⁷⁵

If we opt for a lower number of athletes, we are left to answer the question about how a minority of significantly less than 1 percent of the population could have turned sport into such a prevalent topic in the plastic arts, literature, and social life in general, or why a city like Athens had three public gymnasia and numerous private palestras, or why in the Hellenistic cities the gymnasium became a central architectural feature. Assuming a higher

---

70. Ibid., 90–91.

71. *IG* 2² 964 mentions the children who won at the different events at a local Athenian competition. All children belonged to several of the tribes, except one who is from Smyrna. It is unclear whether he was a metic or he just came to the competition. Because of the local character and the almost Athenian exclusiveness of the competitors, I would be inclined to believe that he was a resident alien. The orator Lysias (445–380) was a rich metic, who presumably received a very good education. Although we do not know what he studied in detail, we are safe to assume that he would have participated in the physical education at school and thus was a potential athlete.

72. Hafez 2015 calculates the number of laborers as 40 to 60 percent.

73. Hafez 2015.

74. Christesen (2013: 221) estimates the growth of active athletes from one thousand to eleven thousand after the establishment of democracy.

75. Crowther (2004: 179–80) calculates that adult competitors at Olympia, where only the best of the best participated, would have varied between 20 men for the running events and 8 men for the heavy events. At local festivals during the imperial era, according to inscriptions that detail six to eight elimination rounds in wrestling, participation can be calculated to be anything in between 64 and 256 men. Boys' events had considerably fewer participants, perhaps only 4 at Olympia, and four to six rounds at local events, i.e., between 16 and 64 boys.

number of athletes may be a more reasonable option to explain the influence that sport had in Greek culture in general.

Comparative data of the European Union shows that in 2013, 15 percent of all men between fifteen and twenty-four years of age exercised regularly, and another 59 percent exercised with some regularity. These percentages dropped with the increase of age. Thus, only 9 percent of men between twenty-five and thirty-nine years of age practiced some kind of sport regularly, and 42 percent did so with some regularity. Among men forty to fifty-four and over fifty-five, the percentage of those exercising regularly dropped to 8 percent. The main difference was that only 22 percent of the older age group versus 32 percent of the younger exercised with some regularity.[76] Although modern data may be misleading when applied to the ancient world, they nevertheless provide a potential maximum number of 15 percent regular participation. It would be difficult to assume that participation in sport in ancient times extended to higher numbers than that. Assuming 15,000 young men in Attica out of a population of 100,000, and assuming about 15 percent of athletes among them, we come to a number of 2,250. This is not a number to disrespect and certainly large enough to be taken into consideration by the cities, which organized events to target them. Whereas these numbers are total speculation on my part, at least they provide an attempt to frame the activity of sport within the general population of a region. Numbers would have varied from city to city, obviously, but certainly they help us assume the presence of more than a few athletes in any given city.

---

76. Data taken from the online dossier published by the European Commission 2017.

2

High-Performance Training

When one thinks of athletes, the very first idea that comes to mind is the competitive, high-performance athlete. In fact, most books and studies dedicated to sport in ancient Greece deal with this type of athlete and the competitions in which he participated. It is, therefore, only logical that I also start the search for the athlete by looking at the evidence that brings us closer to him. In this chapter, I propose that a change in the methods for developing competitive athletes took place during the Hellenistic times and that its implementation was at its highest during Roman imperial times. In Hellenistic times, every area of human activity undeniably underwent a certain degree of specialization, and sport was no exception. Hellenistic armies were composed, by and large, of hired mercenaries rather than citizen-soldiers. A great array of professionals such as cooks, physicians, architects, engineers, scribes, and scholars are known from our sources, and although these had existed all along, there was a formalization process in their professions during Hellenistic times. Thus, the scholars who first developed the model of the professionalization of sport were not entirely mistaken in their assumption that there was a change toward a more specialized practice, which they called "professionalization."[1]

---

1. The most prominent proponent of the model of professionalization for Hellenistic times was E. N. Gardiner, who equated it with decline. See, for instance, his statement that "when money enters into sport corruption is sure to follow.... Thus within a century the whole character of athletics was completely changed. From this time there is little to record save that all the evils which we have described grew more and more pronounced. The festivals became more purely spectacular, the competitions became more the monopoly of professionals and their training more artificial and unpractical, and the result is visible in the deterioration of their physical type" (1910: 103–4).

Nevertheless, what is understood by "professional" still demands an explanation, since athletes of the fifth century who competed continuously over twenty years in numerous contests and made their fortunes from sport cannot be considered anything less than professional. Perhaps we should look to other avenues to explain the change in athletic practices without invoking the ghost of professionalization.[2] I propose a model that explains the changes in the Hellenistic and Roman imperial times based on athletic practices and training methods rather than on social or political concerns, although the changes in training would likely not have been possible without a previous social change. Specifically, I will argue for a change from a training model based on *late specialization* to a model based on *early specialization*. I will argue this from the results at competitions in the periodic games of athletes of classical and later times. The results of Hellenistic and Roman imperial athletes indicate that there was a careful planning of competitions, even for athletes in the children's category. When data is available, it shows that Hellenistic and Roman imperial athletes completed the whole periodic games in a very short amount of time and at a much younger age than the athletes in previous times. The combination of early success and carefully planned careers speaks in turn for a change in methods of athlete development.

2.1 Different Career Paths

Looking at the careers of Greek athletes of the sixth to fourth centuries and comparing them with the careers of later athletes, it is surprising to see how the success at the periodic games of those athletes during Hellenistic and Roman imperial times was very rapid. For athletes up to the middle of the fourth century, retirement tended to coincide with ceasing to participate at the periodic games. This does not seem to be the case for later athletes, who completed the *periodos* in record time while still very young and did not repeat it in most cases. During Roman imperial times, it is not uncommon for young athletes in their early twenties, including wrestlers, to compete and win one *periodos* and then, after the Olympic victory, to compete only in other local games or games sponsored by the emperors.[3] For instance, Marcus Aurelius

---

2. "Specialization begets professionalism and professionalism is the death of all true sport" (ibid., 122). Gardiner's mistake was to identify specialization with moral decline. For criticism of the amateur ideal, see Pleket 2001 [1974] and Young 1985. For a reevaluation of Gardiner's ideas, see Kyle 1990.

3. For data see Knab 1980 [1934]: 50–75.

Asclepiades was approximately twenty-two at his first periodic victory in the pancratium and only twenty-five when he retired in 181 A.D. An inscription details Asclepiades's career.

> I am the son of Marcus Aurelius Demetrius, head priest of the whole union of athletes for life, the leader of the union and director of the baths of the emperor, citizen of Alexandria and Hermopolis, pancratiast, victor of the *periodos*, wrestler without comparison—I, Marcus Aurelius Asclepiades, also known as Hermodorus, the eldest of the temple assistants of the great Sarapis, head priest of the whole athletic union for life, leader of the union and director of the baths of the emperor, citizen of Alexandria, Hermopolis, Puteoli, councilor of Naples and Elis and Athens, councilor and citizen of many other cities, pancratiast, victor of the *periodos*, undefeated, who cannot be thrown down, unchallenged. As many contests as I entered, I won them all. I was never challenged, nor did anyone dare to be challenged by me, never settled for a tie, nor went against [the referee], neither declined nor abandoned a match, neither won a match by sheer luck nor with a bye, but, in all the contests which I entered, I was crowned in the ring and I was tested in all the preliminary rounds. I fought in three parts of the world: Italy, Greece, and Asia. I won all the contests in the pancratium written here: the Olympics in Pisa in the 240th Olympiad, the Pythian Games in Delphi, the Isthmian twice, the Nemean twice (the second time, no opponent dared to face me), the Shield Games of Hera, the Capitoline in Rome twice (the second time, after the first draw no opponent dared to face me), the Eusebeia Games in Puteoli twice (the second time, after the second draw no opponent dared to face me), the Sebasta in Naples twice (the second time, after the second draw no opponent dared to face me), the Actia in Nicopolis twice (the second time, no opponent dared to face me), in Athens five games (the Panathenaea, the Olympics, the Panhellenic, and twice the Hadrian Games), in Smyrna five games (the common Asian Games twice—the second time, no opponent dared to face me—and similarly the Olympics in Smyrna and the Hadrianic Olymipcs), in Pergamon the Augusteia three times (the second time, from the beginning no opponent dared to face me, the third time, after the first draw no opponent dared to face me), in Ephesus three times (the Hadrian Games, the Olympics

and the Barbillea—after the first draw no opponent dared to face me), in Epidaurus the Asclepeia, in Rhodes the Haleia, in Sardis the Chrysanthis, and many more games for prizes, among which are the Eurycleia in Lacedaemonia, the Mantinea and others. I competed in total six years, I stopped competition at age twenty-five because of dangers and envy gathering around me. After retirement after many years, I was forced to participate in the local Olympics at Alexandria and I won the pancratium in the sixth (local) Olympics. (*IG* 14 1102)

According to this, in six years Asclepiades won in thirty-four games. Besides the *periodos*, he won many other games in Asia, Italy, and Greece— certainly a very impressive achievement. He came back, probably at the age of thirty-eight, after twelve years of retirement, to win the pancratium in the sixth local Olympics in Alexandria. The emperor Marcus Aurelius may have founded the Olympics at Alexandria in 176 A.D.[4] In that case it would not be surprising that Asclepiades was forced out of his retirement to participate in one of them. The relation with the Roman emperor is seen in the fact that Asclepiades held the same office as his father, Demetrius: that of overseer of the imperial baths. Like his father, he bears the name of Marcus Aurelius, which may speak to direct support of the emperor in both their careers.[5] The emperor's name may also imply that they were imperial freedmen or were granted Roman citizenship by the emperor, perhaps because of their athletic achievements.[6] Like Demetrius and Asclepiades, several other victors in the *periodos* in the first and second centuries A.D. have the name of an emperor. This indicates that these successful athletes may have been sponsored by the emperors, who most likely were interested in an assured victory.

In contrast to Asclepiades, we know that the boxer Theagenes, who was active at the end of the fifth century, had a career of twenty-two years, in which he achieved thirteen hundred victories. This very impressive record was probably unmatched in all of antiquity. Theagenes participated not only

---

4. Ibid., 43.
5. Marcus Aurelius was emperor from 161 to 180 A.D., spanning the time of Asclepiades's career but not Demetrius's. Demetrius must have been around thirty years old when Marcus Aurelius ascended to the throne, too old for Marcus Aurelius to have shown interest in his career after he became emperor, but not too old to be rewarded for his previous success with Roman citizenship. On the other hand, it would have been normal for foreigners admitted to citizenship to adopt the *nomen* and *praenomen* of the current emperor. See McLean 2002: 15.
6. The emperor Hadrian (117–138 A.D.) admitted Greeks into Roman citizenship, but still this does not explain the imperial surname.

in boxing, he was also a pancratiast and a long-distance runner. In order to come to thirteen hundred victories, he would have had to participate in about nineteen games a year in all three different events.[7] It is obviously hard not to see Theagenes as a professional athlete. Professionalism per se does not explain the difference between him and Asclepiades. Despite his amazing record, it took Theagenes ten years to achieve his first *periodos*. His first victory at the Isthmian Games probably occurred in 490 as a boy, and his Olympic victories did not occur until 480 in boxing and 476 in pancratium. This would also make him Olympic victor at about twenty-five, like Asclepiades. But, unlike Asclepiades, he continued competing in the periodic games even after he achieved a second *periodos* in 476, which this time around took only four years. Even allowing for the fact that there were more local games in the second century A.D. than in the fifth century B.C., this does not explain why a young athlete like Asclepiades at the peak of his career would no longer participate, not just in the *periodos*, but in any other games. The inscription mentions that he retired because of dangers and jealousies that were gathering around him but does not give any indication as to their nature. Perhaps fear of injury was an important factor. An inscription, discussed later in chapter five (*PPAphr* 89), describes the injury that caused the death of a pancratiast as "envy."

That the career paths of Asclepiades and Theagenes are not isolated can be seen by comparison to other athletes in the classical and Hellenistic and Roman imperial times. Set out below are two tables of athletes listing their victories and length of participation at the periodic games. The tables include all the known victors of the *periodos*.[8] Although in some cases the age of the competitors is not attested, if they did not have any recorded victories as children, they were at least eighteen years old when they achieved their first victory. Table 2.1 shows those athletes active during classical times whose careers spanned a long time. The heavy athletes had careers of about twelve years (Milo close to twenty-five). The runners had careers of eight to ten years. It is true that in some instances we cannot tell much about the length of careers, as in the case of Ephudion, who defeated his opponent at Olympia when he already had grey hair and was old, but he might have won the other three periodic competitions in his earlier years.[9] So we need to evaluate the data carefully since the unknown may be greater than the known.

---

7. Knab 1980 [1934]: 21.
8. The list of the victors of the *periodos* is adapted from Knab 1980 [1934] and Moretti 1957.
9. This comes from a scholium found in Aristophanes, *Wasps* 1190. See Knab 1980 [1934]: 27.

Table 2.2 details the participation of athletes at the periodic games during Hellenistic and Roman imperial times.

The first thing to notice is that, starting in the 300s, the majority of athletes completed their first *periodos* in two to three years. What had previously been something achieved only by a select group of runners seems to be much more attainable for every type of athlete. Where ages are known, the age for completion of the *periodos* is in the early twenties. This implies a degree of planning that is unlikely to have been common in earlier times, when the last attested victory at the periodic games for most heavy athletes occurred when the athletes were in their thirties and for runners in their mid-twenties. It might even seem that athletes were now competing to break a record for completing the *periodos* in the shortest time.[10]

The table of the athletes active during Hellenistic and Roman times (table 2.2) also shows that the time to achieve the *periodos* is shorter than in archaic and classical times, but because many of the later athletes are known to belong to athletes' associations, which would generally imply an active involvement in sport, it is not always easy to ascertain whether they had been competing for a long time before they attempted the *periodos*. Some may have completed the *periodos* in three years as a high point to their careers. We do not have information about earlier or later victories in most cases. It is, however, most likely that athletes used the *periodos* as entry to the "professional circuit." Like the case of Aristomachus shows, he completed the *periodos* as a boy and youth but probably kept competing beyond those years. We just do not possess any records of his later career, if there was one.

Archippus of Mytilene completed the *periodos* in boxing by 296 when he was not much more than twenty years old (Pausanias 6.15.1). Titus Flavius Metrobius completed his *periodos* in long-distance running from the years 86 to 89 A.D., Marcus Ulpius Domesticus completed his in the pancratium from 134 to 138 A.D., and Apollonius, probably a wrestler, completed his from 282 to 285 A.D.[11] We do not have an approximate age when these athletes started competing, nor do we possess any evidence as to whether or not they competed in the younger categories. M. Ulpius Domesticus had a son Ulpius Firmus Domesticus who was also victor in the *periodos* between 150 and 153 A.D. Both of them had the name Ulpius and were overseers of the baths of

---

10. See Young 1996.
11. Knab 1980 [1934]: 42–46.

Table 2.1. Victors of the periodic games during classical times

Name	Years at periodic games (B.C.)	Approx. age of first victory at periodic games	Approx. age of last victory at periodic games	Discipline	Times victorious at periodic games (number of games, not events)				Years for first *periodos*
					O	P	I	N	
Milo	540–514=26	14	40	Wrestling	6	7	9	9	7
Glaucus	520–504=16	At least 18	At least 34	Boxing	1	2	8	8	6
Theagenes	490–470=20	14	34	Boxing	2	3	9	9	10
Dromeus	487–479=8	At least 18	At least 26	Dolichos	2	2	3	5	3
Callias	484–472=12	Less than 20	Ca. 30	Pancratium	1	2	4	4	12
Dandis	479–471=8	Perhaps 14	22	Stadium, Diaulos, Hoplito-dromos	2	2	2	5	3
Ergoteles	474–464=10	At least 18	At least 28	Dolichos	2	2	2	2	5
Epharmostus	472–466=6	14	Ca. 20	Wrestling	1	1	3	2	6
Diagoras	470–464=6	Probably 18+, a son by 470		Boxing	1	1	4	2	6
Ephudion	466–464=2		Old and with grey hair	Pancratium	1	1	1	1	2
Telemachus	450–440=10	At least 18	At least 28	Pancratium	1	3	6	5	10
Agias	450–440=10	At least 18	Ca. 28 *akmē*=40 by 428	Wrestling	1	3	6	5	10
Dorieus	438–424=14	At least 18	At least 32	Pancratium	3	4	8	7	6
Dicon	392–380=12	14	26	Stadium, Diaulos	3	3	3	4	6
Sostratus	367–356=11	At least 18	At least 29	Pancratium	3	2	6	6	5
Chilon	330–324=6	At least 18	Died in war in 333	Wrestling	2	2	4	3	2
Astyanax	324–316=8	At least 18	At least 26	Boxing, Pancratium	3	2	5	4	2

O = Olympic Games; P = Pythian Games; I = Isthmian Games; N = Nemean Games

Table 2.2. Victors of the periodic games during Hellenistic and Roman Imperial times

Name	Years at periodic games	Approx. age of first victory at periodic games	Approx. age of last victory at periodic games	Discipline	Times victorious at periodic games (number of games, not events)				Years for first *periodos*
					O	P	I	N	
Antenor	315–308 B.C. =7	14	21; still alive in 280	Boxing, Pancratium	2	2	4	2	3
Pythagoras	305–296 B.C. =9	14	23	Stadium	2	2	5	5	5
Nicon	303–296 B.C. =7			Pancratium	2	2	4	4	3
Archippus	299–296 B.C. =3	17	20	Boxing	1	1	2	2	3
Philinus	270–260 B.C. =10	14	24	Stadium, Diaulos	3	3	6	4	3
Cleoxenus	242–240 B.C. =2			Boxing	1	1	1	1	2
Damatrius	208–200 B.C. =8	14	22	Dolichos	2	2	2	4	?
Moschos	202–200 B.C. =2	14	16	Boxing	1	1	1	1	2
Xenothemis	192–188 B.C. =4	14	18		2	1	2	2	2
Leon son of Myonides	After 189 B.C. =?	14	At least 22		1	3	3	5	?
Epitherses	186–180 B.C. =6	About 18 by 190, so about 22	28	Wrestling	2	2	2	2	4
Menodorus	165–160 B.C. =5	Less than 20	Before 25	Wrestling	2	1	1	3	3
Hagesarchus	118–116 B.C. =2			Boxing	1	1	2	1	2
Isidorus	74–72 B.C. =2			Wrestling	1	1	2	1	2
Straton	73–64 B.C. =9	15	24	Wrestling, Pancratium	2	2	4	5	5
Philippus Glycon	26–20 B.C. =6	14	20	Pancratium	2	2	1	2	6
Hermas	17–12 B.C. =5			Pancratium	2	2	1	2	5
Heras	22–25 A.D. =3			Pancratium	1	1	1	2	3
Democrates	25–33 A.D. =8	At least 8 years of competition		Boxing	3	1	2	2	?
Son of Aristeas	35–41 A.D. =6	Less than 20	26	Pancratium	1	1	1	2	6

(*continued*)

Table 2.2. Victors of the periodic games during Hellenistic and Roman Imperial times (*continued*)

Name	Years at periodic games	Approx. age of first victory at periodic games	Approx. age of last victory at periodic games	Discipline	Times victorious at periodic games (number of games, not events)				Years for first *periodos*
					O	P	I	N	
Ti. Claudius Patrobius	49–57 A.D. = 8	Less than 20	35	Wrestling	3	2 3?	1	2	?
P. Pompeius Eutyches	57–61 A.D. = 4			?	2 x *periodonikes*				?
T. Flavius Artemidorus	77–86 A.D. = 9	Less than 20	Before 29	Wrestling, Pancratium	2	2	3	2	5
T. Flavius Metrobius	86–89 A.D. = 3			Dolichos	1	1	2	1	3
T. Flavius Archibius	92–106 A.D. = 14	14	28	Wrestling, Pancratium	2	4	1	4	9
Aristomachus	115–117 A.D. = 2	14	16	Pancratium	1	1	1	1	2
P. Aelius Alcandridas	115–121 A.D. = 6			Wrestling	2	2	2	2	3
M. Ulpius Domesticus	134–137 A.D. = 3	Older athlete? son 18+ by 150		Pancratium	1	1	1	1	3
M. Aurelius Demetrius	146–149 A.D. = 3			Pancratium	1	1	1	1	3
Ulp. Firmus Domesticus	150–153 A.D. = 3			Pancratium	1	1	1	1	3
Mnasibulus	158–161 A.D. = 3		Died in war in 165	Stadium, Hoplito-dromos	1	1	1	1	3
M. Aurelius Asclepiades	178–181 A.D. = 3	20	25	Pancratium	1	1	2	2	3
M. Aurelius Demostratus Damas	187–193 A.D. = 6	14 (before the *periodos*)		Boxing, Pancratium	2	2	2	2	2
Claudius Apollonius	282–285 A.D. = 3			Wrestling?	1	1	2	2	3
Claudius Rufus Apollonius	299–305 A.D. = 6			Wrestling? Pancratium	2	2	2	2	2

O = Olympic Games; P = Pythian Games; I = Isthmian Games; N = Nemean Games

Trajan.[12] Domesticus the elder appears in a letter from Antoninus Pius to the Heraclean Athletic Victors of Sacred Games and Crowns. The emperor agrees to donate some land in the area of Trajan's bath for the athletes to keep their trophies and records.[13] The letter is dated to 143 A.D. Domesticus was the negotiator on behalf of the athletes' union. This may indicate that he perhaps had a longer career than the *periodos*, but there is no assurance of it. Certainly, he was involved in sport administration after his victories.

On the other hand, we know that Titus Flavius Archibius competed and won victories in the child (*paides*), youth (*ageneioi*), and adult (*andres*) categories. His victory as *ageneios* (aged 17–20?) took place in Naples in the year 94 A.D., and he retired from active competition in 106 A.D.[14] This puts him at a maximum age of thirty-two and a minimum age of twenty-nine. Considering that Archibius was a pancratiast, his career still falls short in comparison to the previous athletes, who competed into their thirties. Asclepiades and Domesticus were also heavy athletes, so the promptness in completing the *periodos* in comparison with the athletes of archaic and classical times really stands out. Even Metrobius's participation at the periodic games seems rather short for a long-distance runner.

The most important change, however, is that there seems to be a careful plan about how to enter the periodic games during later times, whereas we can hardly distinguish a specific plan of training from the dates of the athletes' victories in the fifth and fourth centuries B.C. For instance, the pancratiast Dorieus won his first Isthmian Games as an adult in 438. Then he won at the Pythian and Nemean and again at the Isthmian, and then again at the Pythian, Nemean, and Isthmian until he won his first Olympics six years later in 432. He kept competing at the other periodic games and won his second Olympics in 428. Then he repeated the whole *periodos* and again won the Olympics in 424 and subsequently retired. It is clear that Dorieus did not win the Olympics in 436, so he kept repeating the circuit until he won, not once, but three times. His career spanned fourteen years. Obviously, the Greeks called the games periodic because they constituted a circuit of

---

12. The emperor Trajan (full name of Marcus Ulpius Trajan) was dead by 117 A.D. Someone in the *gens* Ulpia after Trajan must have taken an interest in the athletic career of Domesticus the elder. Another possibility is that he was a successful athlete already by the time of Trajan and that his participation at the *periodos* was the end of his career. IG 14 1109 does not detail his activities. IG 14 1054 and 1055 show that he was already involved in administration of the gymnasium and the emperor's baths in 134 and at least until 143 A.D.

13. *IG* 14 1055b.

14. *IG* 14 747.

competition. Yet, Dorieus's inability to win the first time at the Olympic Games (we do not even know whether he participated or not) did not keep him away from the rest of the games. The pancratiast Callias shows a similar pattern. Callias started his victories as an *ageneios* in the Isthmian Games of 484. He continued achieving victories at the Nemean, Isthmian, and Pythian Games for many years. His Olympic victory came only in 472, when he retired after twelve years of competition. Considering that the Olympics Games were the most prestigious, it is not strange that athletes desired victory at the Olympics as their most precious one. However, not achieving victory the first time around did not keep them from competition.

In the case of athletes during Hellenistic and especially Roman times we get a very different impression. There seems to be a change of mentality from practicing athletics as a way of life for a certain period of their lives to one of having a single-minded objective of winning all the games in the shortest possible amount of time. For instance, the pancratiast Hermas managed to win the Olympics in the year 16 and in the year 12. In between he won the Pythian and Isthmian Games once each and the Nemean Games twice. In fact, he accomplished all this in four years. What stands out among the athletes of Roman times is not only the fact that they won the *periodos* in three years, but also that they did not repeat the *periodos*. The availability of alternative competition all over the Greek world does not explain this alone. During Hellenistic times there were also numerous other games, yet Astyanax competed in both boxing and pancratium from 324 to 316 and in eight years managed to win three times at the Olympics and complete the *periodos* twice, if not three times. Astyanax's career was short for a heavy athlete, yet he competed in two disciplines, which certainly brought another degree of difficulty. The sprinter Philinus almost completed his first *periodos* as a *pais* but was just short of the Nemean Games, which he won as an adult. He completed two subsequent *periodoi* as an adult from 267 to 260. So we can see with these two examples that it was very possible to complete a *periodos* in a single cycle; nevertheless these athletes kept competing for at least another cycle. The sprinter's career of ten years (if we take his success as a child into account) is actually a very good one, bringing his retirement age to about twenty-six.

As noted, around the mid-third century B.C. the list of victors of the *periodos* shows a new trend. From the boxer Cleoxenus onward (242–240) the majority of the winners competed for one *periodos* only, which they achieved within two or three years. They did so even as children, as the case of Moschus shows. Moschus won the *periodos* as *pais* (before 18 years old) in boxing during

202 to 200. The case of Moschus might be significant because even as a child there seems to be a directed plan of action. In order to finish the *periodos* in three years without repeating any games, one has to enter into the Pythian Games, then the Nemean and Isthmian Games (or vice versa),[15] and finally the Olympics as a culmination. Perhaps one could reverse the order of the Pythian Games and the Olympics, but that may not have given as much prestige. Any other order of games would not result in achieving victory in such a short time and without repeating participation at one or even two games. We just saw the example of Astyanax who, even if winning three times at Olympia, managed to complete only two and a half *periodoi*. He started competing at the Isthmian Games and moved then to the Olympics. He then cycled through the Nemean, Pythian, and Isthmian Games, then participated in the Nemean Games and the Isthmian Games again, before finally moving on to his second Olympics—the same cycle occurs for the third Olympics.

The pattern of winning the *periodos* in two or a maximum of three years and afterward moving on to different local or newly created competitions starts around 240 and continues until 300 A.D. There are possible explanations as to why a young athlete would not repeat the *periodos*. With the increase in the number of games, many of them with huge chrematistic advantages, the *periodos* may have lost part of its appeal. During the classical period there were one hundred and forty different games in Greece, and during Roman imperial times the number went up to two hundred and seventy, most of them involving prizes.[16] Competing at the *periodos* became some kind of graduation to the professional circuit. It would be parallel to modern athletes who become professional after participating at the Olympics, for instance, in figure skating. However, even if this is the case, completing the *periodos* in three years or less and then never participating in any of these games again seems planned.

Three inscriptions serve to further exemplify the different career paths of athletes during classical and later times. The first one comes from Olympia and details the achievements of Dorieus, son of Diagoras. It is dated ca. 424 and reads as follows:

Dorieus, son of Diagoras from Rhodes
In the Olympics, pancratium
In the Olympics, pancratium

15. See introduction and introductory table for order of circuit.
16. Scanlon 2002: 29.

> In the Olympics, pancratium
> In the Pythian, boxing
> In the Pythian, boxing
> In the Pythian, boxing without a contest
> In the Isthmian, boxing
> In the Isthmian, boxing
> In the Isthmian, boxing and pancratium
> In the Isthmian, boxing
> In the Isthmian, boxing
> In the Isthmian
> In the Isthmian
> In the Nemean, boxing
> In the Nemean, boxing
> In the Nemean, boxing
> In the Nemean, boxing
> In the Nemean, boxing
> In the Nemean, boxing
> In the Nemean, boxing. (*IvO* 153)

The inscription is repetitive; nevertheless, it does not leave any question as to where Dorieus concentrated his athletic efforts. If we contrast this inscription with the one describing the career of Leon, son of Myonides, a very different impression emerges. The inscription is dated to the second century, after 189. It reads as follows:

> Leon, son of Myonides
> Olympia in the men category, wrestling
> Isthmia in the children, youth, and men categories, wrestling
> Nemea in the children and youth categories, wrestling and pancratium,
> In the men category wrestling and pancratium . . . the first of the Greeks. . . .
> Pythia in the men category, wrestling
> . . . in the men category, wrestling . . .
> . . . in the men category, wrestling
>
> Col. II
> having won the wrestling without falling in many contests,
> The Heraia in Argos in the men category, wrestling,

The Hyacinthotrophia in Cnidos in the men category, wrestling,
The Heracleia in Thebes in the men category, wrestling,
The Theophaneia in Chios in the men category, wrestling and pancratium
The Romaia. LTIONTOU. . . .
Among the Lycians in the men category, wrestling,
The Dieia in Tralles in the men category, wrestling
The Romaia in L. . . . (*SEG* 22: 350)

There are two distinct parts to this inscription. The first column details the achievements in the periodic games, the second in other local games. The Olympic Games are named first because of their prestige, yet the inscription is divided by and large chronologically. Leon participated as a child and youth in the Isthmian and Nemean Games and completed the *periodos* only once, starting as a child and finishing as an adult. Another inscription calls him Achaean, so perhaps this is an indication that children tended to compete in the games closer to their homes and later on moved to participate at further distances (*SEG* 25: 467 [1]). On the other hand, Argos was the organizer of the Nemean Games, but nevertheless, Leon did not participate (or at least did not win) in the Heraia in Argos until he was an adult. Obviously, there were more than geographical reasons to the choice of competitions. He could have participated in less significant local games, but his debut at the periodic games indicates that he was already at a high level of training at a young age. Whereas Leon repeated his participation at the other three periodic games, he either did not repeat the Olympics or he did not achieve victory at them again. Although we do not possess dates for the victories mentioned in the inscription, it seems that the periodic games were a category of their own.

The next notable thing is that, as a child and youth, Leon doubled up in wrestling and the pancratium, whereas as an adult he tried this only twice, in Nemea and at the Theophaneia in Chios.[17] Many boxers and wrestlers competed in the pancratium. This was probably due to a difference in style of the pancratium, where some athletes would be more inclined to use wrestling techniques and some others would be more inclined to use boxing ones, similarly to modern ultimate fighting. Although he might have kept

---

17. The Theophaneia had children's contests as well, as attested in the *Sylloge Inscriptionum Graecarum* (*SIG*) 1064.

participating in both disciplines, Leon may have realized that he had better chances of winning by specializing in one sport, namely, wrestling. By contrast, Dorieus combined boxing and the pancratium throughout his career at the three complete runs at the periodic games, winning both events only at one Isthmian Games. He won at Olympia in the pancratium, whereas all his other victories, except the double one, were in boxing. Perhaps he participated in both events, perhaps not, but certainly he was able to alternate more successfully than Leon.

A third inscription dated to 221–216 helps clarify the progressive specialization of athletes in Hellenistic times. The inscription reads as follows:

> Callistratus Philothaleus
> In the children category: The Basileia, wrestling
> The Lycaia, pancratium
> The Isthmia, pancratium
> The Panathenaea, boxing
> The Nemea, boxing
> The Asclepeia, pancratium
> The Naa, wrestling and boxing and pancratium
> The Rhieia, wrestling and boxing and pancratium
> The Isthmia in the youth and men categories, boxing
> In the same Isthmian
> The Nemea, pancratium
> The Nemea, pancratium
> The Nemea, boxing and pancratium in the same Nemea
> The Isthmian, boxing
> The Pythian, boxing
> The Lukaia, boxing twice
> ... And boxing and pancratium
> Thonias, son of Teisicrates, did it. (*IG* 4 428)

Callistratus was short of the Olympic Games to become *periodonikēs*. However, his record is otherwise very impressive. He participated in many contests as a child, which indicates that he was introduced to competition rather early. As a child he won festivals in all three heavy disciplines. As a youth and adult man, he focused only on two, the pancratium and boxing, unless the last line of his exploits contained a victory in wrestling that is now lost. Callistratus's career exemplifies two things especially: first, the early introduction of children to competitive sport, not just in local games, and second, the move toward specialization at least at the start of the adult career. This coincides with Leon's career path.

2.2 ✍ Specialization in Athlete Development

We read some pages above about how Aristotle considered the ideal age to start rigorous training to be about three years past puberty, so that bodily exercises may not hinder the physical and mental development of youth. The immediate context was Aristotle's attempt to distinguish Athenian education from the Spartan model, which, according to him, made the children animal-like. Aristotle also rejected other models that "train their children in athletics to the exclusion of other necessities," thereby making the children vulgar and useless for the state (*Politics* 1338b). It is well known that the Spartan educational system (*agōgē*) separated the children from their parents at the age of seven and, through very tough physical work and competition among peers, prepared them to be Spartan soldiers.[18] Aristotle pointed out that the Spartans used to surpass others not because they trained their youth in a specific way, but because they were the only ones who trained, whereas their opponents did not (*Politics* 1338b).

If we read Aristotle in modern terms, his rejection of the Spartan system corresponds to most Western countries' rejection of training systems used by totalitarian states.[19] In the former Soviet Union and its satellites, and still in China, athletes were considered a kind of elite among the rest of the citizens,[20] since their victories were used to advertise the supposed superiority of their societies.[21] On the other hand, athletes were seen as disposable once their careers were finished.[22] From a very young age, athletes were given

---

18. Kennell 1995: 5–27.

19. Early specialization also occurs in the Western world with some sports, but what characterized the totalitarian regimes was the use of the early specialization model even in those sports that qualify as late specialization ones, such as the Greek sports were.

20. Riordan (1993: 36) explains how top athletes received two or three times the salary of the average working man.

21. Riordan quotes the chairman of the USSR Committee on Physical Culture and Sport as saying, "Once we decided to take part in foreign competitions, we were forced to guarantee victory" (ibid., 26).

22. "According to the *China Sports Daily*, nearly 80% of China's 300,000 retired athletes are struggling with joblessness, injury or poverty. Many athletes suffer from sports injuries and health problems caused by their training. [Chinese Olympic weightlifter] Zou came out of the system with her own appalling legacy. She says the pills she was required to take made her grow a beard and develop a prominent Adam's apple and a deep voice. 'My coach told me it was a nutrition booster. I trusted him,' Zou says. The steroids also made her infertile" (Xu 2007).

performance-enhancing drugs without any consideration for their future health.[23] Although Sparta did not have the actual means to enhance the performance of their athletes artificially, its children were subjected to a very rigorous training from very early on to the detriment of any other development. According to Aristotle, the fact that Spartans were successful in athletics in the first two hundred years of Olympics was due to the fact that they were the only ones training. Once other *poleis* developed their own training systems, the number of Spartan victories decreased. In fact, between 720 and 580, from the seventy-one victories known to us in the different disciplines, forty-three were Spartan. This is about 60 percent of all victories of the Olympics. From 580 to 400, the percentage of Spartan athletic victories fell to less than 5 percent.[24] From 316 B.C. to 393 A.D., there are only nine Spartan victories attested.[25] There are political, historical, and ideological reasons to explain this decline besides the purely athletic ones.[26] Yet, Aristotle focuses mostly on the athletic reasons by pointing out inadequacies of the Spartan system. Instead, he proposes a system of training that is largely applied nowadays in most Western countries.

Although one cannot be sure, the patterns exhibited by the careers of Hellenistic and Roman imperial athletes might also indicate a change in the training system, one employing not only a proactive strategy but also earlier training for success.[27] All ancient Greek sports fall under what are today called late specialization sports. Late specialization sports are those which admit developing sport-specific skills only after puberty. In these late specialization sports, as opposed, for instance, to modern gymnastics, coaches are cautious about developing the muscles of children too early because this

---

23. Riordan (1993: 38) explains how in the former communist bloc children as young as seven or eight were given drugs manufactured and distributed by the state to enhance their performance.
24. Mann 2001: 121–23.
25. Scanlon 2002: 80.
26. See Mann 2001: 143–62.
27. The most explicit ancient source for the study of training methods are found in Philostratus's work *On Gymnastics*. There he examines what we would today call cross-training (43) and the "tetrad system," which can be described as interval training over a period of four days (47). Lucian discusses running on sand and with weights to strengthen the muscles (*Anacharsis* 27). Modern scholars discuss training in theoretical terms, such as Kyle (1987: 141–42), where he distinguishes the *paidotribēs* from the *gymnastēs*. König (2005: 306–15) also mentions the distinction between the two practitioners and discusses the role of medicine in training. Harris (1964: 170–78) acknowledges that training necessitates the teaching of technique, physical fitness, and mental preparation. He recognizes that massages might have been an important part of the training. He also comments briefly on the fact that the *Hellanodikai* (judges) at Olympia may not have followed the tetrad and may have obliged the athletes to train according to their methods.

would have negative consequences in the long term for the athletes' careers.[28] By the time the young athletes are in their late teens, training becomes more strenuous, usually when athletes have completed their physical growth and are ready to concentrate on competition.[29] One of the consequences that early specialization may have is that athletes burn out rather quickly and desist from pursuing the sport. This was the same in the past as it is today. Aristotle observed that only in a very few cases did children who won at the Olympics continue to have successful careers as adults. He attributes this fact to the children being "robbed of their strength" (*dynamis*). But the word *dynamis* in Aristotle also implies potentiality or capacity. Thus, the implication is that subjecting children to a strict training very early on robs them not only of their physical strength but also of a future ability to be successful in the sport. This assertion of Aristotle is, by and large, correct. We know of a few young athletes who won as children and had successful careers as adults.[30] During the archaic period, Hipposthenes of Sparta had an Olympic victory in wrestling as a boy in 632 and continued to win for the next five Olympics. This brings his total years of competition to about twenty, from an approximate age of 14 to 34. His son Hetoimocles also won as a child in 592 and had four successive Olympic victories as an adult. Like his father, he competed

---

28. LTAD (Long Term Athlete Development) is a Sport Canada initiative started in 2004 and implemented at the federal and provincial levels. It sets out "a progressive pathway that recognizes the distinct phases of physical, mental, cognitive and emotional development based on the maturation or development of an individual rather than chronological age. The Canadian Sport for Life model identifies the needs of athletes at various stages of their development, including coaching, training, equipment, and competition needs. It addresses the appropriate stages for the introduction and refinement of technical, physical, mental and tactical skills" (Canadian Sport for Life 2019). The LTAD is promoted by the Canadian Sport for Life association. Their website has this description of the LTAD: "Canadian Sport for Life (CS4L) is a movement to improve the quality of sport and physical activity in Canada. CS4L links sport, education, recreation and health and aligns community, provincial and national programming. LTAD is a seven-stage training, competition and recovery pathway guiding an individual's experience in sport and physical activity from infancy through all phases of adulthood. CS4L, with LTAD, represents a paradigm shift in the way Canadians lead and deliver sport and physical activity in Canada" (Canadian Sport for Life 2019).

29. "Specialization occurs when an athlete chooses to train and compete in one or two sports exclusively. Specialization is inevitable and necessary for athletes who want to become high performers in their sport, but it must occur at the right age for the athlete to be successful. Sports can be classified as either early or late specialization. Early specialization sports include artistic and acrobatic sports such as gymnastics, diving, and figure skating. These differ from late specialization sports in that very complex skills are learned before puberty since they cannot be fully mastered if taught after puberty. Most other sports are late specialization sports. If physical literacy is acquired before puberty, athletes can select a late specialization sport when they are between the ages of 12 and 15 and have the potential to rise to international stage in that sport. Specializing before the age of 10 in late specialization sports contributes to: One-sided, sport-specific preparation, lack of ABC's, the basic movement and sports skills, overuse injuries, early burnout, early retirement from training and competition" (Canadian Sport for Life 2019).

30. Papakonstantinou 2012: 125.

until his mid-thirties and for about twenty years. Assuming an age of 14 for Hetoimocles's first victory, this bring us to his birth in about 606, six years after his father's retirement from athletic competition at the Olympics of 612. On the other hand, we know about many more athletes who won as children but were unable to win as adults, such as Alcydamas, victor at the Nemean in 475. Even if we do not know the names of all Olympic victors, from those we know Moretti mentions eighty-nine child victors at the Olympic Games from its beginnings to 137 A.D. They competed in several sports. Out of these eighty-nine, only eight had victories as adults at the Olympics.[31] This is, less than 10 percent of them were able to become adult victors. This may not mean that they no longer competed, or that they did not win other local competitions and had, in this way, long athletic careers. But most of them did not repeat their success at the Olympics.

Furthermore, the percentage of those athletes who were victors of the *periodos* as adults and had also previous success as children increases in comparison to those athletes who were victors at only one game. The tables show that about 20 percent of the victors of the *periodos* in classical times had successful careers as children and adults, but the number increases to at least 30 percent during Hellenistic times. Victors of the *periodos* were no doubt exceptional athletes, and they would have been so probably since childhood, both in terms of physical and mental abilities. This could perhaps be the explanation for why there is more continuous success for them than for other athletes less talented, less focused, or perhaps less fortunate.

Athletes in the Hellenistic age after the 300s, but specially after the 240s and in Roman times, were successful at an early age, and then they disappeared from competition at the periodic games, some of them perhaps from competition altogether. The change, in comparison to the careers of the previous generations, may have been due to the fact that these young athletes specialized much earlier. As we saw, Aristotle advocated for late specialization in sports, that is, he championed a system that first develops athletic qualities in general before specializing into a sport. The role of the school system would have been, in fact, that of developing athletic qualities, whereas strict training and diet came later. On the other hand, early specialization occurs when athletes train in one sport to the exclusion of the others before puberty. Early specialization has the advantage that athletes peak earlier, but it hardly leads to a long-lasting career.

---

31. Moretti 1957.

As an example of how early an age Greeks may have started practicing sports, we can read the funerary stele for the eight-year-old boy Hermaeus, which describes the little boy as enjoying sports with other dead children:

> You shall not drink, Hermaeus, the drink of Lethe, nor will this tomb hide you, the house of hateful Persephone, but Hermes of beautiful ankles, having you by the hand, has led you to Olympus, drawing you away from the difficult life of mortals [drawing you away from the life of mortals]. Being eight years old you look at the aether and shine with the stars, going to the horn of the White Goat, now you appear as helper of the children in the strong palestras, the immortals pleasing you in this. (*Miletus* 462, unknown date, written in *koinē*[32])

The inscription may attest that children went into the routine of practicing sport very early, at least as early as eight years old if not earlier.[33] Certainly, it seems that little Hermaeus had a desire to practice athletics from very early on. Whether they specialized at an early age or not it is difficult to say.

An inscription of the second or third century A.D. from Macedonia commemorates the young Aelius Nepos, son of Abascas.

> To Aelius Nepos, Abascantus and Charis, on account of commemoration for the son. "What is your fatherland?" "This one" "Is your name Nepos?" "It is, from my father Abascantus. I became twelve." "What is the crown in the tomb?" "I became a victor not unlearned in pancratium and sacred wrestling. Having been crowned many times in my fatherland, before I dedicated to my parents the crowns, which now, being dead I took with me." (*IG* 10² 1 464)

Aelius Nepos was twelve years old when he died and had already won several crowns in his country, either in pancratium or wrestling. It seems that the young Aelius did not compete outside of his fatherland, but the inscription is certainly an indication that children did compete at a young age in later times.

Another inscription from Attica distinguishes between three groups of ages among the children. It is dated to the year ca. 130. Perhaps this

---

32. *Koinē* is the common or standardized Greek language that developed during the Hellenistic period as opposed to the local dialects spoken and written until then.

33. A look at Moretti 1957 is sufficient to demonstrate that children who won the Olympics came from all over the Greek world during archaic times. Certainly, there is a tendency to have victors coming from further away as time progressed; there seems to be a similar pattern for children and adults. See Bertolín 2002.

could also represent specialization at an earlier age. The inscription reads as follows:

> Greetings . . .
> Doro . . .
> The stadium for children of the first age:
> . . . Son of Timomaches from the Hippothontis tribe.
> The stadium for children of the second age:
> . . . Tonicus son of Dysnicetes from the Hippothontis tribe.
> The stadium for children of the third age:
> . . . son of Timocleus from the Erechtheis tribe.
> The stadium from all the children:
> . . . son of Ergochares from the Akamantis tribe.
> Men stadium:
> . . . son of Cleon from the Aigeis tribe.
> (IG 2² 964)

This inscription is not isolated. There are several inscriptions containing the same age divisions, which makes us think that there might have been an attempt, on the one hand, to make competition fairer by having children of different ages and physical development compete against each other. On the other hand, this might also be an indication of early specialization by separating children into sports from an early age. Interestingly, in wrestling, we have either two brothers of different ages or one boy competing in two age groups, which is probably unlikely. The competition may have been open to resident aliens, since the boy from Smyrna won the overall wrestling, or it may have been open to visitors. There is no indication about the possible age of the children of each category, but certainly if the children were between eight and seventeen years old, age and size diversity was mitigated by separating them into classes. We are ignorant as to whether these children just attended the regular training at the palestra, or whether more specialized training was provided for them. It also remains to be proven whether or not the children mentioned here reappear in some other piece of evidence, either in the same or different sport. So far, I have been unable to find any more evidence to that effect.

Besides starting early in competition, a second characteristic of early specialization would likely be early retirement. Continuing a career past its peak was perhaps not the best decision an ancient athlete could make. Ancient Greeks were not gracious to athletes who did not win, as we can read in Pindar: "When they [the losers] return to their mothers, sweet laughter does not arouse joy, they shrink from the enemies, keeping far away, through the back alleys, bitten by disgrace" (*Pythian Ode* 8. 85–87).

Although we do not have direct and specific evidence of the ancient *periodos* winners' training regime, we cannot just assume that they became so successful purely on their physical ability. These young athletes must have trained very intensively and single-mindedly from their early teens, or even childhood, in order to achieve such important results in such a small period of time. Continuous success implies continuous training, sometimes from a very young age. As we saw, this might have been the case of Asclepiades, who won the Nemean Games in the pancratium at twenty-two and completed the *periodos* by twenty-five in 181 A.D. We also know about Asclepiades that his father Demetrius was also a victor of the *periodos* in wrestling. This would imply, at least, that Asclepiades came from a family of highly athletic people and had some type of natural abilities. But success at such a young age also implies training at a young age.

A system that creates athletes who are consistently successful at a very young age just does not happen without a change in training techniques. We need to assume a shift from the traditional way of training based on late specialization to a new way of training based on models of early specialization beginning in Hellenistic times and especially in Roman imperial times. There are two examples that seem to be important to explain the shift. First, we have the boxer Glaucus of Carystos, who won his first Olympics in 520 and perhaps also in 508 and 504, although it is not clearly attested. According to some, Glaucus went straight into the Olympic Games when he was about eighteen. His father saw him fix a plough with a punch of his bare hands and then brought him to the games.[34]

> There Glaucus, inexperienced in boxing, was wounded by his opponents, and when he was boxing with the last of them he appeared to be fainting from the number of his wounds. Then they say that his father called out to him, "Son, the plough touch." So he dealt his opponent a more violent blow which then brought him the victory. (Pausanias 6.10.2)

---

34. Olympic athletes had to spend a month training in Elis, but they also had to swear that they had been training for ten months previously (Pausanias 5.24.9–10), so Glaucus might have been a beginner, but not totally unacquainted with boxing.

After this first success, Glaucus went on to have a long and successful career, winning the periodic games up to three times. He would have acquired technique as he went along. In contrast to Glaucus, we have Cleoxenus of Alexandria, who was proclaimed victor of the *periodos* in 240. He completed the *periodos* in record time between 242 and 240. We do not have any information about him participating in sport after this. The main difference between him and Glaucus is that he is described as being "not wounded" (*atraumatistos*). There is an implication here that his technique in defense was superior to the others. Or, this may only indicate two different styles of boxing. But besides fighting style, the contrast of the two boxers indicates a change in the approach to training. Glaucus was allegedly untrained in his first Olympics, but Cleoxenus carefully trained and planned his performance to be able to succeed in the *periodos* in the least amount of time possible.

Aristotle directed his advice about training hard after puberty to the education of free citizens. Rules on participation at the Olympics included the restriction that participants must be Greek, free males. This restriction has commonly been interpreted from a social point of view; it was a way to separate Greeks from non-Greeks and from slaves. However, if we take this restriction from the point of view of sport and training, it actually is a very positive one. Having in mind Aristotle's model of late specialization, the fact that the athlete is a free man implies that the state does not have the power to turn children into "medal-making machines," as is the case with totalitarian regimes, which see athletes as their property and allow coaches to destroy character and reshape it. This makes the athletes, who are specialized into sport at a very early age, instruments of the state. Free societies that see their athletes as free men do not propose, in general, a very early specialization but see sport as a part of human development.[35]

One can assume that there was a change in the way of training not just from the results of the victors of the *periodos*, but also by consulting sources like Philostratus's *On Gymnastics*. In this work, Philostratus attempts to separate the art of training from medicine and other arts. He also compares training in former times and his own times. Although one does not gain the impression that Philostratus actually knew much about sport, he nevertheless makes some observations about the change that took place since the classical

---

35. One has to be very careful in assuming that athletes in Hellenistic times belonged to lower classes and might have been, therefore, more susceptible to being manipulated by the cities into risking their health and future in order to gain fame and social mobility early on. There is clear evidence that elite athletes kept participating at all times. See Pleket 2005: 153.

period of Greece. His explanations are not always clear, but he is attempting to explain what he considers a decline in athletics, even if athletes seem more successful than in previous times. His explanations are sometimes confusing and not without prejudice, as is common in authors of the Second Sophistic who express dissatisfaction with the present.[36] He acknowledges right at the beginning of the work that there was what he calls an "old gymnastic" and a new one. He writes, "The [gymnastic] of the times of our forefathers knew many lesser athletes, but also amazing ones and worthy of remembrance. The gymnastic practiced now *has changed* in such a manner the things of the athletes that the majority of people despise those who love gymnastics" (1).[37]

The implication of his words is that in former times (and he mentions Milo and Glaucus, athletes of the end of the sixth century, and Polydamas from the end of the fifth) there were many athletes that were not as successful as the ones in his times, although he still perceives his times as a decline and blames this on the lack of healthy training and strong exercises (Philostratus, *On Gymnastics* 3). He decries professionalization in the sense that the athletes are not accustomed to hard work and simple meals (43), and that they even buy and sell victories for money and are not concerned about glory (45). After talking about the origin of the different events at Olympia, and many other things such as the ideal physiognomy of the athlete (25–40), toward the end of the treatise (46) Philostratus mentions that one mistake that the coaches of his time make is that they train the young athlete (*pais*) as if he were an adult (*anēr*) and subject him to the same regime of training.

> But they also make the following mistake: they strip and train a boy athlete as if he were a grown man, urging him to overload his stomach beforehand, and to walk away in the middle of his training, and belch in a hollow manner. In this way just like poor teachers, they rob the boy of his youthful liveliness and train him in habits of indolence, procrastination, sluggishness, and in the habit of being less daring than his youth would warrant. Exercise should be used here just as in the palestra. (Philostratus, *On Gymnastics* 46)

Philostratus does not have anything good to say about this system. He describes it in very negative terms, as a system that robs the child of his

---

36. Bowie 1970: 3–41.
37. The majority of people did not despise gymnastics. Philostratus is referring to the criticism of the intellectuals of his time, spearheaded by Galen. See König 2009: 253, 267.

youthful desire to move and produces the opposite. Sluggishness and lack of fun in the activity may be a sign of burnout.[38] Philostratus explained in paragraphs 43 and 44 that athletes changed from warriors to those not useful for war, from full of energy to lazy, and from hardy to weaklings. He attributes this to the influx of luxury in athletes' lives. He claims that, in former times, athletes were able to compete for eight or nine Olympics because they alternated training with military service. As we have seen from the list of victors of the *periodos*, eight or nine Olympics is a clear exaggeration. Milo participated in seven and retired after being defeated by his younger countryman. But it is nevertheless remarkable that many of them had careers that spanned close to twenty years, whereas later athletes had much shorter careers.

How can we read Philostratus? As I mentioned above, he does not seem to understand athletics very well, but he observed some changes in training and some behaviors for which he attempts to account.[39] Philostratus attributes what he considers to be the decline of athletics to a change of diet. Yet, more food alone cannot be the reason for the decline of athletics. On the contrary, it should explain the success of more athletes. Philostratus was the first to acknowledge that, in earlier times, there were many athletes that were not as good. He uses the comparative "lesser," which would imply the athletes of his times as a reference point. A way we can read Philostratus is that he considers the athletes of his times to be better in general but having shorter careers owing to luxury in food and relaxation of general practices. Before exercising, these athletes would be full of food, "just as Libyan or Egyptian flour sacks." This would fall under the category of decline.

Although eating more, and perhaps more protein, would have produced much heavier and more muscular athletes, Philostratus still notices that this somehow robs the strength of nature, and that these practices are taking away from nature (*On Gymnastics* 2). Although Philostratus promises to go into the reasons for this, he never does so, at least not in a systematic way. He opposes the hardiness and energy of former athletes to the complacency of those in his times. Obviously, he sees former athletes as participating in the cities' life, especially the military, whereas athletes of his times keep away

---

38. "Burnout . . . is thought to occur when children lose interest as a result of specializing in a particular sport at a very early age and practicing for long hours under intense pressure for several years" (Weinberg and Gould 2011: 524).

39. König (2009: 277, 282) explains that Philostratus is polemicizing with the philosophers and scholars of his time, who despised athletics. He is trying to find a middle ground by acknowledging that there is a better way to train and practice athletics, namely, the one he proposes.

from any other activity. They just train and, when they are not training, eat. From the point of view of athletics, this is probably not bad at all. The success of many athletes nowadays is due precisely to the fact that they have the ability to concentrate on their training without worrying about any other things. Of course, this was seen by the Greeks as an alienation from their civic duties. This would have been a valid criticism of athletes in the classical period, but it is, in a sense, a double standard toward athletes when expressed about Roman imperial times or even Hellenistic times, when civic duties were redefined in comparison to the time of the polis.

Because athletes were free to train and received better food than average, they were more successful. But how can we square this with Philostratus's remark that the nature of the former athletes was superior? Besides allowing for the idealization of the past, to me it is very clear that he sees this in terms of the duration of the careers, which is why he exaggerates the duration of the former athletes' careers (*On Gymnastics* 43). The next remarkable observation that Philostratus makes is that it seems to be a general practice of his time to train children as if they were adults. Although he only mentions the eating, belching, and relaxation part, it is to be assumed that children participated in training as much as the adults. Philostratus observes that the general desire for movement is taken away from the children trained in this manner, the same remark that Aristotle had made. The shortness but intensity of the careers coupled with the fact that children are trained as adults is indicative, in my opinion, of a system based on early specialization. Because there was lot of money to be made in athletics, athletes were trained very hard from a very young age, even with the possible consequence of a short career. Athletes trained so hard would be in constant need of massage and relaxation, which would no doubt contribute to the perception of them as lazy and weak. Wine was also a natural painkiller and muscle relaxant. Athletes were seen drinking wine at all times, and this did not contribute to their reputation, either.

These athletes planned their training and competition schedule very carefully. Asclepiades participated in thirty-four games in only six years, that is, five to six games per year. Some of the games were geographically very far away, from Ephesus to Rome. This implied that he had to account for travel time and training in between competitions. When he was not competing, he was getting ready to compete, and this implied rest and massages as well.

For Philostratus, the movement necessary for children was that practiced at the palestra (*On Gymnastics* 46). With this he is probably returning to the system of training proposed by Aristotle that did not recommend hard training until after puberty, although sports were an integral part of children's education. On the other hand, Aristotle's society was a different one, and its athletes were considered free citizens. By restricting participation to only Greeks, the Greeks were looking for a contest among equals, or equally minded free citizens.[40]

In summary, we can observe that athletes in the Hellenistic and Roman imperial times planned their performance in the *periodos* carefully. It took them perhaps only two or three years to complete it. Whether this was the beginning of their careers or a glorious end to them, it is not possible to say. We find indications of both, although I am inclined to see the *periodos* as a starting point. We have some information about some athletes having more victories beyond the *periodos*. Many of these athletes belonged to associations, which implies that they were professionals and probably competed all over the Mediterranean. Many retired to work in the baths of the emperors and created their own schools of athletics. When we have some figures for their age, it is clear that they completed the *periodos* by their early twenties. In classical times, completion of the *periodos* and retirement age seem to coincide and were placed at the late twenties to mid-thirties.

Periodic games still brought fame and glory, but the many other games brought enormous amounts of money. The proliferation of games turned the *periodos* into just some games among many others. In classical times there were also many games, but the fame of the *periodos* was superior to the others. This may be a reason why athletes active during the fifth and fourth centuries concentrated their careers around the *periodos*, but not those athletes active later. At any rate, whether the *periodos* lost its prestige or was not as appealing because of the lack of monetary rewards and was just seen as initiation into professional sport, the systematic completion of the *periodos* in the shortest time possible—not by one, but by many athletes after the 240s—indicates that something is going on. To me there is a careful planning in the careers of these athletes. Their early success is also indicative of early specialized training.

---

40. Sparta stopped competing in gymnic events rather early, as their system constrained more and more individual freedom. Horse events were popular in Sparta in the fifth and fourth centuries as means of aristocratic display. See Mann 2001: 121–63.

3

The Role of Genetics

It is obvious for anyone who is involved in sport, whether as either an athlete or a coach, that not every person has the same natural capabilities to achieve success. Some people are born with a physique that makes them more apt to the practice of sports, either in general or with regard to a specific one. The Greeks were also aware that natural differences existed among the athletes themselves and between the athletes and the general population. In this chapter, we will look at different ways by which the Greeks came to terms with the fact that, independent of training, some athletes were clearly superior in their nature.

The emphasis on innate talent is also making a comeback in our days. For instance, a recent book by David Epstein[1] moves away from the popular rule of "10,000 hours" of practice in order to master a skill and introduces the question whether "sports genes" exist at all. Epstein acknowledges that nature and nurture are always intertwined when it comes to athletic performance, but throughout the book he brings examples of athletes to highlight what genetic characteristics make them special, whether height, specific types of muscle fibers, higher concentration of red cells, better response to training, or ability to endure pain. The author infers that it is impossible to pinpoint a priori specific sets of genes that would make athletes superior to their peers, since the genetic factor is only revealed by science after the fact that an individual athlete has become successful. Nevertheless, Epstein concludes that genetics are an important factor in the success of elite athletes, although, oftentimes, scholars shy away from addressing it because of fear

---

1. Epstein 2013.

of being labeled as racist or discriminatory. On the other hand, the genetic factor is often present in popular thinking. For instance, the 1992 movie *White Men Can't Jump* highlights racial stereotypes in relation to sport. In it, the protagonist (played by Woody Harrelson) allows black men to assume that they are better basketball players because of their race only to make them lose a bet afterward.

3.1 Eugenics

Like the characters in the movie, ancient Greeks were not uncomfortable with recognizing genetic variants in their athletes and assuming that a person's physique corresponded to his athletic abilities. Some of these abilities were already attributed to the nature of the parents. Philostratus writes the following:

> 26. After I have expressed myself in such a way, let us not consider that exercising follows next, but rather the stripping of the athlete and an examination of his nature, in which way it is constituted and for which purpose . . .

> 27. Certainly, there is also an even older consideration than this one, which also seemed good to the Spartan Lycurgus. For, in order to groom for Sparta athletes for war, he said, "Let the girls exercise, and let them be allowed to run in public. No doubt, this is for the sake of having good children and for the sake of giving birth to better offspring by strengthening the body. . . . And if she is married to a young man who is also an athlete she will produce better offspring, for they will be of good size, strong and without disease." Sparta became so great in warfare because their marriages were handled in such a way.

> 28. Since, therefore, it is appropriate to start from the birth of a person, let the coach go to the boy athlete, examine him first concerning his parents, whether they were young when they married and flawless and free from diseases, as many as affect the nervous system, the seat of the eyes or are common in the ears or the internal organs. . . . It is necessary to "wing" a valid procedure according to which by looking at a naked athlete it seems to us that we are not ignorant about the nature of his parents and how it affects him. The reasoning is difficult

and not at all simple, but it is not beyond the art. And so I will make it known. (*On Gymnastics* 26–28)

Philostratus tries to put a method forward that would allow any coach to determine the athletic ability of a young athlete, perhaps in an attempt not to waste the coach's time and energy if the boy does not have a chance to make it to the crown events. Philostratus selects the children of youthful parents since they would be tall, strong, and resistant to disease and presumably more skilled in comparison to their peers. Interestingly, there is a degree of improvisation needed when the parents are unknown. On the other hand, Philostratus advocates continuing to train even those athletes who seem less talented or are born from elderly parents by using what he calls flattery and what we would perhaps call positive reinforcement. His observations perhaps coincide with the modern distinction between talent selection and talent detection or identification.[2] Talent selection refers to the task of identifying athletes that are already practicing the sport or competing at a high level in order to promote their skills at an even higher level. Talent detection does not rule out those athletes that are less developed at a certain stage, yet it encourages them to participate in those sports in which they are more likely to succeed. Whereas Philostratus does not think that children born of elderly parents should be trained in combat sports, he still wants to train them, presumably in the other sports.

> 29. I have shown what kind of offspring will be produced by flawless origins and youth of the parents. The offspring of parents of advanced age can be identified in this way: Their skin is delicate, their collarbones are hollow like cups, their veins stick out like the veins of those who have exerted themselves, their hips are not harmonious and their muscles weak. One can examine them further while in training. . . . And I do not consider them worthy at all of athletic contests—for they are not strong with regards to manliness—and especially not for pancratium and boxing. For they are easily wounded by blows and hits, since they are not strong with regards to their skin. Nevertheless, they should be trained, yet they have to be flattered by the coach, since they need this when they work out and train. (*On Gymnastics* 29)

---

2. Anshel and Lidor 2012.

What may seem to us a rather primitive method of determining the athleticism of a person by observing the nature of the parents has evolved into a much more complex, yet not less unreliable, method. Scientists have developed ways to map 200 human genes that are associated with athletic performance. Yet, since humans have about 20,000 genes, it is hard to believe that we might be able to map all genes involved in athleticism. Equally, trainers have created tests to determine athletic ability, like the vertical jump test used to measure the power output. Another test measures the distribution of muscle and fat in the body, and still others measure the ability to recover after exercise and the maximal oxygen uptake (VO_2 max). Yet at the end of the day, trainers recognize that one needs to take all these tests with a grain of salt, especially when there is no clear definition of what constitutes athleticism. There are many variants in the measurement of athleticism, such as power, reaction time, ability to recover, or ability to adapt and assess the environment.

On the other hand, looking at the parents' athletic ability is still something that is practiced in our days.[3] One extreme case would be that of the Chinese basketball player Yao Ming. Yao is 2.29 meters tall. His parents were both professional basketball players; the father was 2.01 meters tall, and the mother 1.91 meters. In 2005, a book appeared claiming that Chinese officials had tracked Yao's family for three generations[4] and that his parents were "strongly encouraged" to marry each other. Although Yao's height is great even by basketball standards (for a comparison, Michael Jordan stands at 1.98 meters), nevertheless his years at the professional level were plagued by injuries, which brought his career to a comparatively early retirement. This proves that genetic engineering does not always guarantee continuous athletic success.[5]

3.2 Physiognomy

Besides the strictly eugenic factor, another predictor of athleticism was and still is the selection of athletes because of their body types. In antiquity, interest in

---

3. For genetic inheritance in Greek athletes, see Pomeroy 1997: 85–98.
4. Larmer 2005: 4.
5. There is no doubt that Yao Ming was a successful athlete. He was one of the top scorers of his time, but his career spanned only eight seasons, whereas the top fifty scorers over a lifetime in basketball have or have had careers of about twenty years, during which they have played anywhere from 1,000 to 1,500 games. Yao played only 486. On the other hand, Shaquille O'Neal played 1,207 games during his nineteen years in the NBA. Michael Jordan, who retired after fifteen seasons for reasons outside of his basketball skills, played 1,072 games.

physiognomics ("interpreting character from personal appearance")[6] started already with Aristotle, perhaps going back to Hippocrates or even Pythagoras. But, it is during the Second Sophistic, that is, the second century of the Christian era and the time of Philostratus, when physiognomy became very popular. Physiognomy involved not only the comparison between different human beings but also the comparison between human beings and animals, creating a transference of qualities so to speak between species according to looks. In the next section we will consider the relation between athletes and animals, but first let us discuss briefly the use of physiognomy applied to athletics. Philostratus discusses it in paragraphs 31 to 36 of his *On Gymnastics*.

Philostratus's use of physiognomy has to be put in the context of the general interest of physiognomy for Greek writers. A short treaty called *Physiognomics* attributed to Aristotle, but most likely not his work, describes three traditional methods by which one can interpret character through physique (*Physiognomics* 805a).[7] The first method is to assume one body type for an animal and, if a person matches it, then to assume the same character for both the animal and the person. The second method is to divide human beings according to race and perform what we would call nowadays racial profiling whereby the character of a person depends on whether he is an Egyptian, a Thracian, or a Scythian. The third method is to observe separate physical characteristics and make them correspond to specific character traits. The author of the treatise cautions against the improper use of the first and third methods (805b–6 a) and does not discuss the second method at all in the first part of the treatise. He is conscious that one ought to limit the signs that one needs to observe (806a), but on the other hand, it is the agreement of several of the signs (whether movements, shapes, colors, growth of hair, smoothness of the skin, parts of the body, and so on) that makes an inference true (807a).

The new method that the author of *Physiognomics* proposes for the study of physiognomy is not to make assumptions for the whole of humankind, but to divide humans into specific categories like the brave man, the coward, the easy-going, the insensitive man, and so on (807a–8b). Thus, by using a combination of inductive and deductive methods, one can single out certain traits that reveal specific characters.

6. Evans 1950.
7. Evans 1969: 5.

66   CHAPTER 3

The second part of the treatise (probably originally an independent one imperfectly attached to the first part)[8] deals with the comparison between humans and animals (808b–10a) and then with the meaning of specific human physical traits, such as having thin lips, hairy legs, or fat around the belly (810b–14b). This part of the treatise is less developed and less well argued than the first one, and it goes into some of the mistakes that the first part warned about.

The "science" of physiognomy was well established by the time of Aristotle, and it was certainly practiced by several of Philostratus's contemporaries, such as Galen (†200 A.D.) or philosophers and historians of the previous generation, such as Polemo of Ionia (88 to 145 A.D.) and Suetonius (69 A.D. to after 122 A.D.). Philostratus himself was influenced by physiognomic analysis in his work *The Lives of the Sophists*.[9] On the other hand, I believe that it is an innovative approach by Philostratus to apply physiognomic signs to athletic body types and not to characters. Philostratus is concerned mostly with optimal performance when he describes body types. Certainly, later on he makes the typical comparison between animal and athlete to describe their character, but straight physical signs do not reflect the athletes' character as much as they should be a sign for their ability.

> 31. Let the athlete who competes in the pentathlon be heavier than the light athletes, and lighter than the heavy ones. Let him be tall, well-built, and stand erect, without superfluous muscles but not underdeveloped either. Let him have long legs rather than well-proportioned and his loins should be flexible and move easily because of the turning for the javelin and the discus and also because of the long jump; . . .
>
> 32. The athlete who will be best at the long-distance running should be strong in the shoulders and neck like the pentathlete, but he should have lean and light legs like stadium runners. . . .
>
> 33. . . . The strongest stadium runners—which is the lightest of all the contests—are well-proportioned, but even better than these are those who are not excessively tall but a little bit taller than the well-proportioned. For excessive height damages stability, just as plants which have grown too tall. Let them have a solid build, for the start

8. Ibid.
9. Evans 1941.

of a good running is a good stance. Their ideal body type should be this: the legs should be of equal width to the shoulders; the chest should be smaller rather than proportioned, and with good internal organs; the knees should be light, the shins straight, the hands above proportion. Let their muscles be proportioned, for excessive muscles are chains to speed. . . .

34. The boxer should have large hands and strong forearms, and upper arms which are not without robustness and strong shoulders and a high neck. Thick wrists are heavier for punching; those that are less thick are flexible and strike with ease. Let him also stand on firm hips, for the throwing of the hands brings the body out of balance, unless it is supported on firm hips. . . .

35. Let us go now to the wrestlers. The wrestler according to the norm should be tall rather than well-proportioned, but he should be built just as the well-proportioned athlete, without a high neck nor a neck which is sunk into the shoulders. (Philostratus, *On Gymnastics* 31–35)

Philostratus remains in the physical realm when he describes the ideal body types of athletes. This makes his reasoning much more modern and acceptable to us. We still assume that having the right body type for a particular sport is a good starting point. In fact, talent detection programs start by attempting to integrate body types to specific sports. Talent detection is a strategy used by "sporting bodies of governments that seek national and international status in competitive sport and apply scarce financial resources toward developing potential champion athletes."[10] Although some programs for athlete detection include psychological characteristics,[11] all of them include anthropometric, somatotyping, and physiological variables.[12] From this point of view, it is highly interesting that Philostratus uses physiognomy not to determine the character of the athletes, as was the common use of the "science" of his time, but to focus exclusively on the physical characteristics to detect the ideal athlete, or in his own words "how [the nature] is constituted and for what it is suited."

---

10. Anshel and Lidor 2012: 241.
11. Ibid. The use of psychological measures to determine the potential of young athletes has been called into question because they may depend more on the influence of the coach than on the young athlete's personality.
12. Agdebesan et al. 2010.

On the other hand, Philostratus also expresses cautionary remarks toward believing that one body type is necessarily better than another, since one can find many contradictory assertions in this regard (*On Gymnastics* 42). He concludes the passage on physiognomy with a short discussion on how to train the athletes according to their humors. Choleric athletes are unproductive and come to ruin themselves because of their character. On the other hand, the phlegmatic ones need to be pushed to move as if with a goad. Inclusion of the humor theory within the theory of physiognomy is a reflection of more elaborate theories, such as Galen's,[13] but also reflects that physiognomy was primarily tied to revealing one's personality traits.

3.3 The Athlete as Freak of Nature

When Philostratus wants to discuss the personality of an athlete, he does so by comparing animals and athletes, the more traditional use of physiognomy. He distinguishes between the lion, the eagle, and the bear types.

> 37. Those resembling lions have a good chest and strong arms but are rather deficient at the back. The eagle type is similar in shape to these but hollow in the groins just as the eagle is when in upright position. Both of these types appear daring, vehement, impetuous, but lose heart at any failure, which should not surprise us if we think of lions and eagles. . . .
>
> 40. Those similar to bears are rotund, flexible, corpulent, less articulated, and stooped over rather than straight, hard to wrestle with, slipping out of holds and strong on evading. And these athletes retch the breaths, just as bears do while running. (*On Gymnastics* 37–40)

Just as in the Homeric epics, animal characteristics describe not only physiological traits, but, more importantly, moral characteristics and mental or emotional states. There is a typological identification between the athlete and the animal. For instance, the lion type is daring but lacks mental strength and, presumably, would have a tough time winning a contest when coming from behind. He is the type of athlete that is very successful when things go well but loses confidence in front of a tough opponent. Philostratus does not need to explain why this is so, neither does he offer a way to overcome

---

13. Evans 1941.

this shortcoming through psychological training. He seems to assume that this is the nature of the athlete as much as it is the nature of the animal. The athlete is compared to the animal in the physical aspect, but in the mental, the animal substitutes for the athlete.

Identification of an athlete with animal traits had been conducted for a long time, much earlier than when the "science" of physiognomy was established. Already Homeric heroes are likened to lions, stags, boars, bulls, even mules and donkeys. When Homer wants to intensify or clarify human action, he defers to the natural world. Comparisons with animals offer a view into the external characteristics of a hero but also represent the minds of men. Animal similes are not always positive. They also reflect the dichotomies of praise and blame present throughout the epics.[14] In book 23 of *The Iliad*, Panopeus and Euryalos box for a prize. Panopeus knocks out Euryalos, who is described in very visual terms like a fish that is thrown to the beach by a gust of wind (*Iliad* 23.692). The audience has a chance of imagining Euryalos convulsing before Homer continues describing how his friends carried him away unconscious. This is the only time in *The Iliad* and *The Odyssey* when an animal simile is used to describe an athletic event. The comparison is not positive, but certainly vivid.

Mythical heroes are able to move from the divine to the animalistic in pursuit of their adventures. One of these heroes who changes from the animalistic to the divine to the purely human is Heracles, Greek hero par excellence. He covers himself with a lion's skin and relies heavily on his instincts. He eats, drinks, and has sex in excess but goes where no human being has gone before. Heracles is also the embodiment of the Greek athlete. His statue was often displayed at gymnasia, and he was famous for his athletic prowess. There is no wonder, then, that athletes saw him as a role model and placed their own limits in the mythical sphere. Just as for the heroes of old times, stories were created for athletes that distorted their humanity.

Milo is perhaps the most famous athlete in ancient Greece. Although he was by all accounts a historical figure, anecdotes about his proverbial strength were probably attached to him over the centuries. Thus, the lines between the myth and the reality were erased.[15] There are seven anecdotes about Milo that can be considered as demonstrations of his strength;[16] for

---

14. Buxton 2004: 144–45.
15. See Roubineau 2016.
16. Roubineau (2016: 84–95) discusses how these anecdotes signal a progressive consolidation of training exercises as the concept of physical education emerged at the end of the sixth century B.C.

instance, Milo was said to be able to hold a pomegranate in his hand without damaging it while challengers tried to pry open his fingers. Another anecdote says that he was able to stand on an oiled discus and no one could push him down. Yet another anecdote tells how Milo carried a bull on his shoulders into the Olympic stadium and then ate it all by himself.[17] His gluttony, as that of Heracles, was proverbial, and it made him equal to an animal more than a human being. Roubineau explains that this particular anecdote also symbolizes Milo's exceptional position within the community, since the eating of the bull was part of a communal sacrifice, which Milo performed on his own.[18] Isolation within the community turns Milo into more of a mythical than a historic figure.

About one hundred years later, the athlete Polydamas tried to imitate not only Heracles but also Milo, who had become a hero in popular imagination. As in the case of heroes, athletes sought not only to emulate but also to surpass the feats of their predecessors. Because of this, Polydamas also behaved in an extraordinary, not entirely human way. Pausanias tells the story that, in imitation of Heracles, Polydamas killed a lion with his bare hands (6.5.4–9). Reputedly, Polydamas held a bull by its feet so tightly that the bull was able to escape only by leaving one of the hooves in Polydamas's hand. One ought to take these anecdotes with a grain of salt. Yet, they reflect the popular imagination about persons who were at the same time role models and difficult to emulate. The anecdotes conceive of the athlete as superhuman, having almost no limits.

For Polydamas, Milo, and other athletes the human measure was too small. They needed to be measured against the natural world, even if they failed. Anecdotes about their death emphasize this very clearly. Polydamas died when he tried to hold up a collapsing cave.[19] Apparently, he did so also in imitation of Milo, who actually managed to save his friends from a collapsing roof. Milo's death came when he got his hands stuck in a tree trunk and was devoured by wild beasts because he was not able to free himself.[20] In death as in life, these athletes found their match not with other human beings, but with the natural world. It could not be otherwise, since there were no other human beings stronger than these athletes.

17. Athenaeus 10.412F.
18. Roubineau 2016: 149.
19. Pausanias 6.5.8–9.
20. Pausanias 6.14.8

Pausanias tells us that the boxer Glaucus was believed to be descended from the sea-demon of the same name (6.10.1). This is an obvious construct of popular imagination, which tries to explain an athlete's success in terms of a special genetic gift, in this case monstrous ancestry. Nowadays, the success of certain athletes is partially explained by genetic predisposition.[21]

Most interesting is Pausanias's description of the Olympic winner Damarchus of Parrhasia who, despite Pausanias's disbelief, was thought to have spent nine years as a wolf before winning the crown. Pausanias writes, "Concerning the boxer, by name Damarchus, an Arcadian of Parrhasia, I have no confidence in what wandering poets say about him (except, of course, his Olympic victory), how he changed from a man into a wolf at the sacrifice of Lycaean Zeus, and afterwards in the tenth year he became a man again" (6.8.2).

Even if Pausanias rejects the legend of the werewolf, it was an extended belief that Arcadians who participated in the rites of Lycaean Zeus and ate human flesh were transformed into wolves (Plato, *Republic* 565d–e). What is important in the story is that popular belief made Damarchus both a wolf and a successful athlete. We know about one other similar story, that of Euthymus of Locroi Epizephyrioi (Pausanias 6.6.4–11). Euthymus's countrymen said that his father was not Astycles but the river Caecinus. Pausanias tells how Euthymus had won his competition in boxing and on the way back home fought a demon that demanded a beautiful woman each year to be sacrificed to him. Euthymus defeated the ghost and rescued and married the woman.

> This I heard, and I also happened to see such a picture. It was a copy of an ancient picture. There were a young man, Sybaris, a river, Calabrus, and a spring, Lyca. Besides, there were a hero-shrine and the city of Temesa, and between them was the demon that Euthymus cast out. Horribly black in color, and especially frightening in his appearance, he [Euthymus] had a wolf's skin thrown around him as outfit. The writing on the picture gave his name as Lycas. (Pausanias 6.6.11)

Euthymus is described in partial transformation into an animal or monster with a scary appearance and covered with a wolf skin. The name Lycas may also be related to his transformation into a wolf. Yet, the fact alone that he fights successfully with ghosts makes him something more than a man,

---

21. For instance, Michael Phelps's feet are not only very large, they also bend 15 degrees farther than other swimmers' feet. Thus, he can propel himself more strongly. This is always a controversial topic, because genetic predisposition can be understood as discriminatory racism.

someone who can move between the realms of man, animal, and spirit. The connection of athletes with werewolves should be no surprise since, for instance, a gymnasium in Athens was dedicated to Apollo Lycaeus, god of wolves, and there were also games in honor of Zeus Lycaeus.

An epigram attributed to Philippus also makes a comparison between the athlete, an animal, and a hero. It openly speaks about the athlete being more than a mortal. The epigram is composed in the first person, which implies that athletes may have seen themselves in such a light. It is not just a perception by others, but also one adopted by the athletes. The epigram reads as follows:

> Perhaps, O stranger, seeing me with a belly like a bull and with strong limbs like a second Atlas, you marvel, doubting if my nature is mortal. But know that I am Heras of Laodicea, a well-rounded fighter, crowned by Smyrna and the oak of Pergamon, by Delphi, Corinth, Elis, Argos, and Actium. But if you enquire also about my victories in other contests, you shall number also the sands of Libya.
> (*Greek Lyric Anthology* 16.52)

Not only in literature and the anecdotes is there a comparison with animals. Vases offer another source that juxtaposes the athlete to animals and even monsters. Monsters tend to be composite creatures in the Greek mind. Obviously, the Greeks thought about their famous athletes as some kind of genetic freaks, as figure 1 clearly shows. An unidentified long jumper is presented as half human, half bird and with the face of a lion. The implication is that the athlete is able to jump long because he flies like a bird. Although the vase is dated to the mid-fourth century, I believe that the popular conception of athletes as being half animals and half human beings is present earlier.

Not all artistic representations involving the combination of athletes and animals are as explicit, yet we can observe another similar juxtaposition between athletes, animals, and monsters. Figure 2 presents alternating images of animals and athletes on a vase or cup. The center of the tondo offers an image of a sphinx, a monster that is a composite of lion, eagle, and human being. Let us remark here that Philostratus deals with the lion type and the eagle type in the same paragraph, as if this athlete was in fact more of a sphinx type. The next row of the vase presents roosters and hens. The rooster is an animal that is often associated with athletes and adolescents.[22] Often on Panathenaic vases, the rooster stands on top of the columns that

---

22. Csapo 2006/2007.

Figure 1. Caricature of a long jumper: half human, half bird. Apulian miniature red-figure amphora, dated to mid-fourth century. Artifact held by The British Museum, London (F499). Drawn by the author based on a photograph taken by the author.

frame Athena. Roosters are also present as decoration in many other vases that depict athletes.[23] Roosters were not only fierce animals used in fights, they were also a typical gift among lovers. Perhaps then we should try to see the illustration of this vase not just as depicting competition among rivals but

23. Pausanias (6.26.3) describes roosters as very eager to fight.

Figure 2. Alternating images of animals and athletes. Athenian black-figure cup A, dated to between 550 and 500 B.C. Artifact held by the Antikensammlung, Staatliche Museen zu Berlin (F 1805). Drawn by the author after an image from the Beazley Archive, Classical Art Research Centre, Oxford (302814).

also as illustrating cooperation among equals. The next row depicts several groups of athletes: boxers, wrestlers, long distance runners and sprinters, jumpers, and javelin throwers. There are coaches or officials in between the athletes, separating the different events. Their presence signifies that this is possibly an organized sport contest. In the last row of the cup we can see some lions attacking a deer. There are also two sirens, monsters with the body of a bird and the head of a woman.

In the Homeric epics, the warrior was often compared to a marauding lion.[24] On this vase there seems to be a comparison between the athlete at a

---

24. Lonsdale 1990: 49–69.

contest and the lion. The presence of the mythical figures, such as the sphinx and the sirens, creates an association between the athlete and the heroes of old who battled these creatures. Whereas in the past the battle was against monsters, in the present, athletes have to battle each other. There is therefore a transfer of qualities from the hero to the athlete, but also from the monster opponent to the opponent athlete. Even Galen makes the comparison of athletes to animals, although in his case it is a negative one. In his *Exhortation to the Study of Medicine*, he asks who of the athletes could be stronger than lions or elephants or faster than a hare (9.15–25).

The athlete seems to thrive in the company of wild animals. As much as we see sport as a cultural and social phenomenon, the athlete remains an outsider. Public gymnasia in classical times were situated on the outskirts of the cities, and the young men in their twenties were not entirely full citizens since they had to be older to participate in political decision making. As much as there is an ambiguity in the social position of the athlete, the images and metaphors seem to indicate that there is ambiguity concerning the body of the athlete. His special achievements are something far from the ordinary man. This we saw in the anecdotes about Milo and Polydamas. Their strength, appetite, and courage remained unmatched. But human beings do not eat an entire ox, nor do they stop a chariot running at full speed, as one of the anecdotes claims, only animals and monsters do that. This concept is presented through the vases that parallel the athletes and their activities with the animals. It does not matter whether the athletes are wrestlers, jumpers, or runners, they all display, in a way, characteristics of animals.

But the vases go a step further. There is a comparison not only between the athlete and the animal but also another between the monster and the athlete. As in figure 2, where the central image was occupied by the sphinx, in other vases, athletes appear among griffins[25] and centaurs[26], giving the impression that they are close to this kind of composite being. On archaic vases one cannot make the distinction between primary and ornamental motifs. All motifs are equally important. The meaning is carried by the figure itself in relation to

---

25. See for instance the Athenian red-figure cup, dated to between 525 and 475 and held by the Munich Antikensammlung (J 1238).

26. See for instance the Athenian black-figure amphora B, dated to between 550 and 500 and held by the Paul Getty Museum (88.AE.24) in Malibu, California, and the Athenian red-figure cup A, dated to between 525 and 475 and held by the Toledo Museum of Art (63.28) in Ohio.

Figure 3. Athletes among griffins and centaurs. Athenian black-figure amphora, dated to between 575 and 525 B.C. Artifact held by The British Museum, London (B48). Drawn by the author after an image in the Beazley Archive, Classical Art Research Centre, Oxford (310069).

the other figures. The placement of the figure is what stresses this meaning. There is no distinction between real or imagined creatures.[27]

In other cases, we see perhaps a direct competition of an athlete and animal, as in figure 4, where a runner seems to be racing against a horse. The image of this vase is not isolated.[28] Whether a real or mythical contest, the image expresses the need of men to measure themselves against animals.

The image from an aryballos (or oil flask) recreated in figure 5 shows lions preying on a ram and another pair of lions preying on a bull in the lower level. The lions are placed directly under a pair of wrestlers and under a young man trying to tame some horses. The levels of meaning are multiple. The two wrestlers on the upper level can be seen as the lions. The animals fight among themselves in the lower part of the vase. The wrestlers fight themselves but are like the animals. Also, the young man taming the wild horses can be seen as a fight between man and animal, like the hunters in the lower level. Among the viewers of the action there are two winged figures. These winged

---

27. Isler-Kerenyi 1969: 11–14.
28. See for instance the Athenian black-figure cup, dated to between 550 and 500 and held by the Leiden Rijksmuseum van Oudheden (PC61).

Figure 4. A runner racing against a horse. Athenian black-figure cup fragment, dated to between 550 and 500 B.C. Artifact held by the Allard Pierson Museum, Amsterdam (2157). Drawn by the author after an image in the Beazley Archive, Classical Art Research Centre, Oxford (2759).

Figure 5. Lions preying on a ram and a bull juxtaposed with wrestlers and a young man taming horses. Athenian black-figure aryballos, dated to between 550 and 500 B.C. Artifact held by the Metropolitan Museum, New York (62.11.11). Drawn by the author after an image in the Beazley Archive, Classical Art Research Centre, Oxford (350480).

creatures might be monstrous or divine. They belong to a primeval world and are undefined. Sometimes they appear as bearded men, sometimes they have no beards, and sometimes they appear as women. There is an element of indetermination, which is not always positive.[29]

Perhaps these winged figures are the personification of the contest or *agon*. Winged figures often represent fighting, separation, and decision making.

29. Ibid., 17.

Figure 6. Winged figure, personification of a contest. Athenian red-figure amphora, dated to between 500 and 450 B.C. Artifact held by The British Museum, London (1928.1-17.56). Drawn by the author after an image in the Beazley Archive, Classical Art Research Centre, Oxford (204446).

For instance, winged figures like the goddess Eris (Strife) represent rivalry (or the decision to be made), but Nike and Iris represent the decision that has already been made.[30] There is no clear indication of what these winged figures could mean, but they should certainly be seen in context of other winged figures in vases that depict sports. The interpretation of the winged figures as the contest itself may not be far-fetched since we possess other images of the contest depicted also as a winged figure, that is, as the mixture of man and animal. For instance, this is shown in the illustration adorning a red-figure vase and recreated in figure 6.

Another source for identifying the animalistic character of the athletes is to look at the artistic depiction of the shields of the *hoplitodromoi* (athletes participating in the race with armor). Some shields bear images of other *hoplitodromoi*, other athletes, running legs, or vegetation motifs, but more often than not there are animals depicted on those shields: snakes, birds of prey, dogs, lions, scorpions, and even centaurs. If we understand the representation of athletes on the shields as mirror image of themselves—certainly layered

30. Ibid., 46–47.

Figure 7. Image on a shield, reflecting an athlete's character. Athenian black-figure amphora, dated to between 575 and 525 B.C. Artifact held by the Staatliche Antikensammlungen, Munich (J476). Drawn by author after an image in the Beazley Archive, Classical Art Research Centre, Oxford (310320).

in the image within an image—perhaps we could also understand the image of the animals and monsters as reflections of the character of the athletes that carry them. This is not an uncommon interpretation for shield devices. Aeschylus's tragedy *Seven against Thebes* identifies the warriors and their characters by the devices on their shields. The warriors themselves do not appear on stage. From verses 375 to 675 the messenger and Eteocles exchange words. The messenger explains who attacks each of the seven gates and what his shield device looks like. The messenger interprets the shield device as a pledge by the warrior to take the city. Yet, Eteocles explains it not in the way in which the warrior intended, but as referring to the warrior's own demise. Even if the interpretation of the signs can be ambiguous in terms of who is going to be actually destroyed, the basic idea of destruction is common to both interpretations. The same can be assumed for shield devices that athletes carry. Whether the shield shows an eagle or a lion or a pair of running legs, there is a basic representation of speed and fierceness that the *hoplitodromoi* want to appropriate for themselves and that others may attribute to them.

In figure 7, the runner on the right has an eagle as his shield device. Above the *hoplitodromoi* there is a man, perhaps Heracles, wrestling a lion.

This may imply that the runners see themselves also as heroes. Their feat is comparable to measuring themselves against animals. They also perceive themselves as such.

The vases show that animal metaphors are not only literary and do not only refer to heroes. Athletes, who can achieve heroic status, receive this characterization, which can be positive or negative, just as in the Homeric similes. By perceiving athletes as monsters or animal-like, the average Greek person somewhat justified his lack of athletic success. Who can compare to a freak of nature? This perception of the athlete eliminates the need for training and assuages the general population for not excelling in athletics as others do.

4

Nature versus Training

Today it is common to speak of both natural talent and hard work as two key elements of athletic success. As much as this assertion is unproblematic to us, it was, however, not as clear cut for the Greeks. It is not so much that they did not recognize the need to train hard in order to perform; in fact, some festivals like the Olympics demanded that athletes trained on site for a month and that they swore to have been training for at least nine months previously. Yet, natural talent or genetic superiority for sport was closely connected to an aristocratic ideology that focused around two basic tenets: always to excel and to be the best (*Iliad* 6.208). Whereas excelling often implied effort, being the best could be understood as being born the best. That is what kept the aristocracy a closed circle.

When aristocratic ideology was questioned, the issue of being born into a superior position demanded an explanation. This is why poets like Theognis of Megara (mid-sixth century) could contrast the raising of new generations with the breeding of animals. He complained bitterly about the aristocratic persons of his times marrying lowborn ones because of their money. We can read some of Theognis's complaints in his elegies:

> We seek out rams and donkeys and horses, Cyrnus, that are purebred and everyone wants to acquire (offspring) of good females; but a noble man does not mind marrying the ignoble daughter of an ignoble father if he gives him a lot of money, and a woman does not refuse to be the wife of an ignoble man if he is rich. She wants a wealthy man instead of a noble one. It is money people honor. The noble marries

the daughter of a base man and the base marries the daughter of a noble. Wealth has mixed up the race. (Theognis 183–90)

Incidentally, the expansion of wealth beyond the traditional landed aristocracy could be also an argument for the expansion of the practice of sport to the newly rich. It is, therefore, understandable that the traditional aristocracy sought to maintain the appearance of natural superiority. A way to do so was to attempt to suppress the role of coaches in the success of athletes. In this regard, Nicholson analyzed the treatment given in Pindar's odes to the role of the coaches and of charioteers and concluded how their presence could obscure the role of the athlete or owner of the horses. The fear of the aristocrats that their achievements might not be entirely attributed to them explains why Pindar hardly mentioned these figures in his victory odes.[1]

Pindar's victory odes defend a very conservative attitude about the world, the society, and the gods, even if written already in the fifth century. They intend to portray the grandeur of the aristocracy and align themselves ideologically with previous poets like Theognis, although not in such a simplistic manner. Pindar praised the natural ability or condition of a person as opposed to the learned skills. In order to describe the inborn condition that determined everyone's potential, he used the term *phya* instead of the word *physis*, which Pindar used only in relation to the body.[2] Pindar stressed that all real qualities were inborn and could not be achieved through learning. We read this for instance in the second *Olympic Ode*: "Wise is the man who knows lots of things by nature. Those exuberant ones who have learned by rambling words, like crows, speak idle words to the divine bird of Zeus" (2.86–88).

The opposition between nature and learning is underlined by the opposition of god-given talent versus human effort. Human effort is uncertain and ineffectual and brings at best unsure outcomes, whereas inborn talent is always the best, as we read in the next two examples.

> That which is by nature is completely the best. Many men strive to acquire fame through taught virtue, but without the god, anything is better to be left in silence. (Pindar, *Olympic Ode* 9.100–104)

> A man with inborn glory has great weight, but the one who has learned it is a dark man, breathing something different each time,

---

1. Nicholson 2003: 102–13.
2. Heinimann 1965: 99.

never sure when he treads with his foot, but tastes a myriad of forms of excellence with unaccomplished thought. (Pindar, *Nemean Ode* 3.40–42)

Pindar stresses the aristocratic character of nature by making it a hereditary quality. Thus, nonaristocrats who try to do their best by learning skills are excluded from success. "By nature, the noble inborn desire from the parents is conspicuous in the children" (Pindar, *Pythian Ode* 8.44–45).

Besides the suppression of the mention of coaches and the stressing of the unchanging nature, another way to maintain the appearance of natural superiority was done through the stylization of work and training. The word used to describe the effort that is needed to perform in athletic competitions was *ponos*—toil. This expression was opposed to the word that commonly denotes artisan work—*ergon*.[3] Whereas toil was seen as virtuous, work was seen as negative. Already Pindar makes toil a characteristic of those who are already superior by nature and places it above work. "A man with the help of a god, having sharpened another one who is born for excellence can drive him to mighty glory. Without toil very few take joy, as such it is light for life above all work" (Pindar, *Olympian Ode* 10.20–23).

Toil was necessary to develop virtue and self-control; as such, *ponos* is translated both as "suffering" and as "valorized effort." *Ponos* is a word that applies not only to sport but in general to all efforts directed toward mastery of one's body, be it hunting, war, or being accustomed to hunger and thirst and other hardships. For instance, Odysseus's suffering during his journey home is described often as *ponos*. Thus, *ponos* was used to justify the elite's moral superiority. Whereas in principle everybody was able to display effort and its results, in reality it was only applied to the elite's activities, which were not directly productive other than toward virtue.

On the other hand, toil in sport was related to developing technical and tactical expertise (*technē*), which could be understood as if perhaps natural abilities (*physis*) were not quite sufficient and needed to be complemented. Therefore, a tension ensued between the need for training and the need to maintain an imagined sufficient superior nature. Training also opened up the possibility for those who were not aristocratic to excel in a sport, not because they were of superior birth but because they worked hard. Consequently, the conflict between nature and training resurfaced now and again in literature, the arts, and

---

3. Johnstone 1994.

inscriptions. This is a conflict that can be seen from *The Iliad* to the refusal of Spartan athletes to compete to the Greek athletes in the Roman Empire who claimed that their victory was unexpected (*paradoxos*). Whereas works of literature and art may not represent directly the voice of the athletes, the inscriptions are the closest means we possess that let us grasp how athletes perceived themselves and their victories. It is therefore very significant that athletes in the third century A.D. still embraced much earlier ideas of being good by nature, even if many seem to have belonged to lower classes.

4.1 Homer

Already in Homer one can observe the undervaluing of training. The very first written evidence for Greek athletics, namely, the funeral games for Patroclus in book 23 of *The Iliad*, has been studied from many different perspectives. Some emphasize the continuity or discontinuity from historical ancient Greek sport, some emphasize the social relations of the participating heroes, but as far as I am aware no one talks about the conflict between nature and training that is apparent throughout the description of the games.[4]

The first event of the funeral games in book 23 of *The Iliad* is the chariot race. We are all familiar with Nestor's advice to his son Antilochus to use practical intelligence (*mētis*) to compensate for the lack of natural speed of his horses.

> Antilochus, Zeus and Poseidon loved you, even when you were young and they taught you the art of horsemanship. Because of this, I do not need to teach you much. You know well how to turn around the goal, but for you the horses run slowly. I think this will be your handicap. The horses of the others are faster, but they do not know how to plan better than you. Therefore, come on, dear, and put a complete *plan* in your heart, so that the prizes might not escape you. (*Iliad* 23.306–14)

The opposition between nature and the ability to cut corners is very clear in Nestor's words. The other drivers rely on the strength of their horses, but Antilochus has to rely on his plans. Furthermore, the art of horsemanship is something that he has learned from the gods (perhaps hinting at an innate ability), but also something that Nestor could teach him. It is thus an acquired

---

4. Brown 2003; Kyle 1996: 110.

skill. When Antilochus does exactly as planned, his maneuver is condemned by Menelaus, who makes him swear that he did not impede his horses with a trick or *dolos* (Iliad 23.585). A few verses later he advises Antilochus a second time not to deceive those who are better (by nature) (23.605). Menelaus had explained before that he is careful not to appear in front of the Achaeans as if he took the horse prize from Antilochus because he was mightier in *aretē* and force (23.578). From the words used by Menelaus, it is obvious that he sees himself as superior by nature and therefore deserving of the prize independently of the results. This is not just Menelaus's worldview. Even Achilles recognizes that Eumelus was the best horseman by nature (23.536) and wants to give him a prize despite having lost the race owing to an accident.

A few verses after the description of the race, the boxing match is described (*Iliad* 23.653–90). Epeius stands up in order to claim that he is the best boxer despite being mediocre in war (23.670). Epeius introduces the dilemma that the best athletes and the best warriors are not always the same. This is very much contrary to the aristocratic ideology that pervades *The Iliad* and moves on to later authors who criticize athletes precisely for not always being good soldiers. Epeius further says that a man cannot be knowledgeable in everything (23.671). Again, this is much against the aristocratic idea, especially because he attributes success in sport and war to a skill that can be learned. Epeius is a carpenter, and his name refers to the poetic genre of epic.[5] This relates to the professionals (*demiourgoi*) recognized by Homer: the poet, the carpenter, the physician. These are all trades that need to be learned, whether from humans or from gods.

But Epeius is not just a good boxer and an average warrior, he is also the builder of the Trojan horse, as we read in *The Odyssey* (8.492). Interestingly, the horse itself is described as a trick (*dolos*), not without good reason. What in principle can be seen as a very good practical skill, the art of carpentry, is transformed into a trick, contrary in many ways to the nature of the warrior. Epeius is, therefore, neither the ideal warrior, nor the ideal athlete in *The Iliad*. Furthermore, the prize that Achilles sets for boxing is a "hardworking mule," which is not as valuable as any of the other prizes. Achilles must have known who would participate in the event and thus given a less than aristocratic prize. Epeius competes also in the hurling of the iron, but he loses to the Thessalian leader Polypoites.

---

5. The presence of Epeius at the games is perhaps an indication that already in very early times games were open to nonaristocratic participants, as Young 1985 suggested.

The wrestling match between Odysseus and Ajax (*Iliad* 23.700–737) shows very clearly how ideology is used to cover up reality. The match foreshadows the later fight between these two heroes for the arms of Achilles after his death. As we know from myth, Odysseus won that match, which triggered the tragic chain of events that ended with Ajax's suicide. While Achilles is alive he can make up for Ajax's loss in wrestling, but once he is dead, no one can change the result of the fight for the arms.

In the wrestling match, both warriors are in a lock and unable to move each other with their strength. When the crowd becomes restless, Ajax decides to lift Odysseus, who uses what is described as a trick or *dolos* (*Iliad* 23.725) to bring Ajax down. Presumably while he is in the air, Odysseus manages to kick the back of Ajax's knee, which makes him fall. The score is one to zero for Odysseus. Next, Odysseus tries to lift Ajax, but he can move him only a little from the ground without fully lifting him. Odysseus then bends his knee and both fall to the ground.[6] This would be a call for a referee to decide whether Odysseus fell first (that would be a tie at one apiece) or Ajax fell first (that would be two to zero for Odysseus), or whether it was a double fall and consequently not a point and a win for Odysseus. Achilles seems to interpret it in the first way and interrupts the match without allowing them to wrestle for a third time and declares both of them winners. Where Ajax applies force, Odysseus applies techniques. Yet, Homer characterizes the techniques as tricks, signaling that he is not in favor of them. Achilles makes a decision in favor of strength (nature) and against technique. Odysseus may have won, yet Achilles is reluctant to give the victory to Odysseus, maybe because of personal enmity, but also because he disapproves of trickery, which Odysseus exemplifies.

Agamemnon does not participate in the games until the last event of spear throwing is called. As soon as he stands up, Achilles grants him a prize, declaring that they all know that Agamemnon is the best (*Iliad* 23.884–97). This has been typically explained as a restoration of the social order that was broken at the beginning of the *Iliad* when both Achilles and Agamemnon claimed to be the best. Agamemnon cannot participate in the event because if he loses he might be shown again as flawed.

In *The Iliad*, there is an ideologically charged understanding that the best warrior should also be the best athlete. There is an ideal equivalence between athletic prowess and military prowess. Both of them are conceived as being

---

6. Miller (2004a: 9) translates it as "he hooked his knee," as if he is trying to do a technical fall.

innate. On the other hand, examples like the previous ones show that the Greeks knew very well that this was not always the case and that just being good by nature was not enough to get the prize. Even in *The Iliad* there is a fracture between the reality of athletics and the ideology of the aristocracy, which cannot be ignored, as much as certain heroes would like to.

At the end of the games, nature (and natural social order as understood by the aristocrats) triumphs over the actual sport competition. But *The Iliad* is literature and can represent only a set of ideal competitions. In real life the nature of the athlete was tested and needed to be improved with techniques despite the aristocratic ideology of the superiority of nature.

4.2 Sparta

A few centuries later, Sparta fiercely defended the aristocratic ideology that promoted superiority by nature as opposed to training. This ideology started to be applied extensively after the Spartans had stopped dominating the Olympics at the end of the archaic era. Spartan dominance of sport was almost absolute for the first two hundred years after the origins of the games. Certainly, they were the first to develop a training system, but that system proved obsolete when other cities started to develop their own. Once all other cities had their own training programs, Spartans developed the idea that training was actually cheating and contrary to their nature.[7] Instead of adapting their training, they went back to the distinction between nature and training, equating, of course, training with trickery, while they themselves became proponents of nature in athletic competitions. We read this in several anecdotes and poems.

> They [the Spartans] did not hire coaches for the wrestlers, so that there would be not honor for the craft (*technē*), but for the virtue (*aretē*). For this reason, Lysanoridas, when asked about how Charon defeated him, said: "with many tricks" (*polymēchanía*). (Plutarch, *Sayings of Spartans* 233e)

> Someone said to a Spartan who had lost at Olympia in wrestling: "Spartan, your opponent was better than you," and he said: "certainly not, but more technical." (Plutarch, *Sayings of Spartans* 236e)

7. Christesen 2012b.

> I am a wrestler not from Messenia or Argos, Sparta famous for her men, Sparta is my fatherland. Those are technical, but I, as befits the children from Lacedaemonia, I win through strength. (*Greek Lyric Anthology* 16, 1: [epigram attributed to Damagetus])

The three examples are self-explanatory. In the mentality of the Spartans, technique and training were considered opposite to nature. Excellence was in the domain of nature, and anything that attempted to modify that nature was considered a trick.

Contrary to the Spartan mentality, an epigram attributed to Simonides praises the skill developed through training. In this epigram, the young athlete is described as a "dexterous charioteer of wrestling," an obvious metaphor for a well-developed technique and perhaps quasi-choreographed fight.

> Know Theognetus when you look on him, the boy who conquered at Olympia, the dexterous charioteer of wrestling, most-lovely to behold, but in combat not at all inferior to his beauty. He won a crown for the city of his noble fathers. (*Greek Lyric Anthology* 16.2)

Theognetus was from Aegina and came from a well-established family of athletes.[8] It seems that the Aeginetans were not averse to hiring the services of a coach.[9] Mann speculates that perhaps different aristocratic families of Aegina came together to hire a coach, the Athenian Melesias, which would partly explain why the winning results are more often in the younger categories and limited to the technical sports of wrestling and the pancratium. In this, they differed greatly from the Spartans, who wished to appear as self-taught and using only strength and not technique.

After the Second Messenian War (685–668), Sparta underwent a general self-enclosure in all areas of its life. It is not surprising, therefore, that sport was one of them. The turn it took was to proclaim the excellence of "unadulterated" nature, even if its own previous victories were based mostly on the harsh training of the young Spartans since childhood. The emphasis on nature in sport when the other cities were training hard corresponds further to an abandonment of the idea of the value of sport altogether. The Spartans were the first ones then to undermine the glory of sport in opposition to war. This

---

8. See Pindar, *Pythian Ode* 8.37.
9. Mann 2001: 133. Pindar mentions two Athenian coaches, Menander (*Nemean Ode* 5.49) and Melesias (*Olympian* 8.54; *Nemean* 4.93; and *Nemean* 6.65).

is reflected also in some anecdotes that oppose death in battle to winning the Olympics.

> Another woman, carrying out a public procession, heard that her son had won on the battlefield, but that he died from the many wounds. Not removing the garland, reverently she said to the women near her, "How much more beautiful, my friends, to win on the battlefield and die, than to succeed at the Olympic Games and live!" (Plutarch, *Sayings of Spartan Women* 242a)

The struggle between nature and training is not something specifically Spartan or Homeric. It was present throughout the history of Greek sport and responsible in many ways for the criticism of athletes and their activities. In Hellenistic times, elite sport started to be considered unnatural and the source of many moral and physical diseases, as later medical writers were all too keen to assert.

4.3 Need for Training

Whereas training in sport may have been regarded by some sectors of the population or some cities as an unnecessary and even unethical improvement on nature, it was not a secret that athletes needed to train to be able to compete at a high level. Sport and training for sport became a metaphor for the need to train in other areas. Philosophers like Plato realized that the zeal with which athletes trained could be applied to other areas of life, mostly the realms of the political and the military, for which Greeks needed to train.

Plato, who, according to tradition, had been a keen athlete in his youth and even participated at the Isthmian Games, was very conscious that victory, and even participation at the games, did not come without hard training over a long period of time. He describes the need of many professionals—such as soldiers, cobblers, or artists—to be trained in their specialty, which he refers to as *technē* (craft), as well as being born with qualities for it. In his list of professionals, he also mentions the athletes:

> "How so?" he [Glaucon] said; "are the citizens themselves not sufficient for it [the defense of the city]?" "Not if you," said I [Socrates], "and we all agreed when we were developing our city. We agreed then, if you remember, that it is impossible for one person to work many crafts well." "True," he said. "Well, then," said I, "do you think that

fighting in war is a craft?" "It is indeed," he said. "Must we be more concerned, then, for the cobbler's craft than for that of war?" "Not at all." "But isn't it so that we prevented the cobbler from attempting to be at the same time a farmer, a weaver, or a builder instead of just a cobbler, so that we might have the cobbler's work well done, and also to each single person of the others we assigned similarly one job, the one for which each was naturally fit and at which he was to work to perfection being occupied at it through life, not quitting in the important moments? But we ask whether the things concerning war are not to be worked out above everything else or whether it is so easy that a farmer will be at the same time a soldier, a cobbler, or a worker in whichever other trade, though no man could be competent at draughts or the dice unless he did not practice that from childhood but treated it as hobby? And a man who takes a shield or any other tool or instrument of war on that very day he will become a competent hoplite or fighter in any other form of warfare—though no other tool that is taken will make one become a craftsman or an athlete, nor will it be useful to anyone who has neither acquired the science of it nor has put in sufficient practice?" (*Republic* 374a–d)

It was clear for Plato that a person had to be trained in his profession, whatever that might be. A person could not just come out of nowhere and be an accomplished tradesman, neither could he be an accomplished athlete. The passage not only testifies to a degree of professionalism in athletes of the fourth century, it also makes very clear that athletes needed to train as much as anyone else in their profession. Only ideological prejudices can explain the avoidance by certain sources of admitting that athletes were professionally trained for a long period of time.

Plato in another work uses training in boxing as an indication of the need to train in arms to defend the state.

[In the city] will there not be athletes of the greatest contests, for which there will be thousands of competitors? Certainly, someone may say he speaks rightly. So then if we reared boxers or pancratiasts or athletes in any other of those events, would we have gone straight into the contest without fighting each day in the previous days? Or being boxers, we would have learned to fight many days before the competition and trained thoroughly, imitating all those methods as we were meant to employ fighting for victory, going to the real thing as closely as possible: thus, we would don padded gloves instead of leather straps, in order to practice the blows and the avoidance of the blows as competently as possible. And if we wouldn't have many training-mates, would we fear the laughter of fools and not dare to hang up a lifeless dummy and practice on it? Indeed, if ever we were in a desert, and without either live or lifeless training-mates, would we not dare to shadow-fight against ourselves? Or what else should one call the practice of moving the hands? (*Laws* 830a–c)

Besides giving us important information about how training in boxing was conducted, the paragraph also informs us that nature might not be sufficient and that it needed to be complemented, whether in sport or in life, by long hours of hard work and education. In fact, by the end of the fourth century it was clear for the Greeks that nature without education would not bring a person very far, and those persons who were more dedicated would often do better than those who relied solely on nature.

> Certainly, we know that those having a more lacking nature than others, but who surpass them in experience and dedication, not only become better to their own standards but better than others who had more natural talents but neglected them too much. So that each of these ones may be able to speak and act, but if both things are present in the same person, they will produce someone unsurpassable among his peers. (Isocrates, *Antidosis* 191)

This statement is contrary to Homeric ideas, which probably would not have admitted the possibility of someone neglecting his talents. The statement is much closer to the democratic mentality that allowed for a certain degree of social mobility.

The need for training is also expressed by Philostratus. He mentions in paragraph 11 of his treatise *On Gymnastics* that training is often harder than the competition itself, especially for wrestling. Whereas boxers train by shadow boxing and pancratiasts alternate exercises according to concrete themes for the bouts, wrestlers train in real matches. Therefore, the Eleans also crowned the athletes that trained the hardest.

At the time of Philostratus, training had become so specialized that even coaches could do only one sport. He writes that the coach that knows running drills would hardly know anything about wrestling or the pancratium (*On Gymnastics* 15). The coach that specializes in heavy athletes would not know much about anything else. This is a normal development in sport, but it is in stark contrast to the ideological image of the Homeric heroes who were successful at all events, whether sprinting or wrestling, and all this by nature.

4.4 Greek Athletes in the Roman Empire

When we look at inscriptions of the Roman period, it is clear that technique plays an important part in the development of the athlete, even the very young ones. There is a process of learning that may complement the nature of the young boy. An inscription from Alabanda (Caria), probably dating to the Roman imperial period, has a positive look at technique. It says, "first . . . Polyneices the courageous having glory in arms, ruled the stadium being undefeated twenty times in boxing, not abandoned by technique, but youth prevailed over an old body" (*Alabanda* 26).

Polyneices attributed his success for twenty years to his technique; his final defeat however, had to do with nature. He became old, whereas his opponents were younger. Despite technique being instrumental to his success, the young nature of his opponent prevailed in the end. Nevertheless, the impression of this inscription is that Polyneices was proud of his technique and accepted his age as a matter of fact, but not as the most important trait for maintaining a long career. Polyneices is the name of a mythical boxer. That the person commemorated in this inscription bears his name raises the question as to whether the athlete changed his name when he picked boxing as a sport or whether he came from a family of boxers, who expected him to continue the family line. The association with the mythical boxer would also be a way to assert his superiority.

On the other hand, some inscriptions have throughout a positive view of nature. For instance, an inscription found in Magnesia from Caria and dated to Roman imperial times describes in elegiac meter the victories of Aristomachus, a pancratiast, victor in a very long list of competitions.

> Of those from Maeandrus Magna a child pancratiast, Aristomachus, having won these famous contests. First in Pisa in the game carrying the wild olive of Zeus, then the games of the uncut oak in Ausonia, then in Naples, famous crown, and then in Actia and the games of Nemea that feeds lions, and the sacred crown of the Panathenaia, and in Asia the common games of well-built Smyrna and rich Pergamon

and in the much divine Sparta, the Lacedaemonian fortification, I was crowned in the famous games for Ourania, and twice in Isthmia, once as a child, once as a youth. So what? In all stadia I was invincible. (*Magnesia* 322)

He proclaims at the end that he was undefeated by all in competition. The verb that is used then is not *eimi* (I am) but *phuō* (I am by nature). *Phuō* has the connotation of being born in a certain way (it is from the same root as *physis*). The inscription is metrical, and the imperfect of the verb "to be" has only one syllable, whereas the aorist tense of *phuō* has two. This may be a reason to use the verb, but it also may be a way to underline the success owing to his nature and not to technique and training. The victories as a child perhaps have to do more with the nature of the athlete, since every other child is also a beginner. But there comes a time when nature is not enough and technique and experience take over.

Other inscriptions are not as clear as to whether they value technique or nature or simply good luck, which plays a part in every sport. An inscription found in Ephesus celebrates Artemidorus, a pancratiast, *periodonikēs* and "unexpected" victor. The inscription is dated to A.D. 96–98.

> To Artemis of Ephesus and the emperor Nero Caesar Augustus and the people of Ephesus, Tiberius Claudius Artemidorus, from Caesarea and Tralles and also Alexandrian and Ephesian, pancratiast, victor of the *periodos* and victor in an unexpected way, chief priest of the association and president of the association for life. (*Ephesos* 756)

An inscription from Rome celebrates Marcus Aurelius Demostratus Damas, also a pancratiast, twice *periodonikēs*, undefeated, unexpected.

> The sacred athletic synod around Heracles, living after retirement in Imperial Rome, Marus Aurelius Demostratus Damas citizen from Sardis, Alexandria, Antinoea, Athens, Ephesus, Smyrna, Pergamum, Nicomedia, Miletus, Lacedaemonia, chief priest of the whole athletic association through life, president of the association and of the imperial baths, pancratiast, victor of the *periodos* twice, boxer, undefeated, unexpected. (*IGUR* I 243)

The word that I have translated as unexpected is *paradoxos*. Knab believed that its original meaning may have been no longer well understood and that the term just meant "exceptional, extraordinary."[10] This might have been the case, but nevertheless, it is the fact that something is unexpected that makes it extraordinary. Indeed, it is very surprising that two athletes like Artemidorus and Damas, who had achieved at least sixty-eight other victories, declared themselves to be unexpected winners. It is true that sometimes athletes' performances surpass their expectations in any given day, and we cannot just dismiss this. But in my opinion, both Artemidorus and Damas might not have wanted to be seen as professionals and wanted to emphasize their nature instead of training.[11]

As much as top athletes derive joy from their activity, winning is a very important motivation and goal.[12] And if one wants to win, or at least have a chance at winning, one needs to train hard.[13] The conflict between natural ability and learned skill is an artificial one.[14] And yet the conflict is in a sense

---

10. Knab 1980 [1934]: 13–14.

11. Professional snowboarder Shaun White won the Olympic gold in the half-pipe in 2006 and 2010. White cultivates an image of carefree laissez faire that appeals to the general snowboarder. On the other hand, he had his sponsor Red Bull build a secret half-pipe in the mountains where he could practice his new tricks unseen from his competitors. What seemed an easy, unprepared performance at the Olympic games had months of preparation and millions of dollars behind it. A video presentation describes the project in terms of "pushing the sport further and faster than it's ever been done" (Red Bull 2010). The video claims that the project changed the nature of sport, and that might well be true. White managed to practice in a few months what would have taken years to achieve otherwise.

While White claims to be always pushing the athletic limits, he is also starting a clothing line and has participated in some Hollywood productions and has a video game named after him. His estimated earnings were about 7.5 million dollars in 2010, when he was twenty-three. He was already sponsored at the age of seven and became professional at thirteen. It does not get more professional than this. Yet, the media, and even his sponsors, still speak of a natural talent. Usually, the phrase goes something to this effect: "he has a lot of natural talent, but he still trains very hard," as if the hard work needed to be justified. An interview with CNN Sports was called "Natural Board Talent," making a wordplay to an inborn talent (CNN 2011). It is precisely the appearance that something is effortless that is often misunderstood as natural ability. Certainly, athletes have natural qualities, but champions need to train for hours every day for years to achieve their goals. This is as true for athletes today as it was for athletes during Greek times, even if the number of competitors was perhaps not as high. The more an athlete practices his sport, the more the movements and strategies become "second nature" to him. No one is born innately knowing the wrestling locks and the precise moment when to apply them. It takes instruction and practice, whether one is a professional or an amateur.

12. Sir Roger Bannister was one of the best middle-distance runners of his times, and he soon realized "that although [he] could run fast times on inadequate training, [he] could not be sure of winning" (Bannister 2004: 85).

13. Also, Michael Phelps declared in an interview that "whenever I get out of the car in the morning or in the afternoon, heading to work out, I kind of just replay the song that was playing right before I got out of the car. That just sort of is on repeat in my head throughout the whole entire [2 hours] workout. So it kind of helps me not think about the pain that I'm going through in workouts" (NPR 2012).

14. Bannister (2004: 102) clearly describes the need for training, despite his natural desire and ability to run: "My outlook was quite different from that of the previous year, simply because I was stronger and faster as a result of a better training."

very typical of the Greek aristocratic mentality. Natural ability and inclination may be the reasons for someone's first interest in a sport, but without learned skills and hard work, no one will go very far in the practice of sport.[15] Damas and Artemidorus may not have expected to win because they were not at their best and the competitors looked really strong, but certainly their track record makes us realize that their victories were not as unexpected as they claimed. It also brings to mind that the old ideology that forged sport and athletic success remained alive for much longer time than the political system to which it was originally attached.

---

15. The need for good training is a constant and not a one-time event. Bannister (2004: 37) wrote about a race he attended during his university years after a dance on the previous night: "I managed to stay in second place until the halfway mark, and then my sleepless ill-trained body gave way under the combined strain of the previous night and present exhaustion. I had a violent pain in my side but managed to continue running. I eventually dragged myself over the finishing line in extreme agony in ninth place."

5

Psychological Characteristics of Athletes

It takes more than physical traits, whether innate or acquired, to become a successful athlete. Consequently, it is not a surprise that psychological factors are important to modern athletes and coaches. Scholars and practitioners of modern sport pay a great deal of attention to the psychological characteristics of both developing and elite athletes, as well as to how through psychological techniques athletes can improve their performance. Besides the omnipresent "mental toughness," there are several other characteristics that define elite athletes in modern North America. Gould and Dieffenbach identified the following characteristics associated with athletic success:[1]

1. Ability to control and cope with anxiety
2. Confidence
3. Mental toughness / resiliency
4. Sport intelligence
5. Ability to focus and block out distractions
6. Competitiveness
7. A hard-work ethic
8. Ability to set and achieve goals
9. Coachability
10. High levels of dispositional hope

---

1. Gould and Dieffenbach 2002: 172–204. Their study also concluded that parents and coaches had an important role in the development of these attitudes. Interestingly, they discovered that in general families encouraged participation but exerted little pressure to win.

11. Optimism
12. Adaptive perfectionism.

In 1971, Patrucco wrote an article on the psychology of ancient Greek athletes.[2] Patrucco based his article on literary sources, mostly Philostratus's description of the coach's motivation of the athletes in his *On Gymnastics*. For example, Philostratus asserts that some coaches have "put together" their athletes by encouraging, rebuking, threatening, or using wisdom with them (20). Philostratus then gives a few specific examples of what he describes as a list too long to narrate (21–24). To my knowledge, the initial work of Patrucco has not found much continuation among scholars of ancient sport, although it seems obvious from Philostratus's comments that the ancient Greeks were familiar with the importance of psychological factors to maintain and improve their athletic performance.

The purpose of this chapter is to examine further examples of what could constitute a description of psychological characteristics of ancient athletes, or an indication that Greeks took the psychological development of athletes into consideration. It is to be expected that some of the psychological characteristics of ancient athletes correspond to modern ones.

5.1 Competition and Cooperation

In a previous chapter we saw how Aristotle described the characteristics of youth (*Rhetoric* 2.12.3–12). Among the characteristics that Aristotle attributes to young men, he depicts them as being ambitious for honor (*philotimoi*), but more so for victory (*philonikoi*), which, for him, is a kind of superiority. In modern terminology, we could describe the young men as "competitive." Aristotle stresses the competitiveness of youth when he says that the youths tend to make mistakes because of their excess and vehemence.

Competitiveness is certainly a characteristic of an athlete, someone who measures his performance against that of others. Modern sport psychologists define competition as "a social process that occurs when rewards are given to people on the basis of how their performances compare with the performances of others doing the same task or participating in the same event."[3] But competitiveness goes beyond results and is a trait in one's character that

---
2. Patrucco 1971: 245–53.
3. Weinberg and Gould 2011: 104.

in ancient Greece was instilled in the gymnasia and through the traditional goal of always excelling and being the best (see *Iliad* 6.208). Our ancient sources certainly very much emphasize the competitive discourse. These sources often reduce the concept of competition[4] to winning, as seen very poignantly in Pindar's *Pythian Ode*: "Onto four bodies you fell from above, with mean thoughts; to them, not a happy homecoming similar to yours at the Pythian Games was given" (8. 81–84). This same emphasis on the outcome of competition can be found in an inscription dated around 400–380 B.C. As in Pindar's poem, the dedicator sees his opponents as mere bodies, whereas he names himself twice in a very short inscription:

> Polycletus made it.
> Xenocles, son of Euthyphron
> Mainalian
> Mainalian Xenocles won,
> the son of Euthyphron without falling, the wrestling
> Taking four bodies. (*IvO* 164)

Both these examples epitomize the extreme of competition by dehumanizing the opponents and considering them as mere bodies. On the other hand, no sporting system, especially when it is used for the socialization of youth, is based on competition alone. Competition and cooperation are complementary.[5] Athletes training and working together develop a sense of community and understand that victory depends on many things, some of which they cannot control. Athletes are very conscious that victory or defeat depends on many factors. Whereas people outside of sport may stress the victory or defeat, athletes tend to bond together and to express the idea of competing well and achieving their personal goals or personal best, which might not necessarily be equal to a victory.[6]

There is an obvious discourse of cooperation among Greek athletes, even if the discourse of competition might be more striking. For instance, in

---

4. Weinberg and Gould (2011: 107) explain that there are three subjective components to competition: competitiveness per se, defined as the enjoyment of competition and desire to strive for success, win orientation or focus on winning more than improving personal standards, and goal orientation or focus on improving one's standards independently of the outcome.

5. Ibid., 119.

6. In his autobiography, Bannister expresses very well the tension lived before his race at the Olympics in Helsinki in 1952, and the fact that his expectations were not those of the public: "To come even last in the [Olympic] final should be really regarded as a great honour, but I knew that if I were beaten by inches or feet in one of sport's most exacting events, I should be called a failure" (2004: 119).

vases, athletes are portrayed not only competing against each other but often also training together and perhaps assisting each other.[7] Although vases are silent, the faces of the athletes seem relaxed and sometimes even happy. It is hard to imagine that people working together toward the same goal for many years would not have developed some kind of friendship and would not help each other develop their goals. In our times, it has been shown that cooperation is more effective in promoting achievement than independent or individualistic work.[8] Every athlete needs training partners. Vases allow us to make a hypothesis that athletes may have also lived beyond rivalries and competition and helped each other develop as a group.

Another example of cooperation among athletes can be seen from several inscriptions, which show that young athletes at gymnasia got prizes not only for their results but also for their diligence (*philoponia*), fitness or healthy appearance (*euexia*), and coordination or discipline (*eutaxia*).[9] The contest emphasized the character of the athlete, not just his ability to perform; obviously it needed to be judged over a period of time. The person that put more effort into his training received the prize whether or not this translated into winning an actual athletic event. For instance, in the next inscription, dated to before the mid-second century, we can see how none of the presumably older contestants won more than one event. By contrast, the young Asclepiades won the contest in javelin, archery, and long-distance running, together with the contest in coordination. Probably the combination is not very surprising. On the other hand, his fellow athlete, Apollas, won in combat with shield and in diligence, which was applied most likely to all of the events. Hegemoneus won only the contest in healthy appearance, which did not translate into victory in a sport event.

In the stadium, Demetrius son of Democrates
In the *diaulos*, Aretus son of Minnion

---

7. See just as a small sample the Athenian red-figure cup, dated to between 525 and 475 and held by the Antikensammlung (J803) in Munich, the Athenian red-figure cup, also dated to between 525 and 475, held by the Metropolitan Museum (41.162.128) in New York, and the Athenian red-figure oenochoe, date to between 500 and 450 and held by the Louvre (G242) in Paris. In the Paris vase, two young athletes are disrobing, smiling at each other. It certainly shows that there is a friendship of these athletes, independent of their results at competition.

8. Weinberg and Gould 2011: 111–12.

9. According to Crowther (1991), passing the test in *euexia*, *eutaxia*, and *philoponia* represented the criteria to progress from child (*pais*) to youth (*ephebe*). Although the inscriptions show only one winner, the "passing grade" must have been given to more than one person at a time, especially since the winners in one contest were not necessarily the winners in another.

In *euexia*, Apollonius son of Posidippus
In *eutaxia*, Callidromus son of Exacestes
In *philoponia*, Sopatrus son of Exacestes
In catapult, Mentor son of Zoilus
Of the youngsters:
In wrestling, Astericus son of Astericus
In javelin, Asclepiades son of Democrates
In archery, Asclepiades son of Democrates
In combat with weapons, Sostratus son of Sostratus
In combat with shield, Apollas son of Apollonius
In long distance running, Asclepiades son of Democrates
In the stadium, Sostratus son of Sostratus
In the *diaulos*, Porthesilaus son of Cleogenus
In *euexia* Hegemoneus son of Porthesilaus
In *eutaxia* Asclepiades son of Democrates
In *philoponia*, Apollas son on Apollonius
In catapult, Theocritus son of Theocritus. (*Samos* 168)

Contests in skills other than a sport event or military practice are certainly examples not just of instilling competitiveness in the young men toward achieving results, but also of developing an attitude of constant effort to excel. On the other hand, praising the effort takes away the pressure of winning while rewarding individual diligence and solidarity among athletes. When there can be only one winner, it is important to motivate all athletes to work hard, but also to make them aware that victory is anyone's possibility on any given day and that they all need to improve.

Cooperation between athletes might have also been expressed in the few team events that existed in the Greek festivals. One of them was the torch race. Torch races are known from various festivals, the Panathenaea is perhaps the most famous. This race consisted of a relay involving several members of the same tribe and in competition against the other tribes. An Athenian inscription has preserved the names of nine participants in the race from the tribe of Aiantis who won at the Hephaestia festival in the middle of the fourth century. The inscription commemorates the victory of the young runners and especially the gymnasiarch Epistratus, who directed the youth toward victory.

The gods. It seemed good to the tribe of Aiantis, in the archontate....
Xenophon said: since he won the Hephaestia with the torch races, (we are) to honor Epistratus, son of Tremponus, the Rhamnousian,

gymnasiarch. (We are) to crown him with a crown of flowers because he is a good man and always ambitious for the honor regarding the tribe of Aiantis, for the sake of his goodwill and virtue toward the regular (members of the gymnasium) whenever the young men exercise. (We are) to write this decree on this stele and to donate to the gymnasiarch what may seem good to the tribe members. To write the names of the participants in the torch race: Racers: Aristyllus, Xenocleides, Caliades, Xenopeithes, Pythis, Python, Euthymachus, Mnesicleides, Demetrius. (*SEG* 40: 124)

The gymnasiarch is celebrated because he held dear the honor of the tribe and showed goodwill toward all participants. Certainly, his team won, and that is why this inscription was erected in the first place. Yet, it seems that the nine participants, and probably more since the inscription breaks off, and their families may have also developed a sense of belonging. This is not the only inscription of its kind.[10] Even if somewhat formulaic, it seems it was a sincere recognition of the gymnasiarch's work in bringing everybody together.

Torch races were part of the ephebes' education. The inscription is an example that sport was used as a tool to socialize young men and instill in them civil and cultural values.[11] Socialization of young men implies that they need to develop not just as individuals but also within a group. The torch races were relays, which necessitate teamwork and rapport between all the members. There must have been cheering and encouragement going on as well, thus helping the bonding of the group.

Yet another instance of the spirit of cooperation in the gymnasium can be seen through the cult of Eros.[12] Besides statues of Heracles, an obvious symbol of competition, and Hermes, a symbol of transitions, gymnasia often displayed the statue of Eros.[13] The presence of the god Eros in the athletic festival and the gymnasium exemplified the principle of solidarity and cooperation. Eros represents not only homoerotic relations but also a principle of cohesiveness that every society needs to have in order to function. The explanation that Greeks gave for the presence of Eros at the gymnasia beyond homoerotic unions can be read in a passage of Athenaeus.

10. See *IPriene* 112 among others.
11. Scanlon 2002: 273.
12. Ibid., 264.
13. Ibid., 250–55; 89–90.

Pontianus says that Zeno of Citi assumes Eros to be a god of friendship and concord, even skilled in freedom, like no other. Because of this Zeno said in his *Republic* that Eros is a god who cooperates with the safety of the polis. Also, it is evident that other philosophers, older than Zeno, regard Eros as holy and removed from all shameful by the fact that he is established at the gymnasia along with Hermes and Heracles, the former in charge of speech, the latter in charge of strength. When they are united, friendship and concord are born, and through them the most beautiful freedom grows for their partakers. (Athenaeus 561 c–d)

5.2 Positive Characteristics

The closest we come to a treatise on sport psychology in antiquity is perhaps Xenophon's work *On Hunting*. Although Xenophon never made the link between hunting and athletics explicit, they were both considered part of the old education and aristocratic practices during his lifetime in the fourth century B.C.[14] Furthermore, hunting and athletic competition were activities through which the young man could perform so-called deeds of glory.[15] Xenophon considers hunting one of the branches of education (2.1). At the beginning of the treatise, Xenophon mentions that the appropriate age for a boy to be introduced to hunting is when he is coming of age (2.1). This is probably in the late teens. The ideal age for a hunter is when the young man is around twenty (2.3). Some of the characteristics of the ideal hunter can be transferred to the ideal athlete. Along the first lines of the second book and more explicitly in book 12, Xenophon describes the physical and psychological characteristics that derive from hunting or that a hunter will already possess. Xenophon presupposes a set of natural abilities that, on the one hand, will make the young man a good hunter, but on the other hand, if developed and tamed through the hunt, will make him a good citizen.

Along the first lines of the second book, he describes the hunter as being physically light and strong and mentally competent in order that he may enjoy the tasks of hunting, and as having the abilities to make the effort (*ponos*)

---

14. Galen makes the explicit connection between hunting and sport, especially recreational sport. See *On Exercise with the Small Ball* 5.900.10.

15. Scanlon (2002: 88–89) notices how there is a shift from hunting to the gymnasium as erotic setting. The implication is that the gymnasium takes over the educational role of hunting.

demanded (*On Hunting* 2.3). These natural abilities can be translated in modern terms as "sport intelligence" and "resilience." Besides these abilities, other very important components are commitment (*prothumia*) and keen desire (*epithumounta*) to participate in the activity (2.1, 2.3). This enthusiasm will be transformed into physical and mental fitness and endurance, or being accustomed to hard work (12.2). Xenophon stresses this idea through the use of words like habit (*synētheia*) (12.4). The endurance is created through habit, and then the result is fitness (*eutaxia*) and confidence (*thrasis*) in one's own abilities (12.5). Further, Xenophon believes that the exertion produces a desire for virtue, since it drives away the shameful and the selfish from body and soul (12.9). On the contrary, those who lack the desire to exercise and to learn through toil are driven by pleasures and are by nature bad citizens (12.15, 12.16). Xenophon concludes that the ethics of hard work will benefit the city and the citizenry, for he who works hard for himself will as well work hard for his city (12.10).

With his views on the educational values of the hunt, Xenophon stresses the general value of physical training that was constitutive of the old *paideia* or education. What is interesting in the text of Xenophon is that he espouses the values of the old *paideia* as much as he starts to prepare a psychological profile of the athlete. Besides the physical ability, he considers that it is necessary to have commitment and enthusiasm.

Commitment is probably the psychological characteristic of athletes most quoted by modern sport psychologists, but already Lucian talks about the daring, resolve, and commitment of athletes as being an important part of the pleasure of watching the competition: "If you were seated among the spectators you would see the virtue of men and the beauty of bodies, amazing fitness, skillful experience, unconquerable strength, daring, love of honor, undefeated resolve, indescribable commitment for the sake of victory" (*Anacharsis* 12).

Lucian describes both physical and mental characteristics that separate athletes from nonathletes and spectators. Nonliterary sources, like inscriptions, praise also the commitment of the athletes from a young age and their ability to work hard. For instance, an inscription found in Aphrodisias was dedicated to Callicrates by his fellow athletes, who ask for the erection of a statue in his memory. It is dated to the reign of Hadrian, 117–138 A.D.

> It seems good to the sacred athletic synod of many cities, holy and reverend, and the entire union around Heracles and the emperor Caesar Trajan Hadrian Augustus to send this decree to the most sacred

> assembly of the Aphrodisians and its people. Since Callicrates son of Diogenes, of Aphrodisias, pancratiast, victor of the sacred games and victor in many games turning into the road of virtue since the first age with sweat and toil achieved well-renowned glory . . . among all men in the whole inhabited world he is [sought after?] because of his entire wisdom, which comes from his love for toil. Surpassing with his body all the ancient athletes he amazed nature, he also by occupying his mind, was blessed in its ways. Because of all of this on top of his excellence in glory, slanderous envy crept in and feeling of indignation carried away our common good by twisting the part of the body that is most useful for the pancratiast, the shoulders. Because of this it seemed good to the good destiny to ask for a place convenient to the city of the Aphrodisians so that we may be able to make a dedication of a statue of the great victor of sacred games and of the very manly victor and also [another statue] in the metropolis of Asia, Ephesus. Having these honors, a proper inscription may be erected for Callicrates so that through this decree the graces of honors may restore our fellow athlete to us and the heaviness in spirit because of this inexorable death be easily consoled. (*PPAphr* 89)

There is no question in the mind of his fellow athletes that Callicrates is characterized by his perseverance and focus since the beginning of his career. Sweat and toil contributed to his superior ability in the pancratium, not only his natural abilities. Through hard training he achieved wisdom, perhaps better translated as sport intelligence. Callicrates is described as being the common good of all athletes, as if his achievements were then part of the whole group. The occupation of the mind that the inscription mentions was perhaps a way to combat the prejudice that athletes were not very smart. This prejudice was certainly well extended by the second century of our era.

That commitment, hard work, and mental toughness were found not only in adult athletes but also in children can be seen from another inscription found at Olympia and dated to the year 49 A.D. It commemorates the victories of the young Ariston. The inscription reads as follows:

> Publius Cornelius son of Irenaeus, Ariston, the Ephesian, child pancratiast having won in the 207th Olympiad to Olympian Zeus.
> This one who achieved the age of a boy, the strength of a man, this one whose beauty and strength are visible, where are you from? From which father? Tell me. Having boasted of victory over which

hardships did you stand under the hall of Zeus? Irenaeus is my father, stranger, Ariston my name, the fatherland for both of us is Ephesus, Ionian–born. I was crowned without a bye as a child in the pancratium at Olympia, fighting three contests covered in dust. I will announce it in all of Asia. I am Ariston, that one who was crowned in the pancratium with wild olive. Greece spoke about my feat when it saw me with the age of a child having the virtue of men in the hands. For the crown was not for the good luck of the draw, but far from byes I was made to rejoice by Alpheius and Zeus. For I alone of seven children did not stop in skill (*palama*). Having girded myself always I took the crown away from all. Therefore, I praise my father Irenaeus and my fatherland Ephesus with immortal crowns. Of Tiberius Claudius Thessalus from Coos, victor in many contests. (*IvO* 225)

Like the previous inscription, this too pretends to be the voice of an athlete. It is characteristic that it talks of hardship and hard training. The inscription also reveals that Ariston had already the maturity and toughness (not only the strength) of a man, despite his age.[16] Like Callicrates, Ariston also talks about his superior skills specific to the sport. *Palama* is an ambiguous word and can be translated as the (violent) action of the hand as well as the art or skill to conduct an action. Whether the term here indicated that Ariston did not give up fighting or that he did not stop developing his skill as he fought, both reflect his psychological characteristics more than the purely physical ones. The inscription describes how Ariston managed to find the right level of arousal,[17] whereas his opponents gave up earlier.

The last psychological trait that we can discover from this inscription is that whereas luck is part of the game, Ariston did not sit out in any byes. This is a typical assertion of victors at the games to show how proud they are about overcoming odds. This reflects resiliency and an ability to focus on the task at hand without thinking whether others were, or were not, luckier than themselves. Pausanias mentions how many athletes have won not by strength but by luck of the lot, and therefore omits the description of their statues in his work (6.1.2). Obviously, winning against the odds was considered a great

---

16. Gould and Dieffenbach write that "talent development involves the acquisition of a mature personality during the teenage years" (2002: 176). Teenagers need to be "intrinsically motivated," they need to make difficult choices and come to terms with the implications.

17. Arousal is defined as intensity of motivation at a particular moment. Since arousal falls along a continuum, it is important to be in the right "zone" in order for the performance to be at its peak. Too much or too little arousal usually translates into poor performance (see Weinberg and Gould 2011: 77, 86).

achievement that was possible only by blocking out distractions and not getting anxious about things that lie outside one's control.

Another inscription found at Olympia, dated to the reign of Trajan or Hadrian, also exemplifies the same ability of blocking distractions and of finding the right combination between arousal and anxiety that made it possible for Tiberius Claudius Rufus to win the Olympic pancratium.

Decree of the Eleans:

> Marcus Betilenus Laetus made appear clearly to me that Tiberius Claudius Rufus, an adult pancratiast having participated at the games at Olympia, came to dwell in this city after living in the whole world; he was considered from all testimonies and by all to be a local man on account of his prudence and common good. He restored diligently gymnastic practices in sight of the *Hellanodikai*[18] according to the local custom of the games, so that the hope of the most sacred crown here would be evident. By participating in the stadium in a manner worthy of Olympian Zeus and of the truth and of his present disposition to everybody, he fought greatly and in an admirable manner so that it was worthy to consider to give him an Olympic crown; he fought all rounds without sitting out (in a bye), having been matched with the most famous men. He went into them with such excellence and good courage that, fighting in the pancratium for the crown with a man who happened to have obtained a bye, he considered it more beautiful to neglect life than to neglect the hope for a crown. He endured until night, when the stars were coming up, being moved to fight to the end by the hope for victory, so that he was admired by our fellow citizens and the spectators from all the known world gathered for the most sacred of the events at Olympia. Because of this it was necessary to decree honors for the man in as much as he had enhanced and embellished the contest, and to entrust him to erect a statue of himself at Olympia and an inscription containing a testimony of other contests and showing what he alone among men did on behalf of the sacred games at all times. It seemed well to the magistrates and the people to praise Laetus's proposition and honor Rufus with citizenship and to entrust him to set up a statue at Olympia and an inscription containing what was described above. (*IvO* 54)

---

18. The *Hellanodikai* were the official judges at the Olympic Games.

The inscription describes vividly how Rufus's confidence grew during his matches by defeating his famous opponents, so that he arrived at the final match more tired than his rival, who had received a bye, but more motivated and willing to risk everything for victory. One can imagine that the incentive coming from defeating strong opponents solidified Rufus's intent to win. The hope for victory was his inspiration to tough it out until nightfall. Motivation is defined as both the direction and the intensity of one's effort.[19] Clearly, Rufus maintained his motivation throughout the evening. In the end, his motivation is probably what made him a victor above his physically less tired opponent.

Many other anecdotes reveal that ancient athletes did not fall short on other characteristics as well. Pausanias mentions Eubotas the Cyrenian, who, having been informed beforehand by the oracle in Libya that he would be victorious in the foot-race at Olympia, had his statue made before the race was run and dedicated it on the very same day on which he was proclaimed victor (6.8.3). One can certainly not say that Eubotas was not confident in his ability and hopeful in his victory.

Something that we also find in ancient sources is the fact that athletes do actually derive joy from their activities. The phenomenon called the "runner's high," whereby endorphins and other pleasure-enhancing substances are released during a great, continuous effort, is well known. Endorphins were discovered only in the 1970s, but of course their effect was felt well before that. For instance, Sir Roger Bannister described it in this way:

> I was as tired as everyone else, but suddenly for the first time I felt a crazy desire to overtake the whole field. I raced through into the lead and a feeling of great mental and physical excitement swept over me. I forgot my tiredness. I suddenly tapped that hidden source of energy I always suspected I possessed . . . I had expressed something of my attitude to life in the only way it could be expressed, and it was this that gave me the thrill. It was intensity of living, joy in struggle, freedom in toil, satisfaction at the mental and physical cost.[20]

Since this is a physical response to exercise, Greek athletes must have felt the same. Although Galen was not a proponent of elite sport, he nevertheless asserted that the best sports are those that worked out the body and delighted the soul (*terpein*). He included hunting as a sport and recognized that prac-

---

19. Weinberg and Gould 2011: 51.
20. Bannister 2004: 40.

ticing it "refreshes" the mind, because exertion is mixed with pleasure and delight.[21] Xenophon also mentions the joy that hunting produces, after one is strong enough for such labors (*On Hunting* 2.3). According to Xenophon, physical preparation and endurance come before one starts to enjoy the activity. But as in the case with Galen, this is just a sentence in the middle of their writing, without elaboration as to how one may derive pleasure from physical activity. In one of his works, Lucian lets Solon defend sport in terms of its usefulness and pleasure (*Anacharsis* 6). Solon again mentions that the delight of one's exertions comes only after the unpleasantness of the beginning (10).

Perhaps the word that best characterizes the enjoyment of sport is *philoponia*—literally, love of toil, but probably very close to what Bannister called "joy in struggle, freedom in toil, satisfaction at the mental and physical cost." The word is a general term meaning "diligence," and in addition to being applied to sport, it is applied to war, education, philosophy, or manual work. When the word refers to philosophy it is often used in clear opposition to sport,[22] which ironically attests to the sport context as being the most common for the use of *philoponia*. Philo of Alexandria describes *philoponia* as "sweet and pleasurable toil." He adds that "the sweetness in toil is love, desire, zeal and friendship for the beautiful."[23] Despite this, one is left with the impression that the Greeks saw the joy not so much in the process of exercising as in the result of victory.

5.3 Negative Emotions

Although athletics was used in Greece to create cohesion among the young men, certainly the discourse of competition is more prevalent in Greek sources. This contributed, no doubt, to the "attitude" problem of some athletes. Ancient sources are very clear about the disruptive character of some athletes, who, as Aristotle mentioned concerning youth, are prone to excess and vehemence. In fact, some athletes are clearly selfish and arrogant.[24] For instance, Pausanias tells the story of Theagenes of Thasos, boxer and pancratiast, said to be the son of a phantom of Heracles (6.11.2–9). Theagenes was one of the greatest

---

21. Galen, *Exercise with the Small Ball* 5.900.10.
22. See Isocrates, *Epistula* 8.5.3; Plato, *Republic* 535d.
23. *De congressu eruditionis gratia* 166, 3.
24. Competitive sport can produce self-centered athletes who avoid dealing with real-life issues. See Weinberg and Gould 2011: 103.

athletes of all times in Greece. He won over thirteen hundred victories. His greatness did not exactly make him modest.

According to an anecdote, at nine years of age, Theagenes wrenched up the bronze image of some god from the market place and took it home. The citizens of Thasos wanted to kill him, but one of them recognized his strength and asked him to put the statue back. This anecdote serves to illustrate that Theagenes was perhaps a brat who since a very young age got away with what would have cost others their lives. After he had accomplished many deeds in the heavy events, he switched to long-distance running. According to Pausanias, he did so to imitate Achilles. It is not unusual that athletes measured themselves against the heroes of old. Certainly, Theagenes must have been a man of great ambition and very sure of himself. Pausanias tells us that he entered at Olympia in boxing and pancratium and defeated Euthymus at boxing, the winner of the previous Olympics (6.6.6). He did not manage to compete in the pancratium out of exhaustion after the boxing match. The umpires fined Theagenes because they thought he had entered the boxing to spite Euthymus; this would reveal the destructive character of Theagenes's competitiveness, which made him push ethical limits. Plutarch tells another anecdote on the overemphasis in winning (*Praecepta gerendae reipublicae* 15.7). According to Plutarch, when Theagenes was at a banquet for a hero, after the food had been served he started to fight the pancratium because allegedly no one was allowed to win if he was present. His extreme competitiveness incited a lot of envy, even after death.[25]

As we saw in the previous inscription of Callicrates, envy is an emotion often associated with those who cannot be as good as a certain athlete.[26] Ten curse tablets dated to around 250 A.D. and found at stadia demonstrate not only the envy of which elite athletes were objects but also indirectly the physical and mental characteristics that they possessed.[27] Of the ten tablets, three are directed against the wrestler Eutychianus, son of Eutychia and coached by Aethales. We do not know much about Eutychianus, other than he presumably was a very good wrestler. As is the case in curse tablets, the

---

25. Pausanias (6.11.6–8). Competition can foster interpersonal hostility, prejudice, and aggression, as well as envy, humiliation, and shame. See Weinberg and Gould 2011: 116.

26. Envy of other athletes' performance is not just an ancient Greek obsession. In the early 1990s the sport of figure skating followed the rivalry of Tonya Harding toward Nancy Kerrigan, an attempt to break her leg included.

27. Tremel 2004. There are many more tablets found at circuses (80) and amphitheaters (10). Most of them are directed toward the charioteers and their horses.

name of the mother is mentioned since the mother is always certain and the person cursing wants to be sure to jinx the right individual. The curse is very immediate and intends to work its effect for "this coming Friday." The person speaking the curse wishes that Eutychianus loses his resolve (*gnomē*) and his strength and that he does not wrestle, but if he does, that he does so in such a manner that he would fall and shame himself.

> Borphorbarbarborbabarphorbaborborbaie strong Betput, I give to you Eutychianus, whom Eutychia bore, so that you freeze him and his resolve. (I give him) into your gloomy air and those with him. Bind him onto the darkest eternity of forgetfulness and freeze him and destroy his wrestling which he is about to wrestle in the DH. .EI this coming Friday. And if he wrestles, so that he may fall and shame himself. Mozoune Alcheine Perpertharona Iaia, I give to you Eutychianus, whom Eutychia bore. Strong Typhon Kolchoi Tontonon Seth Sathaoch Ea, lord Apomx Phriourigx upon obliteration and freezing of Eutychianus, whom Eutychia bore, Kolchoicheilops, let Eutychianos freeze and not be well toned this coming Friday, but let him be loose. As these names freeze so shall Eutychianus freeze, whom Eutychia bore, whom Aethales coaches. (*SEG* 35: 213)

The second tablet aimed against Eutychianus informs us that his opponent is a wrestler called Secundus, probably not the dedicator himself, since other tablets mention other opponents. Although we do not know who cursed Eutychianus, it might have been someone who was betting against him or had a grudge against him. The second and third tablets give us a bit more insight into the qualities that made him such a formidable wrestler. The second inscription reads:

> Orphorbabarphorbabarphorbabarborbabaih, strong Betpu, I give to you Eutychianus the one who is going to wrestle Secundus, so that you may freeze Eutychianus and his resolve and his energy, strength, wrestling and (I give him) into your gloomy air and those with him. Bind him into the darkest eternity of forgetfulness and freeze and destroy the wrestling of Eutychianus the wrestler. If you freeze him with respect to Secundus and do not let Eutychianus wrestle, so that he may fall and shame himself, Morzoune Alcheine Peperrtharona Iaia, I give Eutychianus to you. Strong Typhon Kolchloichelops, let Eutychianus the wrestler freeze. As these names freeze so let the

name of Eutychianos freeze and his soul, passion, victory, knowledge, strategy, knowledge. May he be deaf and dumb and witless, guileless, and let him not wrestle against anyone. (*SEG* 35: 214)

The third inscription presents a small variation at the end (*SEG* 35: 215): "Let Eutychianus freeze with respect to his name, soul, passion, knowledge, victory, mind, knowledge, victory, strategy. May he be witless, guileless, without hearing, without passion."

Except for the victory, which is not a quality but the result, the inscriptions insist on two types of qualities, volitive and intellectual. Of these, the intellectual qualities seem to be more important. A good wrestler needs to know well his sport and prepare mentally for it; he needs to perceive the situation well and think on the spot and adapt to his opponents' reactions. The curse is certainly formulaic; nevertheless, the qualities it wishes to obstruct correspond to the reality of sport. Basically, the curses are about mental anxiety. It has been shown that if athletes cannot manage anxiety, it causes a lack of concentration. Tasks that seemed easy before are no longer so, the muscles tense up, and fatigue ensues, making coordination difficult. Also, anxiety affects the visual and other perceptual patterns, memory, and thought control, making athletes doubt themselves.[28] The curses clearly show an understanding of the symptoms of anxiety in a person under stress. The person cursing the athlete was obviously a keen observer of athletic behavior and understood well the dangers of not controlling anxiety.[29]

The insistence on cursing with anxiety is also extended to the runners Aphous and another runner, as seen in the following curse:

> Bind and bind down the tendons, the body parts, the mind, the understanding, the intelligence, the 365 parts and tendons of those around ... whom Taeias bore and (bind) Aphous whom Taeis bore, the runners, so that they not ... nor are they strong, but that they lie awake all night and they vomit all the food to their detriment ... and so that they are not strong to run, but they come last. And you hold them back ... whom Taeias bore and Aphous whom Taeis bore, in

---

28. Weinberg and Gould 2011: 93–94.
29. Controlling anxiety is a very important aspect of being an elite athlete, and pressure can be a great motivator, as Shaun White, an Olympic snowboarder, explained in an interview. "A lot of people, they can't stand the pressure of having to win, of having to feel like people are watching or expecting things. I love it. I like the fact that people are counting on me to do something brand new, something that's never been done before and be the guy. I like that feeling and so I use it as a motivator, I tend to rise to the occasion" (CNN 2011).

all and impede the head and eclipse the eyes so that they might not be strong in the run and they are struck dumb and dim ... by your strength, lord, ... Abrasax.³⁰

These two runners were cursed not only with mental symptoms of stress and anxiety but also with physical ones, such as sleeplessness and an unsettled stomach. The ancient Greeks recognized that anxiety was a major issue in athletes, as we can read in Philostratus, who describes a type of athlete as the "anxious" one (*agoniostēs*) (53). This particular athlete type needs to be influenced in his mind with encouraging and uplifting words. He has to train with those athletes who are insomniac and have problems with the digestion. Obviously, many athletes would have had in anxiety their weak point and the writers of curses knew it well.

Psychological pressure extends also after retirement. Modern sociologists of sport describe as social death the adjustments at the retirement of athletes, when the benefits of being famous and successful disappear. Stories abound about once successful athletes being unable to reintegrate into the society. Many become depressed, abuse drugs and alcohol, and even commit suicide.³¹ Although all athletes that retire require adjustments on a social, physical, and personal level, about 15 to 19 percent of them require considerable emotional adjustment.³²

Not all ancient Greek athletes had difficulties after their careers were over. Most of them went on with their lives, some became coaches, as for instance we read in Pausanias about Iccus, a Tarentine, son of Nicolaidas, who gained the Olympic crown in the pentathlon and is said to have been afterward the best trainer of his day (6.10.6). This must not have been an isolated case. Coaching is still nowadays a good career option for retired athletes.

Nevertheless, as we can read in the famous fragment of Euripides's *Autolycus*, there were some athletes who had difficulties integrating back into their social context.

> Of the myriad of evils that are in Greece, none is worse than the race of athletes. For, first of all, they neither learn to live well, nor could

---

30. Institut für Altertumskunde, Universität Köln, inv. nr 4, lines 13–32.
31. See the recent deaths in strange circumstances of hockey players Derek Boogaard (May 13, 2011), Rick Rypien (August 15, 2011), and Wade Belak (August 31, 2011). It is still not clear what caused the death of thirty-five-year-old Steve Montador on February 15, 2015. Montador suffered from depression after repeated concussions.
32. Wylleman, Lavellee, and Alfermann 1999: 14.

they do so; for could any man being a slave to his jaw and defeated by his belly acquire bliss to surpass his father's! For they are not able to suffer poverty, nor accommodate themselves to fortune; and so being unaccustomed to good habits, they harshly fall into helplessness. In youth they shine and walk about as adornments to the city, but when bitter old age falls upon them, they walk around as cloaks, which have lost their threads. (Quoted in Athenaeus 413c–d)

Euripides complains that old athletes are reduced to almost a beggar status after having spent their wealth. This was certainly a problem not only in ancient Greece. Modern parallels are countless, as a quick internet search reveals.[33] Although ancient sources are mostly silent about the reasons for such behavior, some anecdotes reveal that, in fact, it was not always easy for athletes to come back to a normal life.

Pausanias describes how the pancratiast Timanthes of Cleonae committed suicide after retiring from an active life as an athlete (6.8.4). Apparently Timanthes tested his strength every day by drawing a bow. After a period of time of not practicing, he could not draw the bow and committed suicide by jumping into a fire. Pausanias qualifies the action as madness rather than courage. This act of madness, however, may not be an unusual response by successful athletes toward their retirement or failure to meet expectations.[34]

Cases of unsuccessful reintegration were apparently as common in antiquity as they are today. Pausanias tells the story of Cleomedes of Astypalaea, who killed his opponent in a boxing match by what the umpires thought was foul play (6.9.6–7). The frustrated athlete who had been deprived of the prize and probably of a subsequent career became mad owing to grief. As a consequence of that grief Cleomedes attacked a school and pulled down a pillar, killing sixty children. Why Cleomedes came to attack sixty innocent children is not said. Being pelted by the citizens, Cleomedes took refuge inside a chest, and when the chest was finally opened, he had vanished. The myth represents figuratively Cleomedes's suicide—he went into a chest as if it were a coffin.

---

33. In 2009, a study of *Sport Illustrated* revealed that 78 percent of NFL players were bankrupt two years after retirement. See Torre 2009.

34. Well known is the case of the Japanese marathon runner Kokichi Tsuburaya, who committed suicide because he was injured a few months before the Olympics in 1968 and was conscious that he would not be able to win. His suicide note read, "I cannot run anymore." After Tsuburaya won bronze in 1964 in the Tokyo Games, he became a media star in Japan and the government subjected him to a very strenuous training during which he could not even see his family or girlfriend. Thinking that he would be a disappointment to everybody, he opted for suicide.

The social death of the athlete provokes anger against the innocent and then is followed by the death of the perpetrator. Cleomedes could not be found in the chest, and the citizens realized that he had become a hero.[35] The story again follows a pattern of heroization of dangerous persons, in this case an athlete. Nevertheless, it may still suggest that forceful retirement from elite competition was not always considered in a positive way.

5.4　External Influences

Besides the help of other athletes, in order to develop successful athletes, there needs to be other positive influences. "Talent cannot be developed unless it is valued by society and recognized and nurtured by parents, teachers and coaches."[36] As mentioned above, Philostratus addresses a coach's influence on his athletes (*On Gymnastics* 20–24). Philostratus gives five different examples of athletes who were motivated to win. For instance, Promachus's coach lied to him and said that the girl he liked would give him her love, if he won at Olympia (22). This is a typical example of how extrinsic reward is combined with intrinsic motivation.[37] Some other examples show the confidence that the coach had in the abilities of his athlete and in his own ability to instill them in him. The Egyptian Optatus won the race at Plataea for his second time because his coach was willing to offer himself as bond. According to Philostratus, the law in Plataea was that whoever ran for a second time after winning once was to be put to death if he did not win. This might not be true, but nevertheless it points out that the coach showed his confidence in Optatus, and this gave him the strength and confidence to win.

This passage, although extreme, is a typical example of how the coach's confidence in the athlete can motivate the athlete to perform to his best.[38] Greeks were certainly very aware of the coach's influence on athletes. For instance, Pausanias also narrates some anecdotes in which the influence of the coach was key to victory. Although the anecdotes may not be entirely true, they certainly illustrate more general concepts about motivation of athletes

---

35. Heroization of athletes is not uncommon. See Golden 2013.
36. Gould and Dieffenbach 2002: 176.
37. Weinberg and Gould 2011: 138.
38. Gould and Dieffenbach (2002: 193) state that the confidence that these coaches had and displayed in their athletes helped their psychological development. As one athlete said, "Coach X, I mean, he just believed in me and that is all it takes. You know, I just feel like he cared about me as a person and he believed in me as an athlete."

and coaches. Pausanias tells the story of Artemidorus, who was first too young and too weak and therefore lost his first Olympics. Pausanias continues:

> When, however, the time arrived for the contest held by the Ionians of Smyrna, his strength had so increased that he beat in the pancratium on the same day those who had competed with him at Olympia, after the boys the beardless youths as they are called, and thirdly the best of the men. They say that his match with the beardless youths was because of his trainer's encouragement and also that his match with the men was because of the insult of an adult pancratiast. (6.14.2–3)

It becomes clear from this passage that beating the boys was due to the fact that he was by now big and strong. He might have entered the competition for the beardless youth and the men without expectations, but after winning the boys' category the coach wanted him to try out the next level. Certainly, external influences were key to his victory in the next levels. First the coach encouraged him, and then his own passion was stirred.[39]

Some anecdotes reveal that athletes themselves saw the coach as a positive influence and an important factor in their success. Pausanias tells the story of Cratinus of Aegira in Achaea who was the most skillful wrestler of his time (6.3.6). After his victory over the boys in wrestling, the Eleans allowed him to set up also a statue of his trainer. Even in the case of a very young athlete, the Eleans recognized that the coach was a fundamental part of his success. This is also expressed by Philostratus, who agrees that some athletes' victories can be credited not only to the athletes themselves but also to the coaches (13).

Sometimes coaches may have appeared as overbearing and as claiming too much of the success of the athlete. For instance, Pausanias records the inscription on the statue of the Samian boxer, which declares that the statue was dedicated by his trainer, Mycon, and that the Samians are the best of the Ionians at athletics and sea-fights, but about the boxer himself the inscription says not a word (6.2.9). Perhaps the coach was trying to live vicariously through the success of his boxer.

Ancient Greek athletes found motivation not only in their coaches' words and actions; perhaps the most important influence came from their families, especially their parents. Greek sources offer several examples. Pausanias in

---

39. "I think it is the duty of the coach to encourage resource and initiative in all of us. . . . The mental approach is all-important, because the strength and power of the mind are without limit. All this energy can be harnessed by the correct attitude of mind" (Bannister 2004: 178–79). See also ibid., 162–63.

books 5 and 6 of his work mentions some stories worth mentioning. He tells the story of Daemonicus, who was so eager for his son to win in wrestling that he even bribed the father of the son's competitor (5.21.16). The umpires did not fine the sons for manipulating the results, but the fathers, for they were the real culprits. The story is in accordance with the information about the oath that athletes, their fathers, brothers, and trainers had to swear that they would not do anything against the rules (5.24.9). The Greek wording emphasizes the concern about the members of the family and secondarily mentions the trainers. This is perhaps because they recognized family members to be the greatest influence, both positive and negative, on the athletes.

That victory in the ancient games was a family event is known clearly through the *epinicia* or victory songs of Pindar, in which the ancestry of the athlete is constantly mentioned as proof that the success of one athlete comes from his whole line being favored by the gods.[40] Yet, the encouragement to their children is a more difficult matter to ascertain.

Like today, a number of the athletes were born into an athletic family. For instance, Hippocles, whom Pindar praises in the tenth Pythic Ode for his victory in the double race of the boys, is the son of a two-time Olympic winner. In his seventh Olympic Ode, Pindar praises Diagoras for his victory in boxing and his father Damagetus, who delights in Justice (v. 18–19). The young wrestler Alcimidas, praised in the sixth Nemean Ode, is the grandson of Praxidamas, an Olympic victor, victor five times at Isthmus and three at Nemea. Three of Diagoras's sons and two grandsons were also Olympic victors.

In the case of athletes who stem from an athletic family, it is clear that there is a need for emulation and sense of pride passed on from one generation to the next. It was common that children took over the trade of their fathers, independently of what that trade was. Continuation of trades was easily assumed without any mentioning of parental support. Children were expected to live up to the ideas of the family, and in the case of an athletic family, the children would have followed suit.

In ancient times, as we saw in a previous chapter, the genetic factor was explained in terms of what they called eugenics. For instance, Philostratus describes the mothers of athletes as being robust (17) and manly (23). He talks about the parents of athletes being young and strong when they engendered their offspring (26–29). Besides eugenic considerations, there is an important psychological support that parents could offer their children. Philostratus

---

40. About the poetic celebration of athletes of the child and beardless youth categories, see Howie 2012.

retells the anecdote that Pherenike, daughter of the famous boxer Diagoras and mother of the boxer Peisidorus, also an Olympic winner, not only risked her life by sneaking into the public dressed as a man because she was so robust but did so to coach her son (17). Pherenike must have been truly exceptional, a woman who could not only support her son emotionally and psychologically but also coach him in the technique of boxing.

The influence on the athlete may not have come only from the parents. Brothers and close relatives would also have encouraged each other. An epigram presents to us a group of four brothers who were all successful athletes.

> (1) I conquered the diaulos. (2) and I in wrestling (3) and I in the pentathlon (4) and I in boxing. And who are you? (1) Timodemus (2) and I Cres (3) and I Cretheus (4) and I Diocles. And who is your father? (1) Cleinus (2,3,4) and ours too. And where did you win? (1) at the Isthmus and you where? (2) In the Nemean grove and by the home of Hera. (*Greek Lyric Anthology* 5.13.5)

There is something missing at the end so we cannot know where the last two brothers were victorious. All participated in different sports. This may indicate that they all pursued the sport that may have been more suited to them as individuals, but also it avoided competition among them by their not having to eliminate each other. Cleinus was not only a proud father, he was probably also a very smart man to avoid rivalry between his sons. This probably allowed the children to encourage each other.

Fathers appear also fostering their children's careers even when they were not directly involved in sports. As we saw in a previous chapter, Pausanias talks about Glaucus the boxer, who fixed a plough using his hand instead of a hammer (6.10.1–3). His father saw that and entered him at Olympia. Because of his lack of knowledge in boxing, which implies that his family was not involved in sports previously, he was losing to his opponent until the father called out, "Son, the plough touch!" So Glaucus delivered a powerful blow and with that started a successful career that made him an Olympic victor, twice a victor at the Pythian Games, and eight times a victor at the Nemean and Isthmian Games, respectively. We have to assume that he received some good coaching afterward because Glaucus became the best boxer of his time.

Perhaps because sport allowed social mobility—if not always in economic terms, certainly in prestige—we find that some younger athletes were pressured by their parents to achieve success. As the anecdote about Daemonicus and bribery reveals, the fathers were the real originators of the misconduct.

Taken in conjunction with the oath that fathers needed to swear, we can assume that indeed in some cases there was a lot of pressure placed on the children.

The pressure came also from the mothers, not just the fathers. Pausanias mentions Deinolochus, about whom his mother had a dream while she was pregnant (6.1.5). Deinolochus's mother saw him wearing a crown. Pausanias states that "for this reason he was trained as an athlete." The use of the passive construction indicates that Deinolochus did not have much of a choice in whether he wanted to compete or not. Interestingly, he competed in the boys' events and did not seem to have an athletic career afterward. Are we dealing with a case in which the parents are more interested than the sons in their sports success? Modern psychologists think that successful athletes had supportive parents, but not parents that pushed them into competition. Studies about athlete and parent perception conclude that the attrition rates of junior athletes increase with the emphasis on competition outcomes. These junior athletes perceive their parents to be more upset at their lower performance than parents themselves admit. About one-third of the athletes say that their parents have embarrassed them at competitions, either by yelling, walking away, or even hitting them after the match.[41]

Ancient Greek parents do not seem to be an exception to this perception. The young Deinolochus possibly burnt out after he won his crown; by then he might have thought that his mother was satisfied. Also, the young Daemonicus would have been embarrassed by the misconduct of his father. Sources do not generally investigate more than the anecdote. But it is clear from Pausanias's words that the father wanted the victory more than the son. Significantly, neither the parents of Deinolochus or those of Daemonicus were successful athletes. In the case of Deinolochus this is obvious, since it is the mother who had a dream, but also in the case of Daemonicus there is no indication that the father was a successful athlete himself. It seems it is not only a modern phenomenon that some parents try to live their dreams through their children.

Through our examination, it has become clear that ancient Greek athletes' performance depended not only on physical factors, but very much also on psychological ones. Those athletes who found motivation and controlled their anxiety were more successful than those who did not. Greek coaches and acute observers of athletics were conscious of the need for developing

---

41. DeFrancesco and Johnson 1997.

the proper psychological characteristics. Although not to the same scientific level as today, there was a clear understanding that victory in sport depended on more than physical preparation.

In the previous chapters we have seen that the majority of athletes were boys and young men, since it is during youth when physical abilities and recovery are at their highest. Whereas all athletes trained, competitive, high performance athletes needed to do so at times in an exclusive manner, which created a contradictory attitude toward training. During the archaic and even classical times, training was not deemed suitable to be talked about. Training went directly against the aristocratic idea of being the best by nature alone. During the Hellenistic times and certainly later during the Roman imperial times, there seems to have been a change in the training methods associated not just with internal developments in the sports, but with society in general. Although testimonies about training seem to focus more on the physical aspects, there is no doubt that the Greeks understood that training the mind was an important component of high performance.

In the next section, I will deal with perhaps the most common athlete in terms of numbers, namely, the athlete who practiced sport as part of his school education. For most participants, sport in the school and festival system would have been the extend of athletic participation, but certainly there was a fluid transition between the high performance and the school activity. Although there was a certain amount of competition involved in education, the purpose of this sport was not so much intrinsic as extrinsic, namely, turning the young man into a good man. This is the reason why we can speak of separate categories. We will look not just at sport during the school and ephebate years but also at how the change in education that took place during the fifth century created a change in the understanding of personhood itself, which in turn affected the role of sport and propelled perhaps the change in training discussed previously.

Part II

The Athlete during the Formative Years

6

Sport and Education

It is important not to conceive of sport as a monolithic block, but instead to recognize many levels of involvement in physical activities, just as in today's society. Besides the competitive component of sport, another essential aspect of Greek sport was its use as an educational tool. This is sport that involved children probably from seven years onward and lasted until the young men were about twenty or twenty-one, provided they could afford to stay in school for such a long time. The school sport overlapped in part with the years of entry into high performance competition.

Likewise, the discussion about sport needs to include not only historical and sociological facts, but also attitudes and ideological positions that influenced the training and performance of the athletes and the perception that others had of them. In the previous section, I discussed issues of class and especially issues of age. It became apparent that athletes were in need of instruction because they were by and large young men. In this chapter, I will discuss the dichotomy between body and mind in the study of ancient sport. This is important because the value ascribed to sport depends on the value attributed to the body in relation to the mind. When the person is conceived as a unity of body and mind, there is, generally speaking, equal emphasis in developing both parts. When one aspect takes precedence over the other, its development and training becomes dominant. In ancient Greece, a change in the relation between body and mind took place during the classical times, which affected how sport was conceived in its role of human formation. Since sport was mostly an activity for the young, obviously the changes in the concept of personhood affected how they were educated.

6.1 Dichotomy of Body and Mind

It was clear to the Greeks that human beings possessed both a body and a mind. The very common phrase "words and deeds" reflects the two spheres that humans were supposed to foster. Yet, the relation varied over time. Homeric heroes had an embodied soul (or mind).[1] Their mental activities were tied to their bodies; they were what Long calls a "psychosomatic whole."[2] It is from this original concept of man that the Greeks devised the old aristocratic education (*paideia*) to include the equal development of body and mind. Though there was the attempt to achieve such a goal even in Homeric times, natural differences occurred. For instance, Achilles recognized that there were other speakers more powerful than he was, whereas Odysseus was praised for his intelligence.

With regard to sport, we see the disjunction of body and mind already in *The Odyssey* (8.176–77). In the festivities after dinner, the Phaeacians want Odysseus to participate in their games. Because Odysseus is reluctant to accept, Laodamas accuses him of not resembling an athlete (8.165). Odysseus in turn accuses Laodamas of the fact that his outward appearance does not correspond to his mind; that is, he accuses him of being beautiful in body but weak in mind. This is the first time in the work, but it certainly will not be the last, that such a discrepancy between body and mind is mentioned. The ideal aristocrat is strong in both body and mind: he is an athlete, but also someone able to speak in public without offending his guests. The Phaeacians excuse themselves by saying that they are not really athletes and, therefore, not part of the Greek aristocratic world. They are not excellent in boxing or wrestling, but they are runners and seamen, eager to feast and dance (8.246–52). This confession about their lack of athletic ability still acts as a confirmation of the Greek aristocratic ideology of the unity of body and mind that Odysseus wants to exemplify. Despite his body being battered by the sea and his legs not being accustomed to running, he still retains the superior (natural) ability that silences the Phaeacians' taunts.

In the centuries after Homer, the division between body and mind was emphasized. With the expansion of ideas of the afterlife and the possibility that the soul continued existing after death, despite the body's decay, philos-

---

1. Homer did not distinguish between the body and mind of his heroes and used the same word (*psyche*) for both.
2. Long 2015: 29.

ophers started to consider the soul as the true self.[3] This in turn led to the eventual subordination of the body to the soul. One can perhaps also attribute the shift in the value of the body in relation to the mind to the development of nonaristocratic ideologies during archaic times. Greek society from archaic times on did not perceive *aretē* in general as an imbued characteristic of a person or class but as something teachable. Although there was no consensus about what constituted *aretē*, certainly athletic prowess was a common popular perception of it. Hence, the poets and philosophers, such as Xenophanes of Colophon, criticized the by then already traditional education of physical and mental development. Xenophanes saw his mental abilities as better serving the city than the physical abilities of athletes.[4] He also saw his attempts to reform society falling onto deaf ears. One of the longest fragments that we possess has to do with the criticism of sport.

> But if one were to win a victory by swiftness of foot, or in the pentathlon, where the sanctuary of Zeus lies by Pisa's stream at Olympia, or in wrestling, or participating in painful boxing or in the skilled contest they called the pancratium, he would look more glorious to the citizens, he would win a visible front seat at assemblies, and he would receive banquets at public expense from the city, and valuable gifts to pass on. If he won in the equestrian events, he would get all these things, yet not being as deserving as I am: for our wisdom is better than the strength of men or of horses, yet it is considered inferior. It is not just to choose strength over excellent wisdom. For if there is among the people someone good at boxing, or in the pentathlon, or at wrestling, or in swiftness of foot, which is honored more than strength as far as it goes for the works of men in the games, because of this the city would not certainly be better ruled. Small joy would it be to any city in this case: if anyone competing would win at the banks of the Pisa, for this does not fill the treasures of the city. (Xenophanes, frg. 19)

Whereas Xenophanes decries bitterly that his own worth is not recognized, he is jealous of those athletes who are honored by the city. Xenophanes created a distinction between his art and the ability of athletes. For him, athletes were overpaid and received honors due instead to the intellectuals. The body and

3. Ibid., 56, 89.
4. Harris 2009.

mind dichotomy was perhaps more a creation in the mind of the intellectuals than a reality of Xenophanes's times. But as education changed during the fifth and especially after the fourth centuries and became more academic, sport had less approval from the intellectual elite, yet it remained very popular with large sectors of the population. Thus, a gap was created between the "higher" and "lower" cultures in regard to sport.

The criticism of the cultivation of the body that started in the sixth century was exacerbated in the fifth and parallel to social and political changes, such as the institution of democratic systems in several cities. The new concept of personhood demanded a new education. Jaeger explains this shift when he discusses the role of the Sophists as the first ones to spread the belief that political *aretē* was teachable and did not just come by nature.[5] The question of what type of education was the most effective to lead a person to *aretē* was brought up to the forefront in the democratic city. Whereas the old aristocratic education aimed at developing the whole person in his physical and spiritual aspects, the ideal of manhood that arose within the new political system demanded its own answers. The democratization of aristocratic values implied at first the extension of those values to all citizens more than an actual replacement. For example, already during the tyranny of Peisistratus in Athens in the second part of the sixth century, the first public gymnasia were built, and perhaps, as discussed earlier on, there was a start to the democratization of sport. On the other hand, if virtue was no longer inherited, then it had to be transmitted and taught. During the fifth century, training individuals to serve and lead the polis became the ultimate goal of education. Political leadership was accomplished through the ability to convince one's peers in public by means of rhetoric. This in turn placed the focus on acquiring and transmitting intellectual knowledge. Therefore, the concomitant of the sophistic educational revolution was an intellectualization of learning.

Even if Plato and Aristotle later on "shook the [sophistic system] to its foundations,"[6] they also continued the trend of intellectualized culture and the training of the mind separately from the body. We owe to Plato the consolidation of the model of the separation between body and soul. Plato separated the body from the soul in order to create a concept of a soul that would be less vulnerable to the irrational allure of rhetoric in politics and to bodily desires.

---

5. Jaeger 1945: vol. 1, 286–98.
6. Ibid., 293.

A well-trained soul would temper the impressions received by the senses.[7] In this way, the soul took its place at the top of what was, from then on, considered a hierarchical ordering of the person. It became consequently necessary to train the soul through practice and self-discipline to achieve moral virtues.[8] Although to various degrees, the intellectualization of education changed the attention given to the body in education, and the role of sport in education and socialization of the young was questioned. Once the role of sport was opened for debate, the question was never settled. In fact, it still remains unsettled in our own modern societies. The changing of emphasis is symptomatic of a changing in values.[9]

It is clear that the Greeks saw education as a way to prepare the young generations to eventually assume the direction of society. We can read this in the fourth-century orator Isocrates, who was a proponent of the new type of education based on rhetoric as a means of personal social mobility and societal responsibility.[10]

> You are to give your vote not only about me, but about the occupation (*epitedeuma*) to which many of the young men (*neoteroi*) devote their mind. I suppose that you do not ignore that the older generation hands down the matters of the city to the next generation. Since this cycle continues always it is necessary that the young men are educated in such a manner that the city continues faring well. (Isocrates, *Antidosis* 173–74)

The problem was what to include in the curriculum to best serve the interests of society and the individual. Although Plato and Isocrates differed in the specifics of what education needed to include,[11] both conceived the *paideia* as aimed at developing a complete citizen. Plato offers the following:

> *Paideia* is that training in excellence from childhood that makes one into an adherent and lover of becoming a perfect citizen, knowing both how to rule and how to obey in accordance with justice . . .

---

7. Long 2015: 109–10.
8. Ibid., 123.
9. In the introduction to his *Paideia*, Jaeger expressed that "since the basis of education is a general consciousness of the values which govern human life, its history is affected by changes in the values current within the community" (1945: vol. 1, xiv).
10. For an understanding of Isocrates's ideas on education, see Poulakos-Depew 2004.
11. Gregorio 1999 offers a compact summary of the educational positions of Plato and Isocrates and their divergences.

> whereas an upbringing that aims at money or physical strength or some other cleverness without reason and justice is workman-like, slavish, and entirely unworthy of being called *paideia*. (*Laws* 643e–44a)

Even in Plato's early works such as *Protagoras,* which deals with the question whether virtue is teachable, there is a clear opposition between the body and mind, and yet the art that Protagoras claims to teach has nothing to do with the body, but it is centered on the mind. When one of Socrates's companions wants to entrust himself to Protagoras to be educated, Socrates criticizes the fact that people of his time pay more attention to the body than the mind, thus emphasizing the division.

> After this I said: what now? Do you know up to which kind of danger you are marching risking your soul? If you had to entrust your body to someone, taking the risk to make it better or worse, you would certainly look much around whether you ought to entrust it or not, and would ask your friends and relatives for advice and consider it for many days: but with regard to your soul, which you value much more highly than your body and because the conducting of all your affairs well or deficiently depends on whether your soul is better or worse, you would not consult with either your father or your brother or one of us your friends whether your soul should be entrusted or not to this foreigner who has just arrived. (Plato, *Protagoras* 313a–b)

Despite Socrates's concern, the sophistic education brought an emphasis to the intellect to the detriment of the body. The pale Sophists became a laughing stock in comedy; however, in the long run, their view of education centered on the mind was successful, owing in no small part to the rise of literacy and the abandonment of the traditional, orally based education.

Not all sources that we possess are in favor of the new education. More conservative writers like Aristophanes and Xenophon were proponents of the traditional education that developed the body parallel to a healthy mind. Aristophanes saw the athleticism and self-restraint of the old education being supplanted by deceiving rhetoric and amorality. He summed up the difference in education between the old one based on physical exercise and the new one based on the teachings of the Sophists in *The Clouds*:

> Just Argument: If you do what I tell you and apply your mind to it, you will always have a glistening chest, shining skin, big shoulders,

small tongue, big buttocks, small penis. But if you dedicate yourself to what the modern ones teach, you will first have pale skin, small shoulders, soft chest, big tongue, small buttocks, long thigh bone, long proposals, and he will convince you to consider the shameless beautiful and the beautiful shameless. (1009–21)

Xenophon was also a proponent of the old education. He was also concerned about the separation of body and mind in the education of his time and tried to oppose it. His treatise *On Hunting* is perhaps the most explicit in this respect: "men who are sound of body and mind fare almost always well in success" (12.5). For Xenophon, good men are those who can obey the law, and this happens as a result of good education based both on learning and toil (*ponos*). Toil fosters virtue, and consequently, an education that does not provide toil cannot cultivate good, wise men (12.15–19).

For Xenophon, the toil that is needed for virtue is achieved through hunting. According to this author, every young man out of his boyhood should take up hunting before going into other branches of education (2.1). He proposes, accordingly, to train the body before the mind and explains it most clearly at the end of the treatise (sections 12–13), where he opposes the education that hunting provides to that which the Sophists provide. Besides the general dichotomy of the outdoors and the city, there is as well the dichotomy between the ancestors (12.6), who taught the young virtue through hunting, and the Sophists of his time (13.1). According to Xenophon, these Sophists have not yet made any man good (13.1). On the contrary, hunting has the virtue of making young men healthy. They will also stay young for a longer time (12.1). But Xenophon especially thinks that the bodily development that hunting provides is useful because it prepares young men for war (12.1). The specific advantages that hunting offers for war are discipline, general endurance, the ability to run in different terrains, fitness, and confidence in one's own abilities, up to the point of being able to rout the enemy even in numerical inferiority (12.1–5). Most of these advantages were also attributed to educating the body through sport by the defenders of the old education, who saw the joint development of body and mind as a way to foster good men.

After the Sophists had proposed a new education based on the development of the mind, body and mind were hierarchically ordered. We read this for instance in Isocrates, who thought that the development of one would affect the development of the other, but both parts needed to be fostered in order to create whole individuals.

It is agreed that our nature is comprised of body and mind. Of these two no one would deny that the mind is the leader and is of greater worth. For the job of the mind is to make decisions about the private and the common affairs; that of the body to serve the judgments of the mind. Since these things are in this way, some of our early ancestors seeing that about other things there had been established many arts, but about the body and the mind nothing had been established, inventing two occupations, they handed them down to us: for the body the art of the coach (*paidotribēs*), of which gymnastics is a part; for the mind, philosophy, about which I am about to make this speech. These arts are responsive to each other, coupled together and in agreement with each other. Through these arts, the masters of each prepare the mind to be more prudent and the body to be more useful; both educations do this by not separating much from each other but by using very close methods of teaching both gymnastics and the other disciplines.

For when the coaches (*paidotribai*) take students, they teach the followers the techniques (*schēmata*) devised for the contests; the teachers of philosophy teach their students all forms in which speech happens to be used. Then having made them experienced and giving them an accurate knowledge of them, they make them exercise and accustom them to toil and oblige them to string together what they have learned according to each part in order that they may grasp them more strongly and they may be closer with the theories to the right time (when to apply them). For knowing when to grab the occasion is not teachable, for this escapes the knowledge of all matters. However, those who apply the mind more and are able to foresee the normal consequences will chance upon the right occasion most times.

Taking care of the students and training them in this way the teachers are able to advance them until they are better than the teachers themselves and have a better disposition, some in the practices of the mind, some in those of the body, respectively. However, no one happens to have the knowledge through which to make a strong athlete or strong orator of whomever they wish. They may contribute with a part, but the potential itself is present in those who bring forth perfection with natural abilities and effort. (Isocrates, *Antidosis* 180–85)

Even if Isocrates conceives the person as hierarchically ordered, he does express the need to educate both the body and the mind. He also expresses a training method that can be transferred from one aspect to the other. First comes technique, then physical conditioning and imitation, and then it is up to the athlete to be creative and know when to apply each action. He tries to explain his own trade of educating youth in rhetoric through something that was presumably known to many people, the athlete's development. There is no point in explaining something obscure through something more obscure. The implication is, therefore, that the audience was familiar with the process of training athletes, perhaps more so than with the process of teaching rhetoric to the young men. A second aspect that becomes clear from Isocrates's exposition is that people need both natural talent and effort to be really successful at what they are doing. This is a conciliatory position in comparison to earlier ways of understanding superiority. Whereas natural talent alone is not sufficient, there are things that cannot be taught. One of these is the tactically proper time to do things, either in rhetoric or in sport.

As the nature of the education of a good man was debated, so too was the role of sport. Philosophy took increasingly the role of education and, consequently, attempted to carve a new role for itself in opposition to traditional physical education. As the role of philosophy in education changed, so did the perception of sport. Even proponents of having sport as part of the education curriculum were perhaps inadvertently fostering the opposition between the development of the mind and that of the body, as we saw in Aristotle, who recommended not to exercise body and mind at the same time (*Politics* 1339a). Aristotle argued about the need to practice physical exercise from a very young age, and yet he still considered it more in opposition to the mind than as a complementary subject. Aristotle tries to present the middle way between the traditional education, which fostered sport, and the new tendencies that focused more on academic matters. Nevertheless, his assertions can be understood as evidence for academics having won the battle against sport. Certainly, Aristotle, who considered education as a way to actualize the potential of a person, proposed academic and character education ahead of the physical aspect.[12] In the *Politics* he mentions four areas of primary education: reading, writing (also drawing), physical education, and music (1337b). Both the teaching of physical education and music are supposed to contribute to

12. Collins 1990: 74.

moral maturation; physical education contributes to courage, whereas music contributes to general proper behavior and noble relaxation. But the ultimate goal remained the cultivation of the mind, both in the academic as in the emotional and moral aspects.

Sport, although subordinated to the direction of the mind, was considered an integral part of that education with the goal of creating good citizens, but any training that attempted to create specialized sport was not considered a proper education. In this spirit we see how the gymnasia became not only the places for practicing sports but also for teaching and discussing several matters in the other major areas of education: literacy, music, and philosophy. The education model for the free man aimed at the all-around development of the person, who would then be integrated into the political life of the city. This is a rather elitist concept that presupposes a person who does not have to work for a living and can enjoy the pleasures of culture for its own sake. How many actual persons were able to engage in an entirely liberal education is a totally different question.

The idea that the development of the body contributes to the development of the mind is also seen in later inscriptions. For instance, in the inscription in the Carian city of Mylasa, we read about a certain Chrysippus's contribution to the education of the children in his city. The inscription is an honorary decree for the superintendent (*paidonomos*) Chrysippus. There is no date, but it is written in *koinē*, which means that it is to be dated to the Hellenistic period or later. The inscription reads as follows:

> To the god, carrying the crown, the third after Ariston. He conducted the most seriousness and provision for the care of the children guarding in his return the convenient and proper things since the beginning, so that the children may become more eager toward the study, toward the contest of discipline, and toward the exercise in gymnastics. From all of this came more progress to the children to the advantage of the fatherland. Because of that he also accomplished more sacrifices to the gods on behalf of the health of the children and their safety. For the children and their teachers he frequently paid for sweets and breakfast, wishing to behave in a philanthropic manner. He also paid for a portion of meat for them. He also set frequently the customary contest for the children in the events practiced in the palestra, the footrace, wrestling, boxing, and the pancratium.

Similarly, he set prizes in contests in letters, in reading, calligraphy, and general knowledge. (*IMyl* 909, lines 1–19)

The inscription also emphasizes the need of sport and letters to be taught together as part of the integral development of the individual for the common good. There is no indication of a gradation of values, and both mental and physical education are treated as equally important to the common good. The inscription attests to the importance of the development of body and mind in conjunction and not in opposition. This is obviously not in agreement with our literary sources that tend to value the mind over the body.[13] Literary sources concede that the young man needs to train in sport, but only so that the body is able to carry out the decisions of the mind. This discrepancy between the literary and the inscriptional sources is something to be evaluated in the development and instruction of sport. To me, it shows a general contempt of sports by the intellectuals who, nevertheless, could not avoid mentioning this important social phenomenon. Intellectuals might have been more prescriptive than descriptive in their writings, presenting a world as how it ought to be in their own views more than as it actually was. Again, the different treatment of sport in the inscriptions and the literary sources may also attest to a dichotomy between a lower and a higher culture.

Later authors debate primarily the education of the free-born children in order to make moral adults with the right relation to the gods, the parents, the elders, and the laws. The actual schooling is discussed very briefly by Plutarch. "The same is to be said with regard to virtue: three things must concur toward perfectly just action, and these are: nature, reason, and habit. I call reason, learning, and habit, practice. The beginnings come from nature, advancement from learning, the use from continued occupation, and the culmination from all of them" (Plutarch, *On the Education of Children* 2a–b).

The passage attests to the fact that there are more than natural abilities when it comes to learning. It is very significant that the natural abilities have all been transferred to the intellectual sphere, and there is basically no mention of the training of the body. Plutarch later writes that whereas it is important for the children to be exposed to all branches of general education, it is necessary to make philosophy the head of all education (*On the Education of Children* 7c–d). He does not mention what the branches are, however, and focuses

---

13. Gregorio 1999: 42.

instead on the usefulness of philosophy. He also discusses briefly the role of sport in the education of the youth (8c–d). Sport ought to prepare youth for war and to strengthen bodies in discipline and self-restraint in preparation for old age. At any rate, physical effort should be administered in such a way as not to make the children tired "toward the dedication of education." The phrasing implies that education no longer includes physical exercise but is only academic and that sport is at best a complement to the general education.

Nothing characterizes the change in education better than the construction of the new gymnasium, seen in Vitruvius. Vitruvius describes the ideal gymnasium in his *On Architecture* (5.11). He describes the gymnasium as a place with no less than three porticos where benches can be placed for philosophers and students to discuss their lectures. There would be enough space for people to walk around without being impeded (!) by the athletes. Obviously, the Hellenistic gymnasium saw its function as much more than a place to do sports. Associated with the shift of what happens in the gymnasium is also the placement of the gymnasium in the downtown core of the Hellenistic cities as opposed to the outskirts of the classical ones.

> Even if the construction of the palestra is not Italian, nevertheless it has been handed down to us, so it seems right to me to explain and to show in which way they are built among the Greeks . . . (2) in the three single colonnades there should be built spacious seating, with benches in which the philosophers, rhetoricians, and those who delight in studies could discuss while they sit. On the side of the double colonnade there should be these parts: in the middle of it an *ephebeion* (here too a very large seating area with benches), longer by a third than the width. To its right, there should be a place to practice with the punching bag and then a place to wrestle. . . . (3) But in the outside the three colonnades should be arranged in this way: one as you leave from the peristyle, the other two, one on the right and one on the left, with a running track in them . . . they should be built in such a way that the parts that are around the walls and the columns will have margins, . . . so that those who walk around the margins dressed shall not be hindered by those who, being oiled, are doing exercises. (Vitruvius, *On Architecture* 5. 11.1–3)

By the end of the first century B.C., it had become clear that a public space for education was more important than a space for the practice of sport. Space for philosophers was provided under all four colonnades around the palestra to guarantee teaching all year round, even in bad weather. But more significantly, the running tracks allowed for an empty space around them in order for the students to move undisturbed by those doing exercise. Vitruvius's description makes it clear that it is those who exercise who hinder those who do not, not the other way around.[14] The athletes have been moved to the "periphery," so to speak, of their own space, and the separation between body and the mind has been completed.[15]

6.2 Sport Buildings and Their Users

To discern how sport was integrated within the school curriculum, we need to consider the evidence in relation to the places where sport was practiced, namely, the palestra and the gymnasium. There were two basic buildings in which sport was practiced: the palestra or wrestling grounds, and the gymnasium. Although there were private palestras,[16] it was not unusual for a palestra to be integrated into the architectural complex of the public gymnasium.[17] Besides the palestra, the gymnasium usually included a running track (*dromos*).[18] As time passed, it also included areas for changing, storage, and bathing.[19] The gymnasium was at first outside the city in a sanctuary by a stream, a type of open park. During the fourth century, the gymnasium was built closer to the agora in the city as a result

---

14. Yegül (1992: 23) argues that the change in education caused a change in the way the gymnasium was built. According to him, the new gymnasium reflects a shift from a physical to an intellectual mode of education. The second factor for the change in the traditional building of gymnasia was that the Greek gymnasium was associated with the Roman heated baths. This contributed to the "rising popularity of hot bathing and hydrotherapy."

15. König (2017: 161–64) discusses how the relation between physical and literary activities in the gymnasium was not always "mutually supportive."

16. Olivová (1984: 106) argues that a palestra could be a private school, perhaps in the home of a rich citizen, run by a *paidotribēs*. I do not see why the *paidotribēs* could not have the palestra in his own home, as we see, for instance, in an inscription from Delos set up by an Athenian coach, the first lines of which read, "Staseas, son of Philocleos from Colone, *paidotribēs*, inscribed those from his own palestra among the free children who performed the sacrifices, those who were in charge of the torch race, those who set up the competition and those who were the gymnasiarchs on occasion of the Hermaia games" (*ID* 2595, lines 1–6). A list of names follows these opening lines.

17. Kyle (1987: 66–68) notes the confusion that modern scholars have, since the Greeks seemed to have used the words "palestra" and "gymnasium" interchangeably. For an example of palestra inside a gymnasium, see *SEG* 32: 121: "The measured space to the citizens into the stoa in the palestra in the gymnasium of King Ptolemaios."

18. Gardiner (1930: 72) mentions that the palestra could be a private school, whereas the gymnasium included the *dromos* and the palestra.

19. Kyle 1987: 64–66.

of "increasing [its] civic and educational functions" and the "evolution of the city structure itself."[20] Whereas Athens' three public gymnasia were originally built on the outskirts of the city, Strabo mentions that the gymnasium in Nicaea, a Hellenistic city, was situated in the center of the main intersection (12.4.8). The gymnasium acquired more civic importance as its role as an educational place increased, and it was therefore moved closer to the center of civic activities.

The ideal use called for younger children to train in the palestra, older children and young men under thirty in the gymnasium.[21] Yet, the separation of users of the palestra and the gymnasium is not always strict in the evidence of inscriptions. The famous stele of the gymnasium at Beroea (*SEG* 27: 261) has a section dedicated exclusively to the children (*paides*, lines 14–26 of face B). The inscription states that the young men (*neaniskoi*)[22] are not to interact or talk to the children, and if they do so, they are to be punished by the gymnasiarch. It is obvious from the inscription that the children were at the gymnasium with the teenagers and young men; however, their interactions were prohibited. The purpose of the inscription may have been not only to prevent bullying and mockery of the younger children by the older ones, but also to make people aware that accidents are preventable through the intelligent scheduling of events and flexibility. In fact, the stele mentions different times of training for young men and children: "The ephebes and those younger than twenty-two years old shall practice javelin and archery each day when the children are to oil themselves or similarly if some other learning subject seems necessary" (lines 10–14).

The oiling of the athletes took place before and after the exercise. While the children would be in the changing room, the older participants would be throwing the javelin and practicing archery without the risk of hitting some young boy running around the grounds. It seems that, although the young men and the children share the same physical space, their training is conducted in such a way that it would limit interaction during alternative time slots. The children at Beroea were subjected to physical standards revised every four months, which implies that the children were also expected to compete against each other. Even this seems to imply that there was a rather strict age separation.

20. Yegül 1992: 9.
21. Gauthier 2010: 94.
22. *Neaniskoi* is a technical term for the younger *neoi*. Gauthier-Hatzopoulos 1993: 177.

It might not have been an exception that the young men and the children shared the same space, even if those were not the ideal circumstances. We can see this in an inscription dated to around 275 to 250 and found in Halicarnassus. The inscription is a decree of the assembly and the people for building a gymnasium with permission of King Ptolemy.

> It seemed good to the assembly and the people: a decree of the government (*prytaneon*). In order that the gymnasium of Philip may be reconstructed, since King Ptolemy agreed when the city was ruled by him that the young men may have a gymnasium and the children may regain the children's palestra, which now the young men are using, it seemed good to the people to repair it. Since the greatest works and the majority of them have been built and only a few are missing, he provides the wood and some of the woodworks and with the approval of the people some individuals promise to give the rest to reconstruct the gymnasium, some will lend money with interest and some without interest. (*Halikarnassos* 25, lines 6–21)

The inscription attests to the ideal use of the palestra by the children and the gymnasium by the young men. On the other hand, owing to some circumstances that made the gymnasium unusable, the young men had to move into the children's palestra. What the inscription does not totally explain is if both groups had to share the use of the palestra or if the children were displaced to somewhere else and therefore could regain the exclusive use of their palestra after the construction of the new gymnasium.

The division of a children's palestra from a young men's gymnasium is also attested to in an inscription from Miletus dated to the year 130 that contains a law concerning the cult of Roman Demos and Rome.

> On the eighth day of the month ascribed to him, let (the gymnasiarch) set contests in the children's palestra of the torch races and other athletic things, setting the proper competition. Let the superintendents take care with him of these things and follow up on the contest. The taking up of the set arms among the Romans, let it be according to the former custom in the gymnasium of the young men, and when the sacrifice to Rome is completed, in the Roman gymnasium. (*Miletus* 12, lines 12–22 on side A1)

Access to the gymnasium is set in its upper limit at age thirty. For instance, the gymnasiarchal law of Beroea mentions that the city should choose a gymnasiarch no younger than thirty and no older than sixty (*SEG* 27: 261, lines 22–24 of face A). It also mentions, in lines 55–56 of the second column, that participants at the Hermaea festival have to be younger than thirty. Although there is no direct exclusion from the gymnasium for those older than this particular age, the assumption has been that thirty was the upper limit for those sharing the gymnasium with the younger men and ephebes. On the other hand, we have seen that many famous athletes continued participating in high level competition until their mid- or even late thirties. If that is the case, they would have needed a place to keep up with their training. Two inscriptions may shed some light on that problem. Both inscriptions specifically mention a palestra for older people. Considering that most athletes who competed after thirty were heavy athletes, a palestra is all that they would have needed, leaving the gymnasium for those younger men who had to run sprints or practice their archery and other military training. This implies that the palestra may have remained a place to practice sport exclusively, whereas the gymnasium acquired a new educational role, whether academic or military. The inscription is an honorific decree for the gymnasiarch Histiodorus. It was found in Samos and is dated to the second century. It reads as follows:

> In the archonship of Leucippus on the seventh of the month Lenaeus, it seemed good to those who anoint themselves in the palestra for the old men (*gerontikē*), gathered in an assembly: Since Histiodorus, son of Heroidus, seeking glory from the beginning fulfilled his duty in a friendly manner and provided his own zeal to those senior (*presbyteroi*) athletes, and being gymnasiarch he conducted himself among all since the beginning in a manner that held nothing back in terms of ambition for glory. Since certainly we wish to appear honoring worthily those beautiful and good men who are benefactors to us, it seemed good to the senior men who anoint themselves in the palestra for old men to praise Histiodorus son of Heroidus for his virtue and good will toward those who anoint themselves. (*Samos* 119)

The second inscription was found in Cos and is dated to the years 54–100 A.D. "Under the monthly archons Hermias and Diogenous: those who went to the palestra for the old men (*presbytika*), the gymnasiarch being Tiberius Claudius Alcidamus, son of Alcidamus, the person in charge being Sextus Poppilius son of Sextus." (*Iscr. di Cos* ED 228, lines 1–5)

It is to be noted that the adjectives to describe the main users of the palestra are *gerontikē* in the first one and *presbytika* in the second one. Both adjectives refer clearly to a palestra for a certain age group, much as the palestra for children in the previous inscriptions was referred to as *paidetikē*. This is not the same as an old palestra in terms of the age of the building itself. About that possibility, an inscription at Delos talks about repairing the door of the old palestra, and the adjective there is *archaia* (*ID* 354, line 76). There is no doubt, therefore, that both inscriptions identify a separate user group of men older than thirty. The upper limit of their age is unknown. There is nothing preventing men in their forties and fifties (perhaps older) from participating in physical activities. True, these would not have been athletes seeking competition at the games, but the inscriptions are evidence that there was a whole range of levels in athletic involvement. Not everyone needed to be an Olympic athlete, but it is also difficult to believe that men who had been exposed systematically to the practice of sports since they were little children would have completely abandoned its practice just because they turned thirty. The intensity and the goals of training would have been certainly different, but the "older" men would have liked to spend time with their friends and brothers-in-arms in ways that fostered their well-being and social relations. The existence of palestras for "older" men attests that there is an understanding of recreational sport, at least in Hellenistic times, to which these inscriptions are dated.

6.3 Sport at Schools

Whereas the ideal use of spaces might have been that young children were trained in the palestra[23] and that the older ones were the main users of the gymnasium, together with those young men under thirty, it is clear that this was not always the case. A further complication comes from the different uses at different historical times. We cannot assume that what was valid for Hellenistic times was present during the classical age. During Hellenistic times, education (both academic and physical) became more formalized, which made the role of the gymnasium change in order to admit more academic education. Nilsson connected the development of the formalized school system of the Hellenistic period to the organization of the *ephebeia*.[24] According to

---

23. See Theophrastus, *Characters* 7: The chatterer going into the school and the palestra impedes the children's learning, so copious is his chattering with the *paidotribēs* and the teachers. It mentions both the *paidotribēs* and the teacher as an association, but yet there are different buildings.
24. Nilsson 1955: 29.

Nilsson, the institution of the *ephebeia* would have been established as formal military training in the 330s, but it saw a strong decline at the beginning of the third century and a revival at the end of the second century.[25] The *ephebeia* reappeared then more as an educational institution than as a military one, since the Macedonian conquest rendered the Athenian military unnecessary.[26] Since training of the ephebes took place mostly at the gymnasium, the change in the *ephebeia* influenced the concept of the gymnasium, which was conceived from then on as more of an educational than as a purely athletic place. The move from military to academic preparation also had the consequence that children no longer needed to be fully physically mature to enter the *ephebeia*. During the classical period, the age for entering the *ephebeia* in Athens was eighteen, but during the Hellenistic times the age came down to maybe fourteen or fifteen, depending on the cities. This in turn opened up the gymnasium for younger users. Thus, gymnasia became associated with the youths that had completed their "primary" education, probably those above fourteen years of age, who received physical and military training there.[27]

Greek school education was divided into at least two stages.[28] The young children of six or seven went to learn basic skills in writing and reading, and then, at about the age of twelve, the pupils moved on to analyzing literature and composing their own speeches and poetry. This stage may have lasted from the onset of puberty to twenty-one (Aristotle, *Politics* 1336b). Can we say the same about physical education? Was there a gradation of what type of sport was practiced at the palestra and then later on at the gymnasium? When would the children have specialized and moved on to practice high performance sport leading to competition?

Even if we know quite well how the academic part of education worked and that formalized schooling incorporated physical education, we do not know much about how both interacted. It is clear that not every child was expected to be a competitor at the Olympic games, but they were introduced to sport as part of their school curriculum. Even if asserting that the education directed at the free citizen included sport, we should question whether specialized sport was always part of it. Specialized, high performance sport worked, in fact, against the subordination of the body to the mind and presupposed physical excellence as the ultimate goal. This philosophical discrepancy made it hard to include

25. Ibid., 17–21.
26. Ibid., 26–27.
27. Cribiore 2001: 35.
28. Booth 1979: 1.

sport within the new academic curriculum, which emphasized the superiority of the mind. This new education started to develop in Athens during the fifth century, and it maintained the practice of sport, although its function was conceived of differently.[29] Whereas Kyle believes that there was a variance in the degree of specialization between physical education classes and training for competition,[30] Pritchard argues that, at least in democratic Athens, school training prepared children for competitions.[31] Although I agree with Pritchard that the *paidotribēs* was capable of providing specialized training leading up to major games, I think that he misses the point that Isocrates is directing his education not to the younger children but to the older ones, who may already have been frequent visitors of the gymnasium. Similarly, Pritchard discusses the classes of javelin throwing at the gymnasium as described in Antiphon's speech on the *Prosecution for an Accidental Homicide* (3.1.1), in which the dead person is described as a boy (*pais*), but the perpetrator is described as *meirakion* (young man of an age between a late teenager and twenty-one).[32] Referring to one's son as a boy, independently of his actual age, might not have been unusual.[33] Although I do not question that the *paidotribēs* was in charge of training the younger and the older children, there is no reason to assume that the older children especially received the training only at school and that there was not a higher level of training elsewhere.

From Aristotle's writings, it is very clear that there was at least a difference in intensity of the training appropriate for younger and older children. Aristotle did not recommend that intensive training happen before puberty, but certainly the young children would have attended general classes of physical education conducted by the *paidotribēs*.[34] Aristotle talks about children as young as five being introduced to physical culture through games (*Politics* 1336a). He had, no doubt, a preoccupation with early physical movement and recommended it even for infants. Aristotle mentions that at the age of seven children ought to become spectators of the lessons (presumably both physical and intellectual) that they will have to learn (*Politics* 1336b). However, he later recommends the training of the body before the training of the mind (1338b).

---

29. Pritchard 2013: 47.
30. Kyle 1987: 143. I disagree with Kyle when he bases his distinction on the use of the word *paidotribēs* (general coach) versus *gymnastēs* (specialized coach), but I do agree that there was a different level of coaching.
31. He argues this from a reading of Isocrates (*Antidosis* 181–85). See Pritchard 2013: 48.
32. Dean-Jones 2013: 112.
33. Ibid., 111.
34. See Pritchard 2013: 46–52.

So, children must be handed over to practice "gymnastics and the art of the *paidotribēs*" in order to develop habits for the body and its actions, respectively. Although Aristotle does not mention it directly, the underlying ideology here is that the body needs to be controlled and subject to the mind. Therefore, it needs to be ready beforehand to obey the mind.

Physical education was part of the school system, even if the palestra was at a different location than the grammar school, at which young children would have learned reading, writing, and arithmetic. The palestra was usually integrated into the gymnasium itself. This would be a general education in developing habits of movement. It may not have been specialized, although it did seem to be focused on wrestling in a manner similar to our modern school curricula that introduce soccer or basketball but maintain a sense of general development of motor skills for younger children. From the news of an unfortunate accident at a school in Chios, we know that some of the schools could be rather large. This particular school had one hundred and twenty children, all of whom died, except one, when the roof collapsed (Herodotus 6.27.1–2). An anecdote told by Pausanias (6.9.6–7) mentions that when Cleomedes of Astypalaea returned to his own town, he pulled down the beam that held the roof of the school with sixty children in it. Astypalaea is a small island, so this might have been the only school in town. Not all schools would have been as large, since education was restricted to those who could afford it, and not all children would have practiced at the palestra at the same time, but they would have certainly practiced in groups larger than optimal for individual attention.

One of these group lessons is described by Plato. This instruction in physical education may be conducted by professional instructors and yet still is not specialized on an individual basis and for individual needs, although it seems that this instruction was aimed at competition (*philonikia*, love of victory).

> STRANGER: There are in Athens and also in other cities exercises of sport for a group of men (*anthropoi*), either in running or something else, for the sake of competition, aren't there?
> YOUNG SOCRATES: Certainly many.
> STRANGER: Good, now let us recall again to our memory the orders of those who exercise with technique and are in charge of such classes [i.e., professional trainers].
> YOUNG SOCRATES: How so?
> STRANGER: When they serve, they consider that they cannot approach each one individually, ordering what is convenient

> for each concerning the body, but they think that it is necessary to give orders to the benefit of the body broadly, aimed toward the general and toward the majority.
> YOUNG SOCRATES: Certainly.
> STRANGER: Because of this, they give equal exercises to the whole group, they start together, they stop the running together, and all other workouts for the body. (*Politicus* 294d–e)

Unfortunately, the passage does not give us any indication about the age of the participants. Yet it is clear that the group in this type of lesson is too large to afford individual attention to each athlete, at least on a continual basis. There is no indication in the text about the size of the group, but even a group of ten to fifteen individuals may have been not optimal for individual, specialized instruction. We must then assume that if a school had sixty children, they would have also not received by and large individual attention. Plato's passage does not mention clearly that there were other types of instruction, namely, classes aimed to the particular and the individual. But the implication is that this was the case, just as modern high performance athletes, especially in combat sports, work a lot with private one-on-one lessons. The children that attended the palestra as part of the school education were not necessarily all competitors, but just active kids. Pritchard argues that during classical times technical instruction would have been received just in group lessons as described above and that this would have sufficed for participation at athletic contests. Yet, in my opinion, Plato describes an individual lesson of a running coach.

> And they alone, I presume, could most likely afford to give away their services without fee, if their words were true. For when a man has received any other service, for example, if he has acquired speed from a trainer's lessons, he might possibly cheat him of his due if the trainer freely offered himself and did not stipulate for a fee to be paid down by the other as nearly as possible at the moment when he imparted to him the fast pace he required. (*Gorgias* 520c)

Vases also show individual lessons, and although this may be because of the limitations of the medium, it is most likely because specialization needs individual attention. On the other hand, the fact that even people training within these broad parameters are said to train in order to compete may expand our idea about what the Greeks understood by competition. Indeed, there were the four crown games and other prestigious games, but there was also a whole array of small local competitions that invited a much larger group of competitors as well as regular mandatory demonstration at the gymnasia. So too today it is not the same to compete at the city league as at the regional, national, or international level, and yet participants are all competitors. Some athletes may have been happy just to compete against their schoolmates in the local games and without any intention of pursuing greater goals.[35]

The palestra where boys exercised had a schedule from sunrise to sunset, as we read in Aeschines (*Against Timarchus* 10). There it is clearly stated that, by a law attributed to Solon, palestras were not allowed to be open during the dark. This gives an indication that the palestra might have been occupied at least for about eight to ten hours a day, depending on the season. Different groups must have been scheduled at different times. This is clear in the gymnasiarchal law of Beroea, which mentions that the *paidotribēs* needs to be present twice a day at the time designated by the gymnasiarch. In addition, the *paidotribēs* has to be present at the "appointed time."[36]

We shall assume that not only for the private palestras but also for the gymnasia classes must have been scheduled at different times throughout the day. We know that Athens had three public gymnasia, the Academy, the Lyceum, and the Cynosarges. On the other hand, Socrates's response clearly states that there were many such group lessons. The implication is either that the lessons took place at many locations or that the gymnasia had a whole array of scheduled practice times, conducted for groups and not necessarily specialized. These possibilities are not exclusive of each other.

Fisher calculates that, in regular years, there were thirty *gymnasiarchoi*, that is, rich citizens in charge of financing and organizing the training of teams of athletes and dancers. In the years of the Great Panathenaea, the number increased to fifty.[37] If we consider that the torch race, the typical team event of Athenian athletics, took at least nine participants[38] per tribe, and that there were ten tribes, this gives a minimum number of ninety youth training for the torch races each year. The number was probably much higher, since

---

35. There were certainly games of different levels of competition. Not all games were as prestigious as the crown games, but even within the local games some must have attracted athletes of different calibers. Plutarch gives us a glimpse of this when he describes many of Theagenes's victories as rubbish (*Praecepta gerendae reipublicae* 15.7).

36. Gauthier 2010: 95. SEG 27: 261, B lines 15–20.

37. Fisher 2010: 73.

38. As seen already in the inscription *IG* 2^2 1250.

the best within a team would be selected to run. Fisher also points out that in the period of 334–332, there were between 450 and 550 ephebes.[39] This is a lot for only three gymnasia. The sheer number of youths, boys, and young men using the facilities demanded a well-regulated schedule, most likely according to age. Also, training would have been conducted in group classes, as Plato's *Politicus* point out.

Besides the regular children in school age practicing sport, a large proportion of the users of the gymnasium were already past the school years. The gymnasia became a meeting place for people of several ages where they exchanged ideas[40] or trained. This training was divided, perhaps, not only by age but also by willingness to train harder. The gymnasium was the place that allowed more talented and more committed athletes to pursue specialization in order to move on beyond local competitions.[41] Gymnasia were open for those under the age of thirty and probably over fourteen. Traditionally, they are seen as a place to train the ephebes and younger men, probably between eighteen and thirty (*neoi*), but inscriptions mention the admission of younger children.[42] The Platonic dialog *Laches* seems to indicate that the palestra was frequented mostly by boys in their late teens to age twenty-one (*meirakia*) but perhaps was frequented at different times also by much younger pupils and pupils all the way into manhood (179).[43]

The first time that the contests for children were introduced in Olympia was in 632 (Pausanias 5.9.9), which presupposes somewhat organized physical education throughout Greece.[44] It might as well presuppose specialized sport training beyond what children learned during the school attendance. As seen from the inscription at Beroea, there were revised standards that the children needed to meet every four months. This may be an indication that the level of training performed at the gymnasia, even for children, was higher than that performed at the "mandatory" school palestras. In fact, sport at the palestra does not have the sole purpose of competing but also of educating the body so that the mind can flourish and exert control over the body. We read this in Plato's *Protagoras*:

---

39. Fisher 2010: 71.
40. "I could not hear you clearly because there were many people around" (Plato, *Eutydemus* 271a).
41. Pleket 2005: 160.
42. Pleket identifies three groups of people accepted in the gymnasium: children, ephebes, and young men (ibid., 159).
43. Beck 1964: 131–32.
44. Marrou 1965: 80.

> The whole life of man needs good proportion and good harmony. Certainly, still after these [the music teacher and the grammar teacher] they send the children to the *paidotribēs*, in order that they serve the mind, being the better part, by having better bodies, and they are not compelled to act like cowards in war and in other activities because of the poor condition of the body. (326b–c)

The subordination of the body to the mind is clearly expressed in this passage, as it is also in *Gorgias* (452b), where Plato mentions that role of the *paidotribēs* is to make bodies beautiful and strong.

6.4 Excursus: Coaches

Corresponding with the ideal separation of the use of buildings and the attendance of athletes from different age groups, there was also an ideal division of coaching professionals. According to the ideal, there was the *paidotribēs*, who taught at the palestra, and also the *gymnastēs*, who taught at the gymnasium. Philostratus's treatise *On Gymnastics* is all about what constitutes the art (*sophia*) of the *gymnastēs*, his qualities, his knowledge, and the application of it to the physical and psychological preparation of the athlete. In chapter 14, Philostratus distinguishes between the *paidotribēs* and the *gymnastēs* as professionals for coaching. Both of them are responsible for teaching the technical and tactical aspects of the sports, but the *gymnastēs* would, on top of that, have knowledge similar to that of the physician and would be able to treat physical conditions with diet and massage, developing the body parts healthily and harmoniously by controlling the humors. Sport injuries, such as dislocations or fractures, would be a matter for the physician. The *paidotribēs*, on the other hand, would not be able to apply dietary measures or massages correctly and would do more damage than good.

After this short chapter, Philostratus no longer discusses the *paidotribēs* and concentrates on the *gymnastēs*, even if the description is not always positive compared to the practices of the idealized past. For instance, the *gymnastai* are accused of being responsible for the decadence of sport because of their tendency of accepting bribes (45). Philostratus's description presents a certain prejudice against the *paidotribēs* in favor of the *gymnastēs*. Because of Philostratus's unique role in describing the coaching practices in ancient Greece, we tend to think of *gymnastai* as possessing a level of specialization superior to the *paidotribai* and also as either dominating the profession, or at least being equally represented. The *paidotribēs* is generally presented as a physical education teacher, who would introduce the children to wrestling but was not a specialized coach. He was a professional who conducted the exercises in the palestra.[45]

However, if we consider the information available through inscriptions, we get a very different impression. Inscriptions hardly mention *gymnastai* at all. I have found only three inscriptions containing a reference to a *gymnastēs*:

> Basileides official and *gymnastēs*. (SEG 35: 1309)
> The Delphians to Itulenus Apolaustus from Smyrna, to the *gymnastēs*, because of his *kalokagathia* and the ethical behavior in life and his moderation to the city and its assembly. (FD 1: 220)
> Papias the *gymnastēs* lies here. (Smyrna 656)

The first inscription comes from Amasya in the Pontic region; the second comes from Delphi, although it mentions that the *gymnastēs* was from Smyrna; and the last one comes from Smyrna itself. This raises the question of whether the term *gymnastēs* may have been more popular in some regions than others. But other than that, there is not much information that one can derive from these inscriptions. On the other hand, the number of inscriptions that mention the *paidotribēs* is close to three hundred. Some of them provide a wealth of information that would be otherwise unavailable and certainly do not conform to any stereotypes that the literary sources may create for us.[46]

Whereas sources like Pausanias speak about coaches as being famous retired athletes, some inscriptions reveal coaches who do not seem to have had an athletic career but were just very good coaches. Although people now, and probably then, tend to think that a victor at the Olympics would be a good coach, well-suited to bringing his athletes there, in reality coaching demands a different set of skills. A good athlete does not always make a good coach and vice versa. The inscriptions seem to reflect this.

An inscription from the second century A.D. presents a coach (*paidotribēs*) who was a somewhat successful athlete, but perhaps not enough to mention in which contest he was victorious. The assumption would be that he was successful at local competitions, but certainly none of the bigger ones or he would have made a point of mentioning them by name, as is usually the case. The inscription mentions that he was crowned, but if he had been crowned

---

45. Beck 1964: 130–31.
46. For the social status of coaches, see Golden 2008: 34–39.

at any of the periodic games or Isolympic ones,[47] most likely it would have been mentioned by name.

> Oh stranger, you see the tomb of [Chrysius] who was made proud in many stadia and was crowned. The fatherland honored him. He was superior in beautiful contests of ephebes and all men, the coach. Now old age stopped his life, his wife having died before him, Chrysius having required to be accepted in the same tomb. (*Et. Anat.* 284, 8)

Another inscription, this one from the second to third century A.D. and found in Hermopolis Magna, Egypt, makes clear that there were coaches who did not participate much at any competitions. It is obvious that the coach (also a *paidotribēs*) Hermocrates knew the sport very well, and he might even have participated at local or other competitions. He was familiar enough with competitions to know that competitions entail a lot of hard work and hardships, but he may have never been a victor, as there is no mention of his victories. The inscription focuses only on his ability to teach wrestling techniques to his students. It seems he did a very good job at it. On the other hand, the age of his death informs us that he may have chosen to coach rather early in his life. It was not uncommon for successful wrestlers to compete past their early thirties. Milo was an exception, with a retirement age of closer to forty, but several of the most famous athletes retired in their thirties. It seems that Hermocrates had an established career as a coach, which may have been incompatible with a career as an athlete.

> I Hermocrates, the son of Hermaius, being young lie here.
> Powerful coach, thirty-two years old.
> Because of this also my mother died with me with a sudden death.
> With wretched pain, having her heart torn.
> I alone know many works of the art of wrestling with technique.
> I taught many hardships of competition.
> But no one of the mortals discovered (an escape?) from death.
> It strikes everybody, the way it wants.
> Not Milo, stronger than trees, fled
> Destiny, being defeated when a tree fell with the wind.
> It is for everybody to die and death is for everyone,
> But it is lamentable that the dear son dies before the parents.

---

47. Isolympic games were those games created during Hellenistic and especially during Roman imperial times, which were considered to be as important as the Olympics.

I the tomb, saying these things, hide a mournful body here,
Whom the parents buried being very distressed.
And who do you say this one was, the one who died before his
    parents?
He will know clearly all the letters, having read them.
The dear son of Hermaius was called Hermocrates.
. . . powerful.
This one taught the ephebes wrestling
To defeat everybody and not to fall on the ground.
But he himself fell to the strong wrestling of death.
He lies here having been defeated.
He did not leave any children, for he died before marriage,
Without a bride, having completed a life of only three times eleven
    years. (*Inscr. Métr.* 22)

Another inscription from the Black Sea and dated to the first century B.C. mentions a young coach (*paidotribēs*) with no clear athletic victories:

Pharnakes, son of Pharnakes, greetings.

Oh stranger, look at the stele of Pharnakes, whom grave Hades dragged having chased an unhappy age, in skill a coach, in years young (*neos*), in the fatherland of Sinope going from virtue into darkness. The land of the Bosphorus hides his urn and does not omit the gymnasium lamenting with silent tears. The father Chemation having chosen the tomb with affection preceding him in nature, lying together in the tomb of stone. (*CIRB* 129)

The age of the coach is not mentioned, but generally speaking the "*neos*" category would be still an age when sport is practiced as an athlete. The fact that this young coach died at an "unhappy age" implies that he might have chosen from early on to be a coach without necessarily having a career as an athlete. Perhaps his decision was prompted because of an early injury, or perhaps he could not commit the time and money to train and participate in the games far away from home, or perhaps he was simply not the best athlete around.

Another aspect that inscriptions bring to life is that there were several ranks among coaches (*paidotribai*). We are not sure of how the divisions were created and maintained or the possibility of moving up in the ranks of coaching. But certainly there is a clear distinction among professionals. The first inscription is an ambiguous one. It comes from Cos during the Roman imperial period and mentions either a chronologically older or professionally senior coach: Sextus Allius Epictetus, senior coach (*presbyteros paidotribēs*) (*Iscr. di Cos* [Fun] EF 103/435).

Does the word *presbyteros* refer to his age, or to a possible rank, as in the modern sense? Or does it refer to coaching only the older children? This interpretation would be supported by the fact that other inscriptions mention lists of children in up to three different age groups. Some inscriptions divide the children simply into the younger (*neoteroi*) and the older ones (*presbyteroi*), as the following one dated from between 188 and 160 B.C. does. Perhaps they had different coaches designated with these same adjectives.

> To Hermes and Heracles and King Eumenes, during the *prytanis* of . . . , while Harpalus was the superintendent of education of youth. He . . . son of . . . , son Pantelides, Heracleitus, Gnotas son of Hegetor, Artemidorus . . . To those children who were victors at the demonstration and those children who participated in the contests. Theodotus, son of Apollonides, was the coach, Alexandrus, son of Epicrates, was the grammar teacher, Sotocus, son of Hiero . . . was the drawing teacher, Timostratus, son of Menestratus, was the music teacher.
>
> > Of the younger ones:
> > . . . son of Seuthes, long distance
> > . . . son of Menander, stadium
> > Ptolemaios son of Eupolides, *diaulos*
> > . . . son of Ariston, wrestling
> > . . . son of Menogenes, boxing
> > . . . son of Metrodorus, pancratium
> >
> > Of the older ones:
> > Parthenius . . .
> > Klearchus . . .
> > Metrodorus . . .
> > Artemon . . .
> > Aristarchus . . .
> > S . . . ros . . .
> > (*Ephesus* 684)

The coaches' rank is expressed more clearly in a mid-first century A.D. inscription from Athens that mentions a subcoach or *hypo-paidotribēs*:

Apollonius Menneus, Athenian, having won the torch race, to Hermes, in the archonship of Asclepiodorus, when Meniscus from Colone was the coach, Dioscorides from Colone and Heracleitus Athmoneus were the subcoaches. (*ArchEph* 1973: 176,2)

There are a considerable number of inscriptions mentioning a subcoach, with or without the mention of a coach. The division between the head and the subinstructor also appears in other trades in relation to the education of youths, as seen in the next inscription. It seems that the subofficers might have been paid by the holder of the office.[48]

Col I. 1 To the Good Fortune:

In the second archonship of the most powerful priest of Athena Polias and priest of the Concordia of the Greeks, Titus Flavius Mondonus . . . of Philinus Plyeus, the overseer of the ephebes Aurelius Aphrodisius and Nicon Aphrodisius Sphettius, Roman knight, to those being archons with him and the ephebes during his time, being coach for life Aurelius Socrates, son of Artemidorus Eleusinian, five years, being overseer Aurelius Thales. . . . .

Epctetus, Agathopus, Erotion, Aphrodisius, Iacchus, Hadrianus, Threption, . . .

Col. II. 11 Those for life:

Director Zosas 2, teacher Onesicrates, *hoplomachos* Nymphodorus 5, leader priest Soterichus, sub-coach Aurelius Alexandrus 5, *diaconos* Polydeuces, sub-*diaconos* Eutychas, doctor Iulianos, teacher of grammar Alcibiades, sub-*hoplomachos* Olympios, subteacher of grammar Alcibiades, under Diogenios Nicon, the sling-shot master (*kestrophylax*) Philadelphus, intendant (*lentiarius*) Zosimus. (*SEG* 33: 158)

There were subteachers, sub-*diaconoi*, and even subinstructors in weapons, obviously because one person alone would not have been able to manage bigger gymnasia. In one inscription dated to 38/37 B.C. (*IG* 2^2 2995), there appears to be the same two subcoaches mentioned in another inscription under a different coach (*ArchEph* 1973: 176,2). The inscriptions might be up to a hundred years apart if our dating is correct, which would make it

---

48. Dmitriev 2005: 230.

impossible for them to be the same people. If the dating is not correct and they are indeed the same two subcoaches, it would be a sign of the continuity of lower rank employees, compared to a greater change in the upper rank ones, as is not unusual in our times:

> Ptolemaius, son of Ptolemaius Athmoneus, having won the torch race in the Theseia when Calicratides was archon, to Hermes: the coach being Antiochus from Colone and subcoaches Dioscorides from Colone and Heracleitus Athmoneus. (*IG* 2² 2995)

To give us an idea about how big the classes might have been, we have already seen the previous example of Plato's *Politicus* (294d–e). Perhaps inscriptions are able to illuminate the actual number of participants more clearly. For instance, one inscription mentions that the person making the dedication had fifty friends, who are described as legitimate and spirited (meaning athletic) at the beginning of the inscription and as his own friends at the end (*IG* II² 1969). The center of the inscription contains the names of all fifty of them. Whereas only the dedicator won in the boxing, he made a point of inscribing all of his friends' names, probably training partners or ephebes with him. Lines 24–27 read as follows: "Having won the boxing at the Germanica festival, he dedicated it inscribing his own fifty friends."

A group of fifty would certainly need to be coached and instructed in other disciplines by more than just one person. In this case, hierarchies of coaches would be necessary.

A third aspect that comes forth in the inscriptions is that some of these jobs were elected for a year at a time and some were for life. One inscription mentions the *kosmetēs* of the ephebes, the gymnasiarch, *agonothetai* (or organizers of the competitions), priests, and other designations in relation to the education of the ephebes. "Coach for life: Abascantus son of Eumolpus from Cepheis, 28 years (of career)" (*IG* 2² 2086, column 2, lines 115–16).

Abascantus was a famous coach in Athens during the middle of the second century A.D. Whereas Abascantus was no doubt a good coach, we do not possess any information about his athletic career. Eleven inscriptions mention him.[49] The inscriptions are dated between 125 and 170 A.D. This means that he had a very impressive career of at least forty-five years. His title as coach for life appears first in the year 136. The two inscriptions of the year 125 A.D.

---

49. *IG* 2² 2037, 2045, 2049, 2065, 2067, 2068, 2086, 2094, 2097, 3737, 6397.

just mention him as coach, which means that Abascantus must have become a coach quite early in his life. It might have taken Abascantus ten years of his career and the success of his athletes before he could be declared coach for life, which was no doubt a special honor. Certainly, there is something good to say about the continuation of a coach for more than one year at a time. Apparently, other offices that were held for life were liturgies that could be rather costly but were sought after because of the prestige they brought.[50] If that holds true also for jobs like coaching, it must have meant that Abascantus made a lot of money in ten years so that he could teach the other thirty-five years of his career paying for the honor to coach. It does seem unlikely, however, that a younger coach could demand so much money from his athletes. Higher salaries in coaching would perhaps correspond to more experienced coaches.

Not only could the position of coach be a job for life, even the subcoach is described as being employed for life, which would basically exclude the possibility of a promotion to coach. Of the forty-nine inscriptions that mention the subcoach, only four mention that this is a job for life. One of them refers to a certain Nicostratus Hilarius (*IG* 2² 2113), and the other three to Eutychianus Iacynthius Sphettius (*IG* 2² 2203, 2206, 2223). Eutychianus appears in a total of ten inscriptions dating from 190 to 219 A.D. (a career of twenty-nine years).[51] He is given the title for life only in the ones after 200 A.D. As in the case of Abascantus, this would imply, perhaps, that an assistant coach also needed to prove himself before being hired for life.

On the other hand, the most common procedure seems to have been the public election of the coach for a public gymnasium in a city. The election was most commonly annual. The procedure is best described in an inscription from the year 200/199. It is an honorary decree for Eudemus Thallonius, who established and regulated the administration of a school.

> It seemed good to the people, the decision of the councilors: Since Eudemus Thallionus was elected to be a benefactor of the people and it was announced that owing to his love for honor in order to provide the best commemoration for all time, to give toward the education of free children ten talents of silver, (5) on his behalf and his brothers' Menandrus and Dion, it was voted by the Milesians: to honor Eudemus because of this effort concerning these most noble matters and

---

50. Dmitriev 2005: 220.
51. *IG* 2² 2125, 2130, 2131, 2193, 2203, 2206, 2208, 2223, 2225, and probably *SEG* 18: 55.

these matters to be in the care of the assembly and the people. . . . [lines 9–25 provide details about the distribution of the grant] Those wishing to be coaches and teach letters, shall inscribe themselves with the current superintendent of education (*paidonomos*) for the coming year. The inscription shall be done each year on the first day of the full moon until the twentieth of the month of Artemision, the names of those shall be published in the Antiochean stoa. (30) On the due day of the eighth of the same month, whenever the assembly is gathered there shall be placed on the orchestra a tripod and a censer and sacrifices shall be made, one to Hermes Enagonius in the palestra of the children, one to the Muses and the sacred herald and the young men who have just cut their hair and the about-to-be superintendents of education and to Eudemus while he lives. After this, (35) the oldest of Eudemus's descendants shall burn incense to Hermes, the Muses and Apollo Leader of Muses.

The sacred herald shall make those in the assembly vow to do the best, whoever may vote for the coaches and those teaching the letters, whom they consider best to direct the children, and he may not assign anything contrary to justice because of his desire for honor (40), if not, the contrary. After that let the superintendents give the names of those inscribed to the secretary of the council. Let him introduce each one. Let each one of those marching up and the priests and the sacred heralds swear. Let the oath be for the coaches this one: I swear by Hermes not to have benefited (45) any of the Milesians so that he votes for me. Nor have I ordered any one to benefit on my behalf. Let him be cursed who swearing to be the best, commits perjury toward the contrary. The teachers of letters shall swear the other things accordingly. Let them swear by Apollo and the Muses. There shall be voted and shown from those present (50) four coaches and four teachers. A salary shall be ordered for each coach each month thirty drachmas, for each teacher each month forty. The things concerning their classes and other matters shall be in accordance with the education law. It is possible (55) for those coaches who have been elected in case that they may wish to travel leading athletes to a crown game, to do so by asking dispensation from the superintendent and leaving instead of them a substitute for the children, agreeable to the superintendents. (*Miletus* 42 = *SEG* 36: 1045)

This inscription reveals not only the process of election of coaches, but also the fact that a *paidotribēs* was a professional with sufficient knowledge to bring his pupils to the crown games. The assumption then that the *gymnastēs* would be for high performance whereas the *paidotribēs* had just a basic knowledge of the sport is invalid. As for the election itself, it seems that there must have been more candidates than positions in any given year. This means that it was a competitive job, desired by enough people to need to guarantee by an oath that there was no prevarication.

The last point to reflect on is that the coaches in the inscriptions do not seem to receive a great salary. They are making about one drachma to one-and-a-half drachma a day. Unskilled laborers made one drachma a day. Basically, the salary in the inscriptions signifies that coaches are seen for the most part as unskilled, yet they are able to take the children to crown games. Certainly, there is a huge disjunction between the salary given to a coach (less than the salary of the teacher) and the expectations placed on the job. Yet, the fact that there was competition for it implies that it was still an attractive, somewhat prestigious and secure job.

On the other hand, the salary also reflects the comparative value of intellectual versus physical education. A different inscription mentions the salary for the teacher as six hundred drachmas a year, seven hundred for the citharist, and only five hundred for the coach (*Teos* 41). Though none of these professionals is paid a lot of money, the coach is paid the least, which is symptomatic of the perceived value of the services they are performing.

This, however, does not mean that coaches were not respected in their societies. One inscription reveals that a certain Publius Aelius Tertius, a coach of the middle of the second century A.D., had been elected or appointed member of the council in his city (*Smyrna* 299). Although it does not confirm that he was a rich man, he was certainly a well-respected member of his city, who most likely had more resources than those provided by his coach's salary. By the second century A.D., council members were expected to pay for some liturgies, something that no coach could do from his public salary alone.

6.5 The Extrinsic Purpose of Sport

The dichotomy between body and mind brought to light that whereas the value of training the mind became self-explanatory, the value of training the body needed to be justified. If training the body would not contribute to the creation of a good person, what was sport's role in society from then on? Sport never disappeared from the curriculum in the ancient schools, yet its purpose within education was questioned, at least by the intellectual elite. Sport was simply too important for the society to let go of it, so the Greeks attempted to answer the question of the usefulness of sport by attaching to sport benefits outside of itself, whether real or imagined, as we shall see later on.

Even authors of the Second Sophistic saw sport as part of a traditional cultural practice and therefore included it in their discussions as they reflected on past and present practices. Some things about sport and education become clear through a reading of Lucian's dialog *Anacharsis*, written in the mid second century A.D. The dialog features the sixth-century Athenian lawgiver Solon and the Scythian king Anacharsis, who according to legend traveled to Athens to learn about local customs. In the dialog, Solon explains to the barbarian king the Greek custom of sport. First of all, it is mentioned right at the start and throughout the dialog that the participants in sports are young men (*neoi*) and that sport is part of their education to make them better men and future leaders of society (14–15). Solon recognizes that very few young men are capable of winning at the games, but sport, nevertheless, brings to them as individuals and to society in general a "greater good," namely, freedom, wealth, glory, enjoyment of ancestral festivals, safety for one's family, and all the most beautiful blessings. Solon is thus creating a separation between what can be termed specialized sports and general physical education. Anacharsis remains skeptical of the achievements of sport (either general or specialized) throughout the dialog, so Solon keeps insisting on the ability of sport to make virtuous citizens in peace and strong soldiers in war (20–21).

After explaining the benefits that sport has for war (Lucian, *Anacharsis* 24–28), Solon remarks that sport in times of peace is used to keep the young men occupied and not idle, since idleness may lead to arrogance (31). It is clear from this assertion that Solon conceives of sport as a means of social control. Equally, Anacharsis expresses the same idea. In fact, this is basically the only idea in the dialog that he does not seek to refute. In paragraph 32, he continues poking fun at the usefulness of sport for war. Then he asserts that sports are amusements and pastimes for lazy young men who wish to have it easy. Anacharsis does not conceive of sport as being useful to develop one's character but does not deny that in this way the young men are kept from intervening in political life, although he attributes that to their own wishes. Of course, the political situation in Hellenistic and Roman times was very different from that of the archaic or democratic city, where participation in political life was sought by the young, but access to it was also controlled by the older generations.[52]

This part of the dialog is certainly very interesting from a sociological point of view. The accusation of arrogance is often made against young aristocrats, often because they are both young and aristocratic and want to pursue a life of aristocratic display. Modern scholars agree, by and large, that most athletes were aristocratic.[53] Young aristocrats would be the ones that during the archaic period and most of the classical period were actually trained toward assuming political power. Yet, there were structures in place that guaranteed that this would not happen too early. Some structures were political, like setting a minimal age to enter certain offices. Some of them were social, like pushing back the age of marriage and begetting of children. Another one was in fact sport, which could be seen by many cities as an "escape valve."[54] Sport was an avenue for the young aristocrats to compete against each other without damaging the structures of the society, especially since the most prestigious games took place at sanctuaries far away from every polis.[55]

Whereas the Olympic Games were founded probably at the end of the eighth century, the other three periodic games were founded at the beginning of the sixth century. This is a time of aristocratic infighting for the control of power, both in Corinth and Argos. The Isthmian Games were founded in 582, perhaps with the restoration of oligarchic government after the fall of the tyranny. Also, the beginning of the sixth century is the time of the First Sacred War for control of the sanctuary of Delphi. The result of the war was that the sanctuary did not depend on one city, Crisa, but on several cities allied for its protection in the amphictyony—cities, by the way, which were keen on sending their athletes to the games. [56]

The young aristocrats would find an avenue to display their ideology and excellence outside of their cities, while at the same time the cities controlled, so to speak, the time when a young person was deemed to be ready and the

---

52. Strauss 1993: 137–52.
53. Pleket (2005: 153) argues that even in Hellenistic times aristocratic athletes dominated the scene. David Young argued for lower-class athletes, but his hypothesis has not been generally accepted (1984: 107–62).
54. Müller 1996.
55. As we know from characters all the way from Cylon to Alcibiades and Chairon tyrant of Pellene, aristocrats tried to use their Olympic success to justify their claim to power.
56. "Amphictyony" is the name given to a league of cities (very often neighboring) that defended a common sanctuary.

place where the aristocratic display occurred.[57] For example, Themistocles dedicated his helmet with his name inscribed at Olympia after the battle of Salamis, but a decade later he was ostracized from Athens for his "arrogance." The same display of individual greatness that was allowed at Olympia was obviously received with suspicion in the democratic city.[58]

In order for the establishment of the cities to exert any kind of control on the younger generation, a system of education needed to be in place. Aristotle thus talks about the need for education to be public and not private, as it is a matter of the state (*Politics* 1337a). It is already very significant that the education system is discussed in his *Politics* because it is seen as an important part of civic life. Gymnastics is part of the education system, or *paideia*, because it is deemed to provide manly courage and character (1337b). These qualities would benefit the city, but, as seen in the example of Themistocles, only when displayed through the right channels. For this purpose, a system of public education was one of the best tools.

In this chapter we have discussed the role of sport in education. Although the details of how it worked remain mostly unknown, it is evident that it remained an important part of children and youth's education. The general purpose of noncompetitive sport was to subordinate the body to the mind in order to develop a well-rounded individual. A certainly more cynical purpose of sport in education was expressed by some authors who saw sport as a means of social control. Yet, perhaps the most important extrinsic use of sport was its role as training for war. Whether this was real or not is something that still needs to be ascertained, but certainly the relation between sport and war was present in most ancient discussions seeking a justification of the practice of sport. Another more mythical and more tenuous purpose of sport is its conception as a rite of passage from one stage in life to another. These two extrinsic aspects of sports are going to be considered in the two coming chapters.

---

57. Neer (2001: 273–336) argues that city treasuries at Panhellenic sanctuaries provided a civic frame for the ostentatious displays of the wealthy.

58. Themistocles's rival Aristides was a pentathlete, who also claimed his results in sport as a means to advance his political career.

7

Sport and War

Obviously, an important implication of the fact that athletes were young men is that they were also men of a military age. With the new *paideia* and the questioning of aristocratic ideology, as well as the new hierarchical order between body and mind, the cultivation of the body needed to be somewhat justified. A typical way used by the Greeks to justify the practice of sport was through its association with war, and thus sport was conceived of as an apt preparation for war. This was a problematic validation, which did not satisfy all. Bitter detractors conceived of sport as a hindrance to war, whereas in the past, aristocratic ideology made by and large no distinction between the best athletes and the best warriors, as exemplified by most Homeric heroes. In Homeric times, success in sport was an extension of success in war, except in very few cases.

Pritchard, in his recent monograph *Sport, Democracy, and War in Classical Athens*, argues that athletics constituted an anomaly in Athenian democracy because it did not attract the negative judgment that other elite activities received.[1] He argues that the main reason why sport was not derided was because of its perceived usefulness for war. This usefulness was expressed through a common set of words and concepts for athletic and military activities.[2] Pritchard makes very valid points in his exposition, but to me it is not that clear that the Greeks by and large saw sport as useful with respect to war.

---

1. Pritchard 2013: 136.
2. Ibid., 163.

The relation between sport and war was not an easy one for the ancient Greeks.[3] Some opted to justify sport in whichever way, some preferred not to defend at all the practice of sport. Although sport was accepted and thoroughly enjoyed by the masses, as Pritchard argues, it still received much criticism on the part of intellectuals. Perhaps one can see a dichotomy between elite and popular culture concerning the usefulness and justification of sport. Still nowadays, the relation between sport and war is a huge topic not only in regard to ancient sport but also in regard to modern sport. The question whether the Olympic Games (ancient and modern) are a substitute for war or not is still debated. There are also many theories about whether or not sport is able to control aggression or instead promotes it.[4]

The question about sport and war in modern times seems also to center around the origins of sport.[5] As far as we can ascertain, however, the Greeks did not conceive of the origins of sport as being in a preparation for war. If they had, it might have been simpler to explain sport's role in war. Philostratus might be our only source about what the Greeks believed to be the origin of sport.

> The genesis of it [the art of gymnastics] is the natural ability for men to wrestle, box, and run correctly. For none of these would exist if that through which it came into existence had not been provided beforehand. Just as the genesis of the art of metallurgy is iron and bronze, and agriculture comes from the earth, and seafaring because there is a sea, in that way we consider that gymnastics is inborn and natural for men. A story is told that when gymnastics did not yet exist, Prometheus existed and he was the first one to practice gymnastics. Then Hermes made others practice gymnastics and he was admired because of the discovery. The first palestra came from Hermes. The men being formed out of mud by Prometheus were those who practiced gymnastics in the mud, and they believed that they were formed by Prometheus since gymnastics made their bodies appropriate and fit. (*On Gymnastics* 16)

The fact that Philostratus saw sport as natural to men (and it might be the traditional belief) implies that, in his mind and probably in the mind of many

---

3. Bernardini 2016 discusses topics such as the similar vocabulary between sport and war, the idealization of bodies of warriors and athletes, and the representation in poetry of victory.

4. Pritchard 2013: 20–30.

5. For the theories about the origins of sport, see Sansone 1992.

Greeks, it did not need any justification. The body is predisposed to the practice of sport, and without this predisposition there would be no sport. As I was arguing in the previous pages, sport demands a justification only when it is seen as developing the body in opposition to the mind and when it may risk not contributing to the formation of a whole individual.

Some specific sports lend themselves to an easier comparison with war than others. No one would doubt, for instance, that the modern pentathlon (fencing, shooting, riding, running, and swimming) is related to the fighting needs of the nineteenth century, when the sport was invented. Today, however, is hard to see a relation with twenty-first-century military needs, even if it is still a sport practiced commonly among military people. How the ancient pentathlon (wrestling, stadium race, javelin, discus, and long jump) related to war is perhaps more difficult to grasp. Javelins could be used for hunting, and discuses may have been primitive weapons, but contemporary Greeks did not necessarily see this association. In this chapter I will concentrate on sport's perceived usefulness for war and its usefulness for the military instruction of young men and children.

7.1 The Usefulness of Sport for War

Athletes were occasionally recognized for their military achievements. For instance, Pausanias (6.3.2) tells us about Stomius, who won one victory in the pentathlon at Olympia and three in the Nemean Games. As commander of the Elean cavalry, he challenged a general of the enemy to single combat and slew him with his own hands. Also, Milo is said to have routed the enemy when he appeared at the front of a battle wearing only his Olympic crowns and carrying a club.[6] These examples are, nevertheless, rather anecdotal and do not really illustrate the value of sport with respect to war.

Nevertheless, defenders of sport insist on the general usefulness of sport in the practice of war. Rather typical arguments in the debate between defenders and detractors are presented in Lucian's dialog *Anacharsis*, where Solon explains the usefulness of sport in terms of preparation for war.

> The body, that about which you desire to hear mostly, we train in this way: . . . Then having devised many forms of athletics and appointed

---

6. Apparently other successful athletes also wore their garlands to war and inspired their comrades as having divine favor. See Henderson Munn 2000: 25.

teachers for each, we teach this one to box, that one to do the pancratium so that they may become accustomed to endure fatigue and at the same time to meet the blows and not turn away because of fear of injury. This works in them two most useful effects: they are ready to meet dangers courageously disregarding their bodies, and they become strong and robust. (*Anacharsis* 24)

Solon continues with the usefulness of wrestling: "to those who exercise thoroughly the bodies become more long-suffering and stronger" (24). Also, men trained in such a way will be more capable of throwing their opponents and stand back up if they fall. In general, Solon insists that men trained in sports are stronger, healthier, light, flexible, and, at the same time, too muscular for their opponents. He points out their vitality, courage, elasticity, and vigor and asserts that trained men will suffer less illness and fatigue (25–26). Even runners and pentathletes develop muscular shoulders, arms, and legs (27), which is good in case someone needs to carry his injured comrade out of the front lines (28). Anacharsis is not at all convinced by the explanation and mocks it (31); he recommends training in handling weapons instead of sport (32). Anacharsis advocates training that reproduces real-life situations. So he proposes training with heavy spears instead of light javelins, practicing shooting the bow, and training in combat at close quarters while wearing armor. He is unable to see any skills transferable from athletics to war. Solon replies that the conditioning of sport is very useful for war (34). The two then engage in a discussion concerning general conditioning and endurance levels (35). Whereas Anacharsis believes that it is important to save one's energy until it is needed, Solon explains that the more one draws energy through exertion, the more energy one has at one's disposal. In modern terms this is called raising the aerobic threshold, which is something Anacharsis does not understand.

Solon does not think that sport trains specifically for war maneuvers, but certainly he acknowledges the importance of general conditioning and close combat tactics from wrestling and pancratium in order to be a better soldier. In Greek history, two main examples come to mind. In the first, Athenian soldiers charged at Marathon at full speed, then, after the battle, they raced back to protect their city, which shows that they were certainly very fit and well trained (Herodotus 6.116). In the second, the Lacedaemonians fought at Thermopylae with their hands and teeth once their weapons broke (Herodotus

7.225). These examples show that athletics provided soldiers with an extra edge of fitness and combative spirit.[7]

None of the ancient Greek supporters of the usefulness of sport with respect to war made the point that specialized physical training was good for war. They all mention the general fitness, endurance, and coordination that the practice of sport provides to soldiers. On the other hand, the detractors of sport as applied to war focus on specialized training. And it is this that they decry. As we saw, Anacharsis ridicules the Athenians because they train naked or with a light javelin, and this is not a realistic situation in war (32). It does not matter that Solon explains that just because they train naked, it does not follow that they also go to war naked. But on the contrary, because they are fit and well trained, they can get much better when training with arms (34). This miscommunication or even unwillingness to understand Solon's point is a common thread in Greek criticism of sport concerning its usefulness for war. The best-known piece of criticism of athletes comes from a fragment of Euripides's *Autolycus*:

> Of the myriad of evils that are in Greece, none is worse than the race of athletes. . . . I censure also the custom of the Greeks who, organizing gatherings on account of these, honor useless pleasures for the sake of feasting. For even if he has wrestled well, or is a man of swift feet or has thrown the discus or has hit a jaw beautifully, who has protected the ancestral city having taken a crown? Are they going to fight against the enemies holding a discus or are they going to expel the enemies from the fatherland piercing the shields with their bare hands? No one is so stupid as to stand like this near a sword. It is necessary to crown wise and good men with these wreaths, he who leads the city well, being a prudent and just man, who puts away bad deeds with words removing fights and strife. Such are the beautiful things for all cities and all Greeks. (Athenaeus 413c–f)

The fragment juxtaposes practical virtues like temperance and moderation and other political virtues like justice to the character of the athletes. When it

---

7. Even modern elite troops need to pass fitness tests on a regular basis. They are also trained in a combination of martial arts that include techniques of wrestling and modern variations of the pancratium in order to instill a "warrior ethos." "Today, MCMAP's [Marine Corps Martial Art Program] overarching purpose is to mold and strengthen the USMC collective identity, social structure, and culture. It is a martial-arts system that mandates intensive practice with weapons and unarmed techniques, intense physical conditioning, and the use of established milestone standards" (Yi 2004, 20).

comes to war, the rather ridiculous question, whether the athlete would fight discus in hand, is asked. The speaker in the fragment fails to see that the specifics of sport do not have to apply to war. Though speed in running may not be an asset in hoplite warfare, certainly other benefits that sport provides, like endurance and strength, may be of extreme importance.

In sections 43 and 44 of his *On Gymnastics*, Philostratus contrasts the athletes of past times with his contemporaries. For him, in the "good old times" there was no contradiction between the athlete and the soldier, and sport was considered practice for war, and war practice for sport. However, in his own time, when the infamous "change" occurred, combatants became unable to go into the army, young men full of energy became lazy, and tough men became weaklings. This change came about because luxurious eating triumphed, robbing the stadia of bravery, but mostly because flattery entered the art of gymnastics, making everybody dependent on pampering. Or so Philostratus says.

As we saw from Euripides's fragment, the "good old times" may have been no more than an illusion, even for writers of the fifth century. It is, nevertheless, noteworthy that athletes in the polis were volunteers or drafted to serve when the need arose. The most famous case was that of the pentathlete from Croton, Phayllus, who had won three times at the Pythian Games and commanded his own ship at the battle of Salamis (Herodotus 8.47).

On the other hand, in Hellenistic and Roman imperial times, there was no need for athletes to take up arms in defense of their king, since the army had become, for the most part, professional. The need to be a good soldier was not a priority for athletes, but neither was it for others, in whatever activity they worked. The criticism of athletes because of their diet was perhaps a more justified one, but criticizing athletes as poor soldiers no longer matched with reality when armies were comprised largely of professionals.

Ironically, the rejection of sport as part of military training began in Sparta, when the Spartans started losing at the Panhellenic games. As we saw, this occurred when other cities developed their own training programs and the Spartans' physical superiority was no longer evident. The Spartans soon realized that war and sport demanded specific ways of training and that endurance and strength were not all that was needed. The rejection of specialized physical training as a skill transferable to war may have spread from Sparta to other Greek cities.

Tyrtaeus's most famous poem starts with a tirade against the inadequacy of sports to grant *aretē* to a man and consequently make him an object of song

(12). The poems of Tyrtaeus, composed in the background of the Second Messenian War in the seventh century, signal the shift in mentality that brought about Spartan introspection and their cessation of dominance at the Olympic Games.[8] The Spartans were more concerned about dominating the Messenians and the rest of the Peloponnese through military control than with sport. At the root of the conflict there is a problem of how, and with which purpose, to educate the young men. The Spartans showed an inability to change and adapt their training and education system in order to keep being successful athletes. They were the first ones to have a systematic education plan for their youth, but, because of the Second Messenian War, the Spartans reevaluated their priorities and turned their education system into a military based one, which according to Aristotle turned the young Spartans into animals (*Politics* 1339a). At the same time that participation at the Olympics seem to have been discouraged, or perhaps even forbidden,[9] young men were encouraged to give up their life fighting in the first ranks. Tyrtaeus's poems expressed, for the first time, a criticism of sports in opposition to war. There is a separation between the athlete and the warrior that by and large was not present in the Homeric epics. Sparta is perhaps the first polis to voice this division and consequent censure of the athlete.[10]

The separation between the warrior and the athlete, which is observable in Tyrtaeus, is seen perhaps more drastically in the saying of one Spartan mother at the news of the death of her son in battle: "How much more beautiful, O friends, it is for the victorious to die in formation than for the victor at the Olympics to live" (Plutarch, *Sayings of Spartan Women* 242b).

It is, no doubt, a prominent idea to convey the centrality of war in comparison to every other aspect of Spartan society. That the opposition between the warrior and the athlete is to be considered within the larger frame of the education and duties of the young man is expressed by another saying of the Spartans that makes the young men the bulwark of their city: "[Antalcidas] used to say that the young men were the walls of Sparta, the point of the spears its boundaries" (Plutarch, *Sayings of Spartans* 217e).

Whereas the previous saying reflects the expectations placed on young men, the next one opposes these expectations with participation at the gymnasium, which is considered to be morally damaging: "They reprimanded

---

8. Mann 2001: 121–63.
9. For a discussion on the "boycott theory," see Mann 2001: 123. See also Plutarch, *Moralia* 228d.
10. In other cities, especially in the Ionian world, the conflict will surface as one between the athlete and the intellectual. See Xenophanes frg. 19.

the youngster from the gymnasium, because it teaches the road to Pylaea" (Plutarch, *Ancient Customs of the Spartans*, 239c).[11]

The exact meaning of the expression "the road to Pylaea" is unknown, but nevertheless it is clear that the saying denounces the teaching of the gymnasium as inappropriate for a young man. Of course, this is only in view of the Spartan education, which proposed a military education before the gymnastic. These sayings also exemplify what is expected of the young man, namely, to be a soldier and not an athlete. This is already part of the mentality that views soldiers as an integral part of the polis and athletes as not so important, and in some cases even detrimental, for the cities.

Yet, athletes were still symbols of greatness, especially in the smaller cities, which could not claim military superiority. This might be the reason why we do not hear criticism of athletics and athletes from the smaller cities, but criticism becomes prominent in those cities that aspire to political control of Greece. Certainly, there is a strong political motivation in the Spartan rejection of sport, especially the sport conducted at Olympia. The political rivalry between Elis and Sparta lasted for a long time. In one of the many rivalries for control of the territory, Elis excluded the Spartans from participation at the games in 420.[12] It is no surprise, then, that criticism of sport is linked with criticism of Elis and its control of the Olympic festival. We can also read this in Plutarch: "When some commended the people of Elis because they were very just in conducting the Olympic Games, he [Agis] said, 'What great or marvelous accomplishment is it if they practice justice on one day only in five years?'" (*Sayings of Spartans* 215f).

Although the discussion of the role of sport in war seems to have already started in the sixth century, in Greek cities other than Sparta, it became more prominent as education became increasingly based on intellectual development. In fact, if physical education ceased to be the focus of education in general, then why would it be good for anything, including war, which had developed in ways that did not allow for individual achievements? The development of the phalanx and the new style of warfare that it demanded questioned the role of the individual (and individual glory seeking) in sport. Yet the popularity of sport did not wane.

---

11. Although Spartans never ceased to practice sports and encouraged their performance, they rejected specialized training.

12. Roy 1998: 360–68.

7.2 Paramilitary Sports

Despite all the criticism and rejection of sport with regard to its usefulness for war, the Greeks had some contests that mimicked war. Most important, perhaps, was the race in armor (*hoplitodromos*), which was introduced in 520 at Olympia, and perhaps earlier at Nemea. The race was common in main festivals, such as the Panathenaea, but also in many lesser festivals. The participants initially wore the helmet, shield, and greaves, but, as time progressed, only the shield remained, although the norm might have varied from festival to festival. The distance of the race varied as well, depending on location. In most festivals it may have been the *diaulos*, but in some, longer races were preferred.[13] Philostratus discusses the race in armor in *On Gymnastics*, where he relates the anecdote about the origins of the race in Olympia as involving a hoplite from Elea who ran into the stadium to announce the victory of the Elean army (7–8). Although Philostratus does not seem to give credit to this anecdote, he does not doubt that there is a relation between the race in armor and war. Philostratus also assumes that the herald and trumpeter contests are related to this race and war.

The Panathenaea was also host to another type of contest that resembled military practice. It was called the *apobatēs*, and it consisted of the contestant dismounting and remounting a moving chariot. Both the driver and the runner wore armor.[14] Demosthenes describes the *apobatēs* contest in his *Erotic Essay* (23–29). His description is also a criticism of sports, which were not perceived as having a direct application to war. Thus, he starts by saying that running does not add to courage or morale, and boxing and other heavy sports destroy the bodies and minds of those who practice them. He continues by saying that the *apobatēs* is the best type of sport because it is similar to what one may encounter in war and also imitates Homeric heroes.

Certainly, the contest may be a recreation of Homeric warfare, but it had absolutely nothing to do with the type of war waged in Demosthenes's time. The same goes for running in armor. Heavily armed hoplites were not able to run very far, nor very fast. The battle of Marathon is the first time when hoplites charged against the enemy, and it was a surprise move done in order to avoid arrows and not give the Persians a chance to form their lines. If hoplites had to run for their lives, the first thing they got rid of was their shield,

---

13. Ibid., 9–21.
14. Ibid., 42–55.

contrary to the rules of the athletic contest, which were modified to take off the helmet and the greaves, but not the shield (Pausanias 6.10.4).

The existence of these sports shows that, despite efforts made to justify sport as part of war, we are left with the distinct impression that the Greeks saw sport and war as two different things. It might be that originally the warriors were the same athletes as we see in the Homeric funeral games for Patroclus and other literary descriptions, but soon they separated. The Homeric boxer Epeius confesses that he is not the best warrior and already creates a distinction in Homer between warrior and athlete. Athletes during archaic and classical times had to perform military duties, and in general they did not shun war. When war became professionalized during the Hellenistic period, athletes were no longer required to enlist.[15] Any criticism about athletes being poor warriors is not founded in reality; they may have made equally good soldiers as farmers, potters, or tanners, or perhaps better since their bodies were trained to endure fatigue. But athletes were regarded in a special manner and were not exempt from jealousy and envy.

It did not help that Sparta, which had achieved unmatched athletic prestige at the onset of the archaic period, turned around to despise athletics in favor of war. The perceived luxurious lifestyle and nonproductive life of the athletes contributed to increasing prejudices against them.[16]

7.3 Military Instruction for Youth and Children

The gymnasium became the place to teach the ephebes how to handle weapons: archery, javelin, and sword and spear fighting. Whether or not sport may have been understood as training for war, certainly the place for sport included military instruction. This instruction, however, was not just for ephebes but also for younger children. There is both literary and epigraphic evidence for this.

There are numerous testimonies about the presence of youths in the gymnasium and whether or not training in arms was a useful pursuit. For instance, in his dialog *Laches*, Plato has Lysimachus and Melesias ask Nicias,

---

15. Certainly, this seems to be the case during Roman times, as a letter from Mark Antony to the athlete Artemidorus attests (*P.Lond.* 137). Artemidorus asks that athletes be exempted from military duties. See also Gardiner 1930: 107.

16. Philostratus decries that in previous times war used to be practice for gymnastics and gymnastics for war, but in his own times this has changed because of flattery, medicine, and excessive eating (*On Gymnastics* 43–44).

Laches, and Socrates about the role of weapons instruction in the education of the youths (179d–84c). The terms used to describe the youths alternate between *meirakion* and *neaniskos*, which, especially the latter, refer to an undetermined age, perhaps between ephebate and full adulthood.[17] Nicias argues that such training is a worthwhile pursuit for free young men in their leisure time, in order to strengthen the body (181e–82d). He argues that, although it is a good skill to have during the fighting in formation, it is most useful when the formation breaks. Nicias sees the training in arms as a stepping-stone to learning the art of commanding troops. This might not be an exaggeration, as we know for instance from Xenophon's *Constitution of the Lacedaemonians* that instructors in weapons also taught maneuvers and not just the individual use of weapons (11.8).

Laches, on the other hand, argues that weapon instruction is a skill that does not need to be learned, and he gives as an example that instructors in weapons do not go to Sparta to teach it (Plato, *Laches* 182d–84c). He also comments on how instructors in weapons are not necessarily distinguished in war. The discussion moves then into the nature of courage and whether or not it is teachable. The dialog, however, brings up the important distinction between nature and nurture that seems to permeate all of Greek activities. How realistic, or even convenient, it was to have an army of untrained personnel is a different question. Yet, again, hand-to-hand combat was probably mostly used, if at all, when the phalanx formation collapsed. Thus, it might have been perceived as something more fanciful than practical.[18]

Plato makes reference in another dialog to a discussion at the Lyceum where Socrates and Crito were with a group of young men (*Euthydemus* 271b–73c). The very beginning of the passage attests to the difference in physical build between youths (*meirakia*) of the same age, which would have been an important consideration for coaches and instructors. Then two characters are presented, Euthydemus and his brother Dionysodorus. They are not only teachers of armed combat but also teachers of speech. Although Socrates ridicules them as sophists, he uses play and sport metaphors throughout his speech. Even if Socrates does not take the brothers seriously, the passage attests to the education given in the gymnasia as a combination of intellectual and physical lessons.

---

17. Golden 1990: 14–15.
18. Pritchard (2013: 161) argues that most cities in Greece did not have state–subsidized military training. Consequently, cities would not need to fear their opponents, except the Spartans.

What I consider more interesting is when those training in arms (at least sword and spear fighting, not archery or javelin) are children and pre-ephebic youth. We see them in inscriptions detailing the contest of *hoplomachia*, competition in weapons. This has been perhaps hinted at in both of Plato's dialogs where potential students are described as not completely physically developed. *Hoplomachia* contests are attested for several cities, most of them are for ephebes, some of them mention a group of young men and even men (see *ISestos* 1). But a few inscriptions detail the participation of children.

The first inscription does not tell us at which festival or occasion the contest in weapons was performed. There is a division here between children of different ages common to other sports events. Although we cannot be sure of the ages of the children, we can assume that some of them might have been rather young, perhaps as young as twelve. Assuming, for instance, a two-year division of the three age groups will give us an age range of twelve to fourteen for the first group, fourteen to sixteen for the second, and sixteen to eighteen, or right before the ephebate, for the third age group. Twelve would be a good starting age since the youngest participants at competitive sport events might have been about that age.[19] Also, children younger than twelve may have been too small to hold the spear or sword in one hand and the shield in the other. The shield generally had a diameter of about seventy-five to one hundred centimeters, clearly too heavy and big for a young child. If children also had some kind of protective gear like helmets or breastplates, even if they were not of bronze, the whole exercise might have proven too difficult for them. Perhaps the size of the weapons was adapted to the size of the children. It is certainly not unthinkable, but whereas we have found shields varying in diameter by a few centimeters according, probably, to the length of the forearm of the bearer,[20] as far as I am aware, we have no archeological remains of smaller, child-sized shields. Without weapons adapted to their size, child competitors could not have been much younger than twelve or thirteen years of age. Here are some inscriptions detailing the *hoplomachia*.

> Children contests of the fight in arms in round shield and spear, of the third age:
> Xenocles son of Aristocleus of the Pandionis tribe.
> Children in the fight in arms in rectangular shield and sword, of the first age:

---

19. Pausanias 6.2.9. Damiscus of Messene was the youngest Olympic victor at twelve.
20. Anderson 1970: 17.

Aristodemus ... tribe.
Children in the fight in arms in rectangular shield and sword, of the second age:
... crates ... tribe. (IG 2^2 962; Attica c. 140 B.C., frg. b, lines 1–8)

The round shield (*aspis*) was designed for the battle tactics of the phalanx, and that is why training in it was accompanied by the use of the spear. The rectangular shield (*thyreos*) was a Hellenistic development and carried over to the Roman army.[21] Military instruction as described here was probably aimed both at physical education and actual combat.

The next inscription comes from the Athenian festival of the Theseia. This festival was a common place for contests in the *hoplomachia* and in heralding, sounding the trumpet, torch races, manliness (*euandria*), ability to use weapons in formation (*euoplia*), and the usual sports.

Frg d-p Col. I, 25–66
In the archonship of Anthesterius these persons won the contests of the Theseia:
Manliness of the picked soldiers: the Attalis tribe won.
Ability to use weapons: Ptolemais tribe.
Manliness of the general companies: the unit of Homilus won.
Manliness of the knights: the Aigeis tribe won, being leader of the tribe Alexander son of Alexander Erchieus.
Ability to use weapons: Leontis tribe, being tribe leader Deimachus, son of Deimachos Leukoneus, cavalry commanders Nicogenous son of Nicon Philaedus and Ophelous son of Habron from Bata.
Trumpeters: Aristocrates son of Aristus of the Attalis tribe.
Heralds: Nikok ... son of Socrates of the Leontis tribe.
Torch race of the children: from the palestra of Timeus, Dexiphon son of Kaliphanous from the tribe of Oneis
Torch race of the ephebes: Demetrius son of Antinemes of the Kekropis tribe.
Torch race of the men in the Lyceum: Asclepiades son of Zenon from the Attalis tribe.
Children long distance from the third age: . . . .
Children long distance from all categories: . . . . .

21. Ibid., 14.

Men long distance: . . . Athenian
Children of the first age stadium: Dionisius . . .
Children of the second age stadium: Callistratus . . . Attalis tribe
Children of the third age stadium: . . .
[Col I 67–89 and Col II 26–46 include a list of events in different age groups and disciplines]

Col II, 47–63
Hoplite: Asclepiodotus son of Hermias, Athenian.
Fighter in arms of the first age in round shield and spear: . . . son of Demetrius of the Ptolemais tribe.
Fighters in arms in rectangular shield: Eudoxus son of Eudoxus from the Hippothontis tribe.
Fighter in arms of the second age in round shield and spear: . . . from the Akamantis tribe.
Fighters in arms in rectangular shield: . . . from the Aigeis tribe
Fighter in arms of the third age in round shield and spear: Epicrates son of Arcesas from the Oeneis tribe.
Fighters in arms in rectangular shield: Epicrates son of Arcesas from the Oeneis tribe.
Fighter in arms of the ephebes in round shield and spear: Aristocrates son of Procles from the Oeneis tribe.
Fighters in arms in rectangular shield: Charinus son of Diocles from the Oeneis tribe.
Javelin from the ephebes: Heracleides son of Apollodotus from the Pandionis tribe. (*IG* 2^2 957 [Attica 158/57 B.C.])

This inscription shows that military instruction for children may have started rather early. Only the children's events in sports were divided into first, second, or third age groups, as seen in previous inscriptions. The division in ages in the uses of arms, even if there is no direct mention of the children, can refer only to children. The ephebes and adult men are mentioned as separate categories.

Little is known about the training in arms of children, and even of men, in Greece outside Sparta.[22] On the other hand, we know that Athenian troops, and presumably troops from other cities, were well trained. This, of

---

22. Asclepiodotus's book on military tactics has portions on the different sections of the army, their disposition on the battlefield, and commands, but there is no mention of individual training.

course, implies that there was some kind of instruction going on. Athenians may have not wanted to talk about it owing to ideological reasons,[23] and specifically to oppose Spartan education, but nevertheless, their troops did not look amateurish. In fact, no one can hold an empire without some kind of professional troops.[24] It takes several years for someone to master the skills of fighting with shield (two types), spear, and sword. In case of an emergency, it is true that anyone could hold a spear, but if Greeks were to fight professional or semiprofessional armies, they would have to match their opponents if they wanted a chance at victory.

What may seem strange is that the Theseia festival, which started probably in the middle of the fifth century at the height of Athenian military expansion, maintained the training-in-arms contests long after the Athenian army was if not vanished, at least not relevant. This is probably a survival from the time of the creation of the festival. On the other hand, the festival reflects the fact that there was somewhat regular training in arms for children, even if just for public display and physical education. The actual chances of most of these Athenian children making use of military skills during Hellenistic and Roman times would be rather small.[25]

On the other hand, an inscription from the island from Teos and dated probably to the first half of the third century brings perhaps a different view of the training of children in handling weapons.[26] The inscription contains a law regulating the education of children.

> To be shown also after the election of the gymnasiarch that the superintendent is no younger than forty. So that all the free children are educated according to the foresight of Polythrous son of Onesimus it was announced to the people that he would set up the most beautiful memory of his desire for honor. He donated for this purpose 34,000 drachmas to be assigned each year in the election of the magistrates after the election of three grammar teachers who shall teach the boys and the girls. It shall be given to him who is elected

---

23. See Pericles's funeral oration: "If we turn to our military policy we also differ from our antagonists ... we trust less in system and policy than in the native spirit of our citizens" (Thucydides 2.39.1).
24. Anderson (1970: 87–90) explains that Greeks were drilled in a few standard movements. He also mentions how Brasidas attacked the Athenians troops when he saw them being disorganized. A bad drill was synonymous with bad soldiers.
25. Kennell (2009: 332) argues that military training outside of Athens during Roman imperial times was practically nonexistent.
26. Hauvette-Besnault and Pottier 1880: 110–21.

in the first round 600 drachmas a year, to the one elected in the
second round 550, and to the one in the third round, 500. Two coaches
shall also be chosen, to give each of them a salary of 500 drachmas
a year. Also, a citharist or a harpist shall be elected with a salary to
be given to the chosen one of 700 drachmas a year. This one shall
teach the children whom he appoints to judge verses and he shall
teach those who are younger than those by a year music and cithara
playing and harp playing, and the ephebes music. About the age
of the children let the superintendent judge. Even if we have an
intercalary month let the agreed salary for the month be given to
them. The superintendent and the gymnasiarch shall pay the teacher
of arms and the teacher of archery and javelin from the taxes from
the demos. Let them teach the ephebes and the children for whom
it is prescribed to learn music. Let the salary given to the teacher of
archery and javelin be 250 drachmas, and that for the arms teacher
300 drachmas. The teacher of arms shall teach for a period no shorter
than two months. So that the children and the ephebes practice in
the lessons carefully let the superintendent and the gymnasiarch
take care according to what is assigned to each one according to the
law. If the grammar teachers discuss among each other because of
the number of students let the superintendent decide and let the
others obey as he disposes. Let the grammar teachers do as many
demonstrations as needed in the gymnasium and teach music in
the council room . . . the penalty if they do not pay it down, let it be
possible to oblige them. Concerning the teacher in arms and the
person teaching archery and javelin, let it be accomplished according
to what is written above. (*Teos* 41, lines 1–40)[27]

The inscription is certainly a very interesting piece of evidence. First, we learn
that girls received public education at least at the basic level, if not the more
advanced one involving music and the interpretation of poetry. The girls also
did not receive physical education, but presumably they might have shared the
school, perhaps even the classroom, with boys their age. Grammar teachers
could put forward disputes about the sizes of the classes. There were three
grammar teachers. Does this mean that boys and girls were split among the

---

27. The second part of the inscription (ll, lines 40–72) deals with penalties in case the money donated is not used for its original purpose.

three classes or that the girls were in only one class? We lack evidence to confirm either possibility. Grammar teachers could also conduct as many demonstrations (public examinations) as needed. There is no mention in the inscription whether girls would be able to participate in them or not. If they were regular members of the class, perhaps they could indeed have participated in them. Again, our evidence is too limited to answer positively in any way.

A comparison of the salaries also brings significant points forward. The salaries are similar to, yet higher than, the ones we encountered in the famous inscription of Miletus (*Miletus* 42). Assuming a year of 365 days and that the instructors were paid for every day including holidays, the salaries of the grammar teachers vary between 1.3 and 1.6 drachmas a day. The coaches' salaries were the lowest at 1.3, and the citharists' the highest at 1.9 drachmas a day. The comparison of the salaries indicates the perceived value of the education. The citharists were more specialized, and this influenced their pay rate. On the other hand, the fact that the job called for either a citharist or a harpist indicates that schools were not too concerned about which specialist to hire as long as he could teach poetry and music.

It is very clear from the inscription that the children that are to be instructed in the handling of the weapons are not only the ephebes, but also the younger ones. They are old enough to be past the elementary schooling, but not yet ephebes. Although there is no specific number, the children that received instruction in weapons were probably between twelve and eighteen.

A comparison of the salary for the teachers of weapons makes clear that whereas teachers were paid by the donation of Polythrous, the specialists in handling weapons were paid from the taxes of the demos. The salary raises some problems that are difficult to answer. If the salary of the javelin and archery teacher is only 250 drachmas a year (that is, 0.68 drachma a day) and that of the teacher of weapons 300 (or 0.8 drachma a day), their salaries are extremely low in comparison to the other instructors. However, the inscription talks about the instruction given at least for two months. If the teacher in arms taught for only two months of a year, then his salary would be very high. Kennell argues that teachers of weapons were itinerant professionals outside of Athens and that they were hired for a few months at a time only.[28] Obviously, they were in high demand to manage to negotiate such high salaries.

Teos was subject to constant pirate attacks during the Hellenistic era. It successfully negotiated territorial inviolability (*asylia*) with several cities at the

---

28. Kennell 2009: 333.

end of the third century and came under the auspices of the Seleucids for its protection.[29] We do not have a firm date for our inscription, and the date of the middle of the third century is a conjecture by the editors, but if it does indeed come from about fifty years prior to the inviolability, we can assume that this was a period of much piracy and high insecurity. Instructing the older children in the use of weapons may have been seen as a necessity, paid by public money at whatever price.

---

29. See Strang 2007 about pirate attacks on Teos (173–207) and about *asylia* (208–46).

8

Initiation Aspects of Historical Sport Practices

In the previous chapters, we have established that athletes were young men and, therefore, in need of education and other integration mechanisms. In addition, the intellectual revolution during the fifth century displaced the balance of body and mind in favor of a preeminence of the mind and caused the role of sport to be questioned. A common explanation for the continuous practice of sport was its use as part of war training. In this chapter, we will explore another common explanation given for sport in order to justify its role, namely its ritual role.

8.1 Initiations

In general, when scholars try to elucidate the origin of sport, they elaborate theories that are either anthropological (mostly in reference to hunting and war practices), psychological (need to prove one's superiority) or simply physiological (people do sports because there is the desire to move). Following these theories, organized sports, which involve set rules of competition between individuals or teams, are explained as a secondary development. Presenting a theory based on initiatory practices has the advantage that it unites sport and competition from the start, as well it offers a combined anthropological, physiological and psychological explanation.[1]

---

1. Sansone 1992: 15.

Sport was an integral part of Greek education and transmission of values (*paideia*). In that sense, one can speak of one of the functions of sport being that of introducing the young men into adulthood. This would constitute a kind of initiation. Whereas there might be difficulty in conceiving the ritualistic aspects of sport as remnants of ancient initiatory rites,[2] nevertheless, in historical times athletics was used as a kind of rite of passage from youth into adulthood.[3] Scholars debate not so much the initiatory value of sport as much as the antiquity of such a practice, in other words, whether the ritualistic elements of sport come from a prehistoric period or from a historic one.[4] Although Scanlon doubts that we can set Greek athletics in a context of prehistoric initiation, he nevertheless asserts that sport was used for the formation and transmission of civic and cultural values.[5]

One does not need to argue that sport in its origin was related to initiation practices directed to the socialization of the young in order to explain its use as a generational bridge in historical times. On the other hand, by stressing sport's function as initiation, one can explain the segregated position of athletes in their society. Several other elements in Greek sport permit us, indeed, to make a connection with initiation practices for the transition from marginal youth to integrated adulthood. This means that sport itself represents a transitional stage for youths.[6]

In his book *Paides e Parthenoi*, Angelo Brelich described many Greek, especially Spartan, institutions as initiatory and catalogued Greek practices that can be understood as initiations.[7] However, he did not make a specific connection between these initiatory practices and athletics, although many of the Spartan customs involved physical competition. In the festivals for Apollo (the Carneia, Gymnopaedia, and the Hyacinthia) it was common to have a race and a resistance challenge.[8] Best known of these challenges is when young men were whipped at the altar of Artemis Orthia so as to cover the altar with blood.

---

2. Scanlon 2005: 69–72.

3. Scanlon 2002: 64–97.

4. Scanlon (2005) argues for a historic type of initiation, whereas earlier scholars such as Brelich (1969) and Jeanmaire (1939) argue for a prehistoric one.

5. According to Scanlon, the diet, the dress, and age categories were established in historical times for pragmatic reasons (2002: 69).

6. Sansone 1992: 33–35.

7. Brelich 1981.

8. For a detailed description and function of Spartan festivals, see Pettersson 1992.

Generally speaking, initiation is a process through which an individual is transformed into a different one according to the norms of the society.[9] The transformation is biological (in the case of puberty rites), social, and cultural. The individual leaves behind a former identity and receives a new one. In that sense initiation represents usually a symbolic death and rebirth. It is a rite of passage from one state to another. Frequently, initiation supposes the separation of the initiates from the society. They have a style of life different from both children and adults, characterized by a special diet, nudity or body markers, either permanent or temporary, and often maltreatment and even torture. At the end of the initiation, there is usually a test of physical strength. Often initiation implies a change in the sexual life of the individual, and therefore the process can be characterized by an inversion of sexuality and by homosexual practices.[10]

It is not difficult to see that all these elements of initiation correspond to practices associated with sport. Athletes had a special diet, and they competed naked,[11] underwent arduous training, and could even be subjected to maltreatment by the coaches and officials. This point, specifically, was misunderstood by later Greek writers, who could not conceive that a free man could submit to being flogged without retaliation. Another aspect that may have initiatory character is the practice of running toward the altar. This has been explained as a substitutive sacrifice.[12] On top of that, the victorious athlete adorned himself with ribbons and wreaths in the manner of the sacrificial victims and prehistoric hunters.[13] In fact, even the vocabulary of athletic exertion—*ponos* and *kamatos*—implies not only the exertion but also the maltreatment of the athlete and, by extension, the death of the athlete.[14]

Another practice that could be initiatory is the temporary infibulation of athletes, whereby athletes would tie their genitals with a string so as not to expose the glans. Scholars have wondered what the meaning of the infibulation

---

9. Brelich 1981: 23–35; Scanlon 2002: 65.

10. Scanlon (2002: 67–68) discusses the theories around pederasty and athletics as initiation rituals. He divides the theorists in two groups, those like Dover and himself who think that the association between sport and pederasty is a seventh-century phenomenon, and those like Sergent and Bremmer who think that it is an old Indo-European institution.

11. Christesen (2003) argues for two types of nudity: one associated with initiation and another associated with civic equality. Scanlon (2005: 67–73) denies that Greek athletic nudity had anything to do with initiation and argues for a connection of nudity and pederasty.

12. Also, the covering of the altar with blood at the festival of Artemis Orthia can be explained in a similar manner.

13. Sansone (1992: 37, 75) defines sport as the ritual sacrifice of physical energy.

14. Nagy 1994: 139; Johnstone 1994: 235–39.

could be.[15] According to Scanlon, the infibulation is a marker in the body of the stage of transition as much as it is part of the change in sexuality. Sansone explains it not only as a means to symbolize chastity (whether temporary or permanent) but also as a ritualized element of sport. He thinks that the athletes may have believed that by tying their foreskin they would perform better.[16] Certainly, the infibulation may represent a transitional stage in sexuality, characterized by chastity and restraint. It is well known that athletes participating at the Olympic Games had to abstain from sex for at least a month while they were training at Olympia.

On the other hand, inversion of sexuality is also a characteristic of initiation and athletics. In Greece, pederastic practices are associated closely with the gymnasium, as seen for instance in Plato's dialog *Lysis* or in Eros being one of the gods of the gymnasium.[17] Homoerotic liaisons (and the god Eros) emphasize the cooperative aspect among the group of athletes, as opposed to the competitive nature of sport.[18] Yet, there were strict prohibitions against homosexuals and male prostitutes entering the gymnasium, as in the gymnasiarchal law of Beroea (*SEG* 27: 261).[19] This would hint at the acceptance only of a transitional homosexuality in the passage from young man to adulthood.[20]

The fact that at some early point in Greek prehistory athletic games may have been considered a type of initiation could be responsible for the image of the athlete as perpetual youth, which in turn implies that he is unable to achieve full participation in the society. Athletes belonged to an intermediate stage between childhood and full adulthood, characterized by marriage. Historically, athletes were perceived as abiding in a limbo where there were no other responsibilities but their own training.[21]

---

15. Scanlon 2002: 234–36.
16. Sansone 1992: 120.
17. See Plato's *Lysis* 204b and 206e–7a; *Charmides* 153d–54a; and *Symposium* 217b–c. Scanlon argues that "athletics and homosexuality rose contemporaneously in a context of heightened social competition for status" (2002: 68) in the seventh century.
18. Scanlon 2002: 89–90.
19. Plato warns readers that gymnastics and *syssitia* (communal meals) promote civil strife (*Laws* 1.636b). The implication is that there must be restrictions about who is allowed to enter the gymnasium.
20. Sergent (1986: 49–54) compares Greek pederasty with homosexual practices in other traditional societies from Africa and the South Pacific. He considers Greek pederasty to be an ancient Indo-European institution that characterizes male groups and that does not arise from a lack of opportunity for heterosexual sex but from a rejection of such sex as a way to transmit male values. He argues that homosexuality in a group of men is a way to expunge men of their female portion and relations. It also solves the intergenerational tension.
21. The inability to function in practical life is still a modern concern of young athletes, who seem to prolong their "childhood," so to speak. See Houle 2011. Neyer (1994: 1) mentions that some scholars suggest

8.2   Marriage

Levi-Schmitt explains that youth is a transitional stage for human beings, independent of class or gender. It is a period of liminality between childhood and adulthood, between dependence and independence, between social, intellectual, physical, and sexual immaturity and maturity. It is a period in which things are always changing, full of potential and expectations, but at the same time a period of mistrust, both of the youth toward established society and vice versa.[22] Societies devised ways to introduce young persons fully into the established adulthood. The most clear indication of arrival into adulthood was marriage.

The age of the athlete was opposed by authors such as Solon, Plato, or Aristotle to the age of marriage. Their assertions helped us conclude that most athletes during archaic and classical times were single. This was another source of ambivalence in the perception of youth and young men. By placing the age of marriage after the age of competitive physical activity, the Greeks were emphasizing the liminal character of sport.

Aristotle even asserted that the practice of men marrying late had to do with maintaining social peace by avoiding a generational conflict.[23] Generational conflict was feared in many societies in antiquity, as seen for instance in God's commandment given to Moses to "honor your father and your mother." This is the first commandment that relates to human interactions with other humans.[24] Greek society was no exception to this fear. In Athenian society, the conflict became more prominent during the second half of the fifth century.[25] Yet, it is known since the beginning of Greek society itself, as presented through the succession myth in Hesiod's *Theogony*. The fear of generational conflict tied to the ambivalence toward youth was ultimately responsible for the

---

"that there is considerable developmental delay among student-athletes." Others conclude that "the career maturity of male intercollegiate scholarship athletes in revenue-producing sports was no higher than that of the average ninth-grade student."

22. Levi-Schmitt 1997: 1–5.
23. Bertman 1976.
24. Reinhold 1993: 23.
25. Strauss (1993: 130–78) explains how, especially during the Peloponesian War, young men disposed of more money and commodities than their fathers did when they were young, how they were educated by the Sophists, and how there were because of the epidemic in 430–427 many more young men in their twenties than in their thirties. All these factors contributed to the promotion of more aggressive, self-conscious young men.

need for social control.²⁶ Some of this control was reinforced by the existence of rather strict age divisions²⁷ and exerted through sport. On the other hand, sport was construed as a bridge into the established society and a vehicle to transmit societal values.

One of the most important initiations that individuals underwent in Greek society was, of course, marriage. Certainly, this was the case for women, but also for men. Athletics are associated with marriage and the choosing of a capable husband.²⁸ There are many myths about choosing the right husband through a race, such as Atalanta's and Hippodameia's stories. The latter is even associated with the foundation of the Olympic Games.²⁹ Other narratives describe Olympia as the place to choose the right husband for one's daughter.³⁰ For instance, Herodotus (6.126–30) tells the story of the marriage of the daughter of Cleisthenes of Sicyon. Although the marriage did not take place at Olympia, it was announced at the games that suitable young men could become suitors of Agariste. In Sicyon, Cleisthenes had a racing track and wrestling place built where the suitors competed against each other and were tested for a year in their temper, education, and manners. The final test was conducted at the banquet, however, where Hippocleides danced away his marriage.³¹

Other selections of suitors may not have been as elaborate, but Pindar's odes certainly confirm that Olympia was a good place to choose a husband. His first and ninth *Olympic Odes* mention winning the hand of Hippodameia as prize for Pelops's victory in the chariot race (1.88; 9.10).³² The proem to the seventh Olympic ode is perhaps more explicit about the connection between marriage and victory.³³

---

26. Jones (1977: 168) explains how in traditional societies, the term "social control" indicates a process of incorporation or accommodation to the community. He also attempts to place leisure between the dichotomy of class expression and social control.

27. Kennell (2013) denies that there were age-class societies in ancient Greece despite the existence of certain age restrictions for certain activities.

28. Nimas 2000: 221–40.

29. Hippodameia was the daughter of King Oenomaus. The king used to challenge his daughter's suitors to a chariot race. If they lost, he killed them. Finally, Pelops defeated him and married Hippodameia. To commemorate the victory, the Olympic Games were established.

30. Raschke (2013: 101–20) argues that marriage is a metaphor for peace and unity of the Greeks and puts forth artistic evidence at the temple of Zeus at Olympia to support her claim.

31. See Herodotus 6.129–30.

32. The tenth Olympic ode compares the victory celebration to a man who is no longer a young man, desiring a child by his wife (v. 86–87). This would emphasize the opposition between the age to marry and the age of doing sport. As in the celebration ode, marriage and child rearing comes after the victory.

33. Brown 1984.

Just as someone taking a cup from a wealthy hand, a cup that bubbles inside with the dew of the vine, gives it as a present to his young son-in-law, making a toast from one home to another, the cup is all golden, the best of his possessions, [5] honoring the grace of the symposium and the new marriage, in the presence of his friends, he makes him enviable for his harmonious marriage-bed; I, too, sending to victorious men poured nectar, the gift of the Muses, the sweet fruit of my mind, I propitiate (to the gods) [10] for those who won at Olympia and at Pytho. (*Ol.* 7.1–10)

Brown interprets the father of the bride (the person lifting the cup) as "analogue to the Muses," that is, as the source of the gift.[34] Brown argues that the bride, the victory, and Pindar's song all represent the athlete's hope of immortality. The athlete is described in this ode with the word for young man (*neanias*), which can be anything between twenty and thirty years of age, when he was in full physical strength.[35] If the father-in-law is equivalent to the Muses who grant the song after the victory, then marriage is equivalent to the victory song and also follows victory.

Pindar's ninth Pythian ode is very explicit about the connection of marriage as a prize for sport.[36] It is dedicated to Telesicrates of Cyrene, victor of the race in arms (*hoplitodromos*) in 474. Only men could participate in the race in arms. This makes any of the participants a potential husband. The ode narrates the marriage of Cyrene and Apollo. Cyrene was not a woman inclined to womanly things but preferred to spend time outdoors, much like Atalanta, but unlike her, she married Apollo. Telesicrates was a descendant of the offspring of such a union and as such not only an accomplished athlete, but also a very desirable husband and son, as explicitly mentioned in verses 97–100: "Each young woman who saw you, Telesicrates, in the annual festivals of Pallas prayed, though voicelessly, that you could be her dear husband or son."

The poem finishes with the description of two races for a bride. The first race is that organized by Danaus, who found husbands for his forty-eight daughters in this way. The second race is that organized by the Libyan ancestor of Telesicrates, who offered his daughter in marriage. A young man by the name of Alexidamus won the race, as he had won many victories prior

---

34. Ibid., 40.
35. Ibid., 47–48.
36. Woodbury (1982: 245) believes that perhaps the young Telesicrates might have been promised in marriage since the topic is so pervasive in this ode.

to this one, a fact that underlines marriage as the culmination of an athletic career. The bride is described as the "highest goal" (*telos akron*), perhaps a pun on Telesicrates's name, but the words certainly can refer to the finish line.[37] As well, in a more metaphorical meaning, *telos* is the purpose or goal of an action, its highest degree of accomplishment. This would explain the purpose of running and sport in general as finding a bride.

The long period of being an athlete can be seen as a period of training toward marriage, the ultimate initiation. During this period the athlete was separated from society since it was a time of proving himself. On Crete, the young man who was not allowed into public exercises was called the *apodromos*, "he who is banned from races." This probably represented a youth in his teens. On the other hand, the young man, perhaps in his early twenties, who had already some civic responsibilities and could get married, was called the *dromeus*, the runner. [38]

In this section we have discussed the athlete as a young man in need of education. Education is not just academic but includes the physical, military, and general patterns of integration into society, which culminate in the eligibility for political office and marriage. The traditional *paideia* was based on the equal value of body and mind, but that equality eventually shifted to reflect the prominence of an academic education. Although sport never disappeared from the curriculum, the gymnasium incorporated within its walls lessons of various kinds, which turned the athletes almost into outsiders in their own traditional space.

In the next section we will have a look at the last type of athlete, namely, the recreational athlete. The practice of sport in this case is neither linked to competition or education; it is just for the joy derived from the physical activity.

---

37. The finish line is usually called *terma*, but *telos* has the general meaning of fulfillment.
38. Willets 1955: 9–12, 19. Even if married, the young man did not live with the wife probably until the age thirty. Sexual intercourse was only furtive and sporadic.

Part III

The Recreational Athlete

9

The Rise of Recreational Sport

The motto "mens sana in corpore sano" (a healthy mind in a healthy body) has come down to us as an ancient expression for what we nowadays call "wellness."[1] After the fitness craze of the 1980s, now it is preferable to talk about "being well" instead of "being fit." Wellness includes physical, mental, and spiritual health. The inclusion of the mental and especially spiritual aspect has motivated the spread in the West of new disciplines, such as yoga, which promise something that Western sport supposedly no longer provides. At the same time that recreational sports are considered almost as a necessity for a "healthy lifestyle," we are witnesses to the unprecedented success of professional sport. In any area of sport, new records appear, whether in performance, length of careers, or wages. Consequently, the gap between professional athletes and persons that just want to be responsible toward their bodies is not getting any narrower.

The gap is maintained despite the efforts of organizations regulating sport. As mentioned earlier, in Canada, the recently introduced program of Long Term Athlete Development (LTAD) embodies a theoretical model in which "training to compete" begins with boys when they are sixteen years old and with girls when they are fifteen. As the model states, this is when "things get serious." Although a very well-considered and well-intentioned program, the LTAD aims to develop people to be "active for life" (i.e., to be well) perhaps more than to develop professional athletes.[2] Which gymnast will

---

[1]. For an explanation of what the sentence means and how it was popularized, see Korenjak 2012.
[2]. That is at least how Hockey Canada understands it, and consequently it has developed its own plan in response to the LTAD. They call it the Long Term Player Development (LTPD). It claims to adopt a "player-

make it onto the international scene if she has to wait until fifteen to receive "world class training"? When the best of soccer players in the world are already professional by the age of sixteen,[3] can someone really think that it can "get serious" only between the ages of sixteen and twenty-three for boys? If a boy is not professional by eighteen, he will probably never make it into the major leagues. Even in sports with no money involved, athletes specialize at a very young age, as the creation of the Youth Olympic Games (for athletes between fourteen and seventeen years old) for the first time in August 2010 testifies. The theoretical model and the reality do not always coincide. Whether we want it or not, in our modern society there is a big gap between professional (or at least seriously specialized, high performance) athletes and the rest.

9.1 Definitions

Despite this gap, the modern study of sport includes recreation among its values. There are three basic terms that scholars try to separate from each other: play, leisure, and recreation.[4] The classic definition of play was given by Huizinga in his study of play in culture. He defined play as follows:

> A free activity standing quite consciously outside "ordinary" life as being "not serious," but at the same time absorbing the player intensely and utterly. It is an activity connected with no material interest, and no profit can be gained by it. It proceeds within its own proper boundaries of time and space according to fixed rules and in an orderly manner. It promotes the formation of social groupings which tend to surround themselves with secrecy and to stress their difference from the common world by disguise or other means. (Huizinga 1970: 32)

Leisure is usually defined as the time that is used neither for work or work-related activities nor basic life-maintenance like sleeping, eating, or

---

centered approach and not treating the development of all players the same way." It also reinforces the idea of competition at the highest level. For this they offer a more competitive model starting at the age of eleven. By the time their peers in other sports are still learning to train, the young hockey players are expected to be learning the set of sport-specific skills in competition. See Hockey Canada 2019.

3. Cesc Fábregas started playing for the English team Arsenal at sixteen; Lionel Messi was seventeen when he started playing for Barcelona FC. Bastian Schweinsteiger played his first international game at eighteen.

4. McLean-Hurd 2012.

personal care. It is a time dedicated to voluntary activities that may imply self-improvement, pleasure, affiliation, and relaxation.[5] Recreation is then defined as the activities or experiences that take place during leisure time. Recreation also refers to the emotional state resulting from these activities.[6]

Play and recreation are certainly not only modern concepts. Plato, in the seventh book of his *Laws*, opposes the concept of seriousness (*to spoudaion*) to that of play (*paidia*) and asserts that one ought to spend one's life playing (i.e., sacrificing, singing, and dancing) (803c–d). He also makes a pun with play (*paidia*) and education (*paideia*), both of which he considers the most serious matters. The seriousness of children's play had been established already in book seven of *Laws*, when the Athenian explained that, whereas legislators tended to accept that children would change their games and manners of play, they did not realize the danger that this implied, namely, that children who innovated in their games would be prone to innovate in laws and institutions (798b–c). Thus, Plato establishes play as the foundation of education and of political life.

Plato offers, perhaps, a definition of recreation in the seventh book of *Laws* (814e–15e). There the Athenian stranger describes two functions that the wrestling schools have. On the one hand, they need to teach wrestling itself, and on the other, they teach the movement of the whole body, which the Athenian stranger classifies as "dancing" (*orchēsis*). The word "dancing" is not to be understood in the common modern sense, but rather as general physical activity.

This classification of wrestling and general physical activity is, in turn, divided into subsequent categories. There is a serious (*spoudaios*), beautiful dancing and a negative, shameful one. The shameful dancing that the Athenian stranger rejects is associated with the Bacchic rites, especially when performed drunk (*Laws* 815c). Within the noble "dancing," there is a subdivision between the movement that is appropriate in the context of war, vigorous and for brave souls and traditionally known as *pyrrhichē*, and the movement that is appropriate in "peaceful" conditions. The definition of this peaceful movement is then elaborated (815d–16c). This movement type was traditionally called *emmeleia*—harmony, grace. It is supposed to be performed by men who have left behind their toils and dangers and moved into a prosperous, favorable state. It is meant for a temperate soul living in prosperity and enjoying moderate pleasures.

5. Ibid., 22–24.
6. Ibid., 29.

Emmeleia is perhaps the type of physical activity that could be called recreational. It is supposed to be practiced by people who are no longer toiling but are enjoying the positive outcomes of their previous toil. The movements are moderate and lack the vigor of both wrestling and war-like movement, yet the greater the joy a person is experiencing, the greater his movement. Although Plato conceives of joy as the source of the movement and not as its result, I believe that the intention of qualifying a physical activity not linked directly with any practical effect other than joy speaks for this activity as recreation. The assumption that this type of activity is to be practiced by those who do not need to worry either about war or about the earning of a livelihood seems to tie in with the concept of leisure as understood in modern times.

It has become clear that for the study of ancient sport it is important to notice that the Greeks in the fourth century recognized specific kinds of physical movement as being part of leisure. On the other hand, some other physical activities were recognized as being good for building excellence in the person, without implying high-level competition. In fact, Plato mentions it in book seven of the *Laws*:

> The person aiming at a victory at the Pythian or Olympic Games leads a life of total lack of leisure (*ascholia*) toward the other matters in life, but the life that is called life most correctly is twice, even more than twice, full of occupation concerning completely the care of the body and soul toward excellence. (807c)

Plato intends to regulate every aspect in the life of every freeborn person, even when and how much to sleep (*Laws* 807e). Therefore, the distinction in this passage between the occupation of the high-performance athlete and the rest of the citizens in his ideal city is not to be based on the contrast between competitive involvement in sport versus recreation, but exclusively between competitive versus general fitness. It is only in a later passage that, as discussed above, the concept of recreation comes up. There is consequently a triple distinction in the writings of Plato:

1. Sport as high performance that is incompatible with any other activities. It is clear from Plato's writing that attempting to win the Olympics or any other such games is a full-time occupation without room for anything else in life. Plato is describing a "professional" athlete, whether paid or unpaid.

2. Sport as part of education or as part of instilling virtue in the citizen. Although sport served as part of education and was conducted as an occupation, it could hardly be considered recreational, especially in the very regimented lifestyle that Plato proposes.
3. Sport as the "recreation" of the virtuous citizen, who has already fulfilled his civic duties. The last type of sport is for people free of other duties, whether personal or public. This is practiced on certain occasions, not necessarily on a regular basis.

In order to align it to the modern world, I will call it "recreational sport." The first two types of sport are sport with a purpose, whether intrinsic (to win the Olympic Games) or extrinsic (to become a good citizen). The third type has a more diffuse purpose of expressing joy for one's well-being.

Furthermore, when one thinks of leisure in Greek times, usually the concept of *scholē* as expressed in Aristotle's writings comes to mind. The term *scholē* that we usually translate as "leisure" did not receive this meaning until the fourth century B.C.[7] *Scholē* meant until then "(free) time" but did not necessarily have the positive connotation that it acquired later and that we modern readers attribute to "free time."[8] The negative connotations of *scholē* can be seen still in Plato. In *Laws*, he opposes the state of a lazy lifestyle, where one can be fattened just like an idle beast, to the life that lacks leisure (*ascholia*) as it is directed to bringing about bodily and spiritual excellence (807a–d). According to Anastasiadis, it was Aristotle who invested the concept of *scholē* with positive connotations and idealized it as a supreme good.[9] Aristotelian *scholē* allows free time to be involved in political life or in learning. Yet, Aristotle also offers a view of leisure as a break and rest from the daily obligations.

> Even if both are necessary, leisure is preferable to business and a goal in itself. We must find out why leisure is necessary for those who work. For certainly it is not for those who play. For it would follow that the necessary goal of our lives is play. But if this is not possible, and games should be employed rather in business (for the one who exerts himself needs rest, and games serve rest: business comes with work and tension), then it follows that it is necessary to introduce the

---

7. Bertelli 1988: 98.
8. Anastasiadis (2004: 61) argues that *scholē*'s original meaning was "time with no purpose," which is often an impediment to fulfilling one's true purpose. So Prometheus ironically complains in Aeschylus's *Prometheus Bound* (818) that he has at his disposal more *scholē* than he wishes.
9. Anastasiadis 2004: 69.

use of games at the right moment considering that we are applying them as a medicine. For such a movement is relaxation of the soul and a break because of pleasure. (*Politics* 1337b)

In this passage Aristotle opposes leisure to business and introduces the reason for recreation, which needs business, since those who toil need rest, whereas those who do not toil obviously do not need rest. He is conscious that the activities associated with games are pleasurable and bring a rest and a break to our routines. The word that I have translated as games is *paidia*, which is the same word that Plato used to define activities that should be conducted when something is not serious. Like Plato, Aristotle (*Politics* 1336a33–34) considers that play should be in imitation of future serious endeavors. He considers that play is the main activity of children, but nevertheless, it is incompatible with the activities that bring happiness to the adult man. On the other hand, he recognizes that some type of play brings rest to the busy man.[10]

As we saw in the previous chapters, we cannot speak of the so-called rise of professional athletes in a simple manner. Athletes that competed for twenty years in the fifth century were as professional as those in the third who competed for only ten. As in any other field of human activity, there is a process of specialization and concentration during the Hellenistic period. This does not imply that athletes in previous times were not as committed and dedicated to sport as those in Hellenistic times, or that they did not make a living from the competitions. The difference between earlier and later athletes lies more in a social change, not at all exclusive to sport, which has as a consequence a change in perception of athletic activities. Therefore, the question that scholars need to ask is not about the rise of professional sport, but about the rise of recreational sport, or better yet, the consciousness of its existence and the expansion of its practice. Obviously, Plato and other previous writers knew about this type of sport. Its existence is also implied in the gymnasia for "older" people (i.e., people over thirty), who were definitely too old to start a competitive career or, if they ever had one, were winding down. During Hellenistic times this type of recreational sport acquired a new status.

Recreational sport is to be understood as separated from its traditional roles of education and competition and conceived exclusively as leisure, especially the leisure of the elites, who may or may not be politically engaged.[11]

---

10. For the role of play in the education of children, see Rodriguez 2017.
11. I insist on separating this modern concept of leisure from Aristotelian *scholē*, which is defined as "free time" in order to pursue primarily political or intellectual activities, but not physical ones.

Recreational sport developed in opposition to competitive sport, which in Hellenistic times was more and more restricted to professionals. Likewise, it was also separated from the school curriculum. This allowed for a double opposition. On the one hand, there was the opposition of sport practiced as an exclusive occupation to earn an income and sport practiced by the free, independently rich individual. On the other hand, there was an opposition between tending the body and tending the mind, which intensified as schooling became more academic. We have already discussed that in the previous pages, so we will discuss only the second opposition in connection with the perceived lack of political participation by athletes.

9.2 Recreational Sport and Sport as Occupation

Athletes in the archaic and classical periods were citizens of their *poleis* and involved in decision-making processes. In fact, many of them used their success at the games to influence politics in their cities.[12] On the other hand, athletes in later times may not have been generally involved to the same degree with politics. This is not something restricted to athletes; it is a sign of the times. Cosmopolitanism is concurrent with a lack of involvement in one's own city. Many athletes who won at the games of some cities were given honorary citizenship in them.[13] Thus one could not expect that they would be politically involved in any of them.[14] Citizenship was an honorary award not necessarily attached to political expectations. The famous Asclepiades (*IG* 14 1102) was a member of the council of several cities. Whether membership in the council signaled belonging to the elite or reward for athletic success,[15] active participation in more than one city's council seems improbable. Especially later on, when there is a well-set circuit of competitions and athletes become itinerant performers, many associated in guilds, there is no room for involvement in local politics, at least during one's active career. Involvement

---

12. The most famous cases are the Athenians Cylon and Alcibiades. Cylon attempted a coup in 632 B.C.; over two hundred years later, Alcibiades still intended to make his Olympic success justify his claim for power.

13. Inscriptions show this very clearly for Roman imperial times. For instance, one inscription mentions Marcus Ulpius Domesticus being a citizen from Ephesus and Athens (*IG* 5 1, 609); Gaius Licinius Inventus is a citizen of Tralles, Smyrna, Alexandria, Athens, and a Lacedaemonian (*Tralles* 95); and Marcus Aurelius Chresimus is a citizen from Ephesus and Tralles (*Ephesos* 1131).

14. To my knowledge there is no study yet that specifically concerns the political participation of athletes during Hellenistic times.

15. Golden 2008: 35.

in politics was probably centered around the sport guilds themselves and advocacy for athletes.[16]

The disenfranchising of the athletes from the political and social life of their cities and the resulting focus on their careers had consequences for the ways in which they were perceived by the intellectuals. The prejudiced dichotomy of strong body/weak mind started to be verbalized very strongly during Hellenistic and Roman imperial times. For instance, Diodorus Siculus, who flourished between the years 60 and 30 B.C., commented on the death of Milo and Polydamas (9.14.1–2). He questioned the usefulness of strength if it is not used in the proper way, although he does not explain what this would be. The death of Polydamas from a collapsed cave was an excuse for Diodorus to notice how precarious it is to have great strength but little sense. What in other times had been understood as a heroic action, or at least an attempt to imitate the heroes, later on was considered a simply foolish action.

As the political system changed and elite members had no political benefits from direct participation in sport, they withdrew by and large from competitive sports, except as sponsors and benefactors, where they could, in fact, obtain many political benefits.[17] In Hellenistic times, sport became a way for young professionals—some perhaps from lower classes, some slaves—to generate income either for themselves or their masters. The number of available games increased and, with it, the number of available prizes. These men were trained to be winners and then disappear from the public sphere. At most they became supervisors of the imperial baths, but it remains to be studied in a conclusive way whether they participated generally in political affairs of their cities after retirement from active competition.

We do not know for certain the social class of athletes during archaic and classical times. The consensus is that they were mostly aristocrats and wealthy individuals.[18] It would not be entirely surprising that during Hellenistic times lower-class individuals would be participating in competitions.[19] This might have started by the fourth century. Isocrates's speech *On the Team of Horses* is a defense speech for the younger Alcibiades, son of the famous one, who

---

16. Miller (2004b: 167) cites the London Papyrus 137, which contains a letter from Mark Antony to his friend the athlete Mark Antony Artemidorus confirming his benefits of being exempt from military service and public duties.

17. We have to assume that individuals from the elite classes always participated at the games, yet percentage-wise their participation might have declined.

18. Kyle (2014) shows that the debate is centered on whether sport was exclusive to aristocrats or not and the likelihood of accessibility of nonaristocrats to sport.

19. Pleket 2012: 103–5.

participated at the Olympic Games in 416 with seven teams of horses. Supposedly, not all the teams were his, and he was accused twenty years later of having stolen a team. His son was sued and needed to defend himself and his dead father. In the speech, Isocrates wrote, "He [Alcibiades] despised the gymnastic competitions, knowing that some of the athletes were of humble birth, inhabitants of small cities, and of low education" (33). The passage refers to the situation at the end of the fifth century but may reflect the circumstances of the beginning of the fourth. At any rate, we know that many athletes did in fact come from smaller cities, which were not as culturally sophisticated and wealthy as Athens. Even if their athletes belonged to the local aristocracy, this might not have looked like much to the wealthy Athenians. We may never be in a position to answer whether they were actually low class or not.

One papyrus from Egypt, dated probably to the mid-third century, contains a private letter from a person called Hierocles to another called Zenon (*P.Mich.Zen.* 59–60).[20] Zenon had entrusted the boy Pyrrhus to Hierocles's supervision. Hierocles was to train him only if he was certain that Pyrrhus could win, for money was not to be thrown away. In the letter, Hierocles reassures Zenon of Pyrrhus's potential. There is no indication that either of the men is related to the boy. It seems to be a case of private sponsorship and investment in someone's athletic career with the hope to regain what was put in and obtain further benefits. Most likely the young Pyrrhus did not belong to the elite, or he would not be in need of sponsorship. Indeed, Hierocles asks Zenon to provide swim trunks. On the other hand, the young Pyrrhus might have not been a slave, since the letter talks about the importance of him continuing his studies. Probably this is seen as a way to offer an alternative career if athletics does not pan out, which seems perhaps too much to offer to a slave. The social status of Pyrrhus is not clear, other than he was not elite.[21] Incidentally, the letter also indirectly testifies to the separation of athletic and academic careers.

There is a distinct possibility that athletes in the late classical period and Hellenistic times did not belong to the upper classes.[22] More important, however, than their actual social status was the perception of athletes, who were perceived increasingly as slavish. This is mostly understood in terms of athletes lacking virtues and usefulness to the state. The lazy, gluttonous

---

20. As quoted by Miller 2004b: 166.
21. Golden (2008: 43) argues that Pyrrhus was a slave.
22. Christesen (2012a) argues for nonelite athletes already during archaic and classical times.

athlete becomes a topic in literature. Philostratus criticizes what he calls the effeminate nature of athletes who are not active, eat too much, are accustomed to luxury, and given to sexual impulses (*On Gymnastics* 44–45). But the perception of the athlete as somewhat slavish starts much earlier and is not always in relation to the alleged lack of manly virtues as much as it is in relation to the voluntary subjection to strict rules and regulations about diet, training, sexual conduct, and every other aspect of their lives. Athletes who broke the rules could also be whipped by coaches and officials, and allowing this was the ultimate behavior of a slave.[23]

Dionysus of Halicarnassus, a Greek scholar contemporary to Augustus, commented in his *Ars Rhetorica* on how the athletes that accepted bribes were similar to prostitutes (7.6.45–60). The whipping and the punishments were proper for slaves, not free people, and yet slaves were judged unworthy of competition. Even so, athletes took upon themselves the mark of slavery. Dionysus did not understand this obvious contradiction that a free man would subject himself to such strict rules, even for the prize of glory.

As specialization came along, so did the demand for stricter training. The more the athletes subjected themselves to strict rules, the more they were perceived as slaves.[24] Free citizens would then make an effort of differentiating their sport from the professional one. They did not want to be seen as behaving like slaves, and with this came the elite's relegating of the practice of the traditional sports (perhaps with the exception of wrestling) in favor of less strenuous ones, such as ball playing.[25]

9.3 Ball Playing and a New Lifestyle

Ball playing was a traditional pastime in ancient Greece. Nausicaa and her maidens played ball in book 6 of *The Odyssey* as they were waiting for their laundry to dry in the sun. The Spartans called their youth just coming out of the ephebate "ball players" (Pausanias 3.14.6). They also had a rough team

---

23. Golden (2008: 55–57) discusses the whipping of the athlete as punishment for slaves, but also as an opportunity to show aristocratic behavior by being silent when beaten.

24. Golden 2008: 46. See Plato, *Lysis* 208e–9a. Socrates wonders why the young aristocrat Lysis is treated as a slave since he has to be subject to everybody else's rules. Diogenes Laertius (6.2.33) relates the anecdote about Diogenes of Sinope that when someone boasted that he had defeated men at the Pythian Games, Diogenes replied: "I defeat men, you defeat slaves." There is an additional anecdote about Dioxippus's victory at Olympia, and Diogenes replies in similar terms (6.2.43).

25. Crowther 2007: 154–59.

game of ball. We also know about another ball game called *episkyros*, which might be the same as the Spartan game.²⁶ There is also one stele, very famous after it was popularized by the Soccer European Championship in 2004, that depicts a young man bouncing a ball on his knees.²⁷ Apparently, there was some kind of contest consisting of how many times the young man could bounce the ball. Some depictions of a game called *ephedrismos* represent a man carrying on his back another who attempts to catch a ball thrown in the air (see figure 8). But the game represented in this image is not clear, since the *ephedrismos* usually involved throwing balls or pebbles at a stone in an attempt to overturn it. The player who failed to do so was blindfolded and had to run to touch the stone while carrying the winner on his back (Pollux 9.119), as seen in an Athenian red-figure *lēkythos*.²⁸ Obviously, there might have been variations in the games and many more games that we do not know about.

Ball playing was used during archaic and classical times as a game for women and children or as a part of training.²⁹ The existence of games, not just ball games, implies that even in earlier times, the Greeks practiced physical activities for recreation, even if recreation was not the focus of the practice of sport. During Hellenistic and Roman times, as the focus shifted to recreation as separate from specialized sport, ball games acquired an exceptional importance as a pastime of the elite. Why precisely ball games took over as an elite pastime is something that we may never be able to answer. Certainly, the devaluation of sport made it necessary for the elite to redefine its tastes, but this redefinition could have fallen on any other game or activity.

Most ball games involved a team and not just a direct opponent as in wrestling or boxing.³⁰ In the individual sports, the responsibility for winning or losing falls on only one athlete, who needs to be ready to accept the possibility of both. In team sports the responsibility is shared and the individual's level of performance can be somewhat compensated by that of the teammates on any given day. Common belief aligns introverted people with individual sports and extroverted people with team ones. But psychologists realize that

---

26. Ibid., 156.
27. Athens, National Museum 873.
28. Athenian red-figure *lēkythos* housed at the Louvre (CA 1988) in Paris.
29. O'Sullivan (2012) comments on the erotic character of ball games that involve girls. She also mentions that both in Sparta and Macedonia, ball games played a very important role as part of military training, since the ball games were played in teams. The team event contrasts with the individual pursuits of regular sport events and separates them ideologically.
30. See Galen, *On Exercise with a Small Ball*; Atheaneus 1.14f–15a; Pollux 9.103–7. All mention teams or players in the plural.

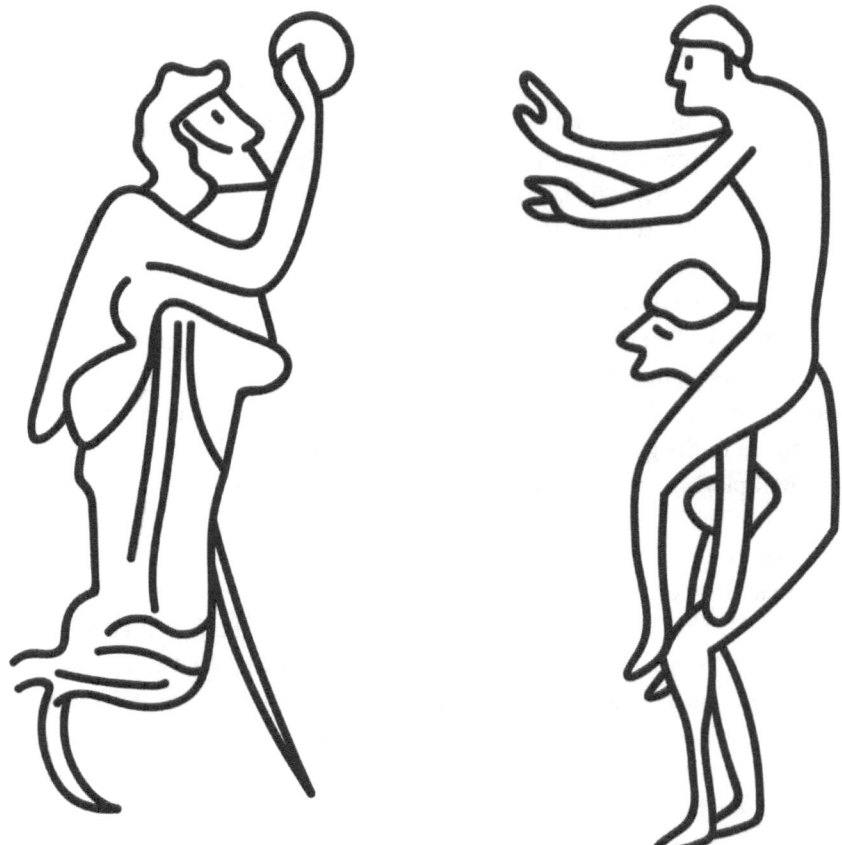

Figure 8. The game *ephedrismos*. Athenian black-figure lekythos, dated to between 525 and 475 B.C. Artifact held by the Ashmolean Museum, Oxford (1890.27). Drawn by the author after an image in the Beazley Archive, Classical Art Research Centre, Oxford (380847).

the equation is not a simple one. Team sports need reliable, thoughtful, and less bold athletes, all traits that are usually associated with an introverted personality. It is highly unlikely that the shift from individual to team sport happened because of a major shift in the personalities of the elite male. The change ought to have been more social than personal.

There is then a clear distinction between competitive sport and the social practice of sport. Remijsen points out that in Hellenized Egypt the construction of gymnasia extended to smaller cities and villages and that the gymnasium was a place for Greek military and royal functionaries to meet their peers and cultivate the Greek way of life.[31] Obviously the new social elite did not have the time nor the interest to practice athletics as an exclusive way of life. At the same time that these Greek expatriates were meeting in the gymnasium, international events were full of Egyptian athletes.[32] The smaller places could not afford to organize anything other than local competitions, whereas the great centers like Alexandria produced a plethora of high performance athletes and set international contests. Perhaps Egypt is the clearest example, but other places all over the Mediterranean had the gymnasium as a marker of Greek identity. Participating in the life of the gymnasium implied a self-selective cultural and political elite. Perhaps the best example is the gymnasium in Jerusalem, which was meant to symbolize attachment to the Hellenistic kings.

9.4 Medical Writers

The change in the choice of sport was introduced because the elite needed to differentiate its practices from those who practiced sport as a profession. Furthermore, the rise of recreational sport was fueled by the medical writers, who increasingly saw specialized sport as physically unbalanced and not conducive to health. Already Aristotle in his *Politics* had expressed the purpose of sport as being conducive toward health and strength (1338a). But some competitive sports, especially the combat ones, could hardly be regarded as healthy. This can be seen for instance in the Hellenistic and imperial epigrams poking fun at boxers. Here are three of them, especially poignant:

> Olympicus here, who now looks so terrible, Emperor, once had a nose, a chin, brows, ears, and eyes. Then he entered a boxing contest and lost them all. He did not even receive his part of his father's inheritance. His brother had a picture of him and showed it to the judge, who judged that it was another man, who did not resemble him at all. (*Greek Lyric Anthology* 11.75)

> In every boxing contest organized by the Greeks have I, Androleus, participated. In Pisa I had one ear left, in Plataiai one eyebrow. In Delphi I was carried off knocked-out. My father Damoteles and my

---
31. Remijsen 2014.

32. Moretti (1957) includes twenty-seven Olympic victors from Alexandria from 296 B.C. to 201 A.D. This averages out to one victor every eighteen years. This is a continuous production of victors for five hundred years. This in turn implies many more athletes, who may not have been as successful.

fellow-citizens were summoned by the herald to carry me out of the stadium, dead or mutilated. (*Greek Lyric Anthology* 11.81)

Aulus the boxer who fought at Olympia has collected his bones piece by piece and has dedicated his skull to the god. If he also survives the Nemean Games, Lord Zeus, he will soon dedicate to you the vertebrae that he still has. (*Greek Lyric Anthology* 11.258)

Boxing was no doubt a brutal sport. Since many heavy athletes doubled in boxing and the pancratium, boxing could be placed last in the order of events because it was considered more dangerous than the mixed martial arts. By the fourth century, the thongs used earlier primarily to protect one's hands had evolved into something to hurt the adversary.[33] Also, if we are to take the accusation of gluttony seriously, we can probably assume that athletes were becoming heavier. With these changes, it does not come as a surprise that elite members were by and large not keen in participating in this type of sport and risking injuries and permanent deformation. Even if elite members participated, which they probably did,[34] the perception of them by their contemporaries was not a positive one. Also, other sports that did not involve as much physical risk were perceived as unhealthy because of the specialization of certain muscle groups over others. This was seen as an imbalance in the body and therefore as unaristocratic.

Traditionally, for archaic and classical sport, the rise of high performance is associated with developments in medicine. Athletes from the city of Croton dominated the Olympics from 588 to 488 B.C., mostly in the stadium race and wrestling. The training school of Croton, linked possibly to Pythagorean teachings,[35] introduced stricter methods for training and nutrition. In this way, they were able to bring forth better performances.[36] According to Mann, the influence of Pythagoras on the cities of southern Italy brought them many intellectual enemies, such as Xenophanes of Colophon,[37] whom we have seen as introducing the dichotomy strong body/ weak mind at the time of Croton's athletic success.

---

33. Poliakoff 1987: 70.

34. Pleket (2005) and Golden (2010) argue that there were always elite members involved at all sports, including combat sport.

35. Roubineau (2016: 132–42) attempts to reconcile the fact that Pythagoreans were vegetarians with the fact that the success of the Crotoniates was linked to a diet based on meat.

36. Mann 2001: 164–81.

37. Ibid., 187.

Even in anecdotes, athletic success is sometimes linked to medicine. Pausanias (6.3.10) tells the story of the pentathlete Hysmon. Apparently, when he was a boy a fever settled on his sinews, and for this reason he practiced the pentathlon in order that by hard exercise he might grow to be a sound and healthy man. He became a victorious athlete. The consideration that exercise was good for health was nothing new in Greece. Neither was the connection of medicine and athletics.[38] What represented a great change is that the medical schools of the Hellenistic and Roman periods rejected the specialization of sport, seeing it as unhealthy.

By the second century A.D., the most durable criticism of sport started to come from the medical profession. We have already seen some of the writings of Philostratus, whose purpose in writing the treatise on gymnastics was to separate medical art from sport, as expressed in his introduction. But the person most influential in the intellectual perception of sport at the time was doubtlessly Galen, who turned the opinion of medical writers against athletics. Ironically, Galen started his career and won his reputation as a physician for gladiators, who considered themselves professional athletes.[39] Galen was not the first one to criticize sports, but certainly he was the most influential. His enormous impact extended directly until the Renaissance and the Baroque eras, and in many ways is still perceptible. The idea of keeping active for life, so prevalent in our times, was expressed clearly in Galen's writings. On the negative side, Galen was responsible for articulating about sport and athletes some prejudices that have survived to our days. The most important of these is that athletes are considered weak in their minds.

In *Exhortation to the Study of Medicine* (or *Exhortation to the Study of the Arts, especially Medicine*), Galen counsels his disciples to study the human arts, such as rhetoric, music, philosophy, astronomy, geometry, architecture, but especially medicine. He advises his disciples to avoid three other professions: the profession of "gentleman by birth," who does not work and lives from the money of his ancestors; the male prostitute; and the athlete. The choice of professions to avoid is more than symptomatic. The reasons for not becoming an athlete occupy about two-thirds of this short essay.

> In nature's goods there are those goods pertaining to the soul and those pertaining to the physical body. Besides this, there are no other

---

38. See Plato's mention of Herodicus, who supposedly mixed gymnastics with medical practice to prolong his life (*Republic* 406a–b).

39. Golden 2008: 68–104.

known types of goods. For it is clear to everyone that athletes, even in a dream, do not participate in any of the goods of the soul. To begin with, they do not even know if they have a soul, so much are they lacking in knowing logic. For they always bring together a great amount of flesh and blood and they have completely extinguished their mind as in great filth. Their mind is not able to know anything with accuracy but remains unthinking similar to the irrational animals.

Perhaps athletes may disagree, thinking that they participate in the goods of the body. Do they disagree thinking that they possess health, the most honored good? But you may not find anyone else in a more dangerous condition of the body if we trust Hippocrates when he says that fitness in exaggeration, which they pursue, becomes dangerous, and especially that exercise toward health is to eat without satiety and to work out without exhaustion. This wise saying of Hippocrates is praised by all.

Athletes practice exactly the opposite, overexerting and overfilling themselves, ignoring fully the word of the old man like senseless Corybants. For he suggested that the healthy diet is exercise, food, drink, sleep, sex, all in moderation. But each day they practice gymnastic beyond what is convenient. And also they carry out feeding by force and frequently they extend their eating until the middle of the night. (11.1–20)

Galen quoted Hippocrates for the injunction to practice sport in moderation. What Galen could not know at the time is that the treatise attributed to Hippocrates where he talks about practicing athletics in moderation (*Nutriment* 34) is actually not a fifth-century treatise but a Hellenistic one.[40] Galen had expressed similar ideas in his treatise on hygiene (*De sanitate tuenda* 6.41.1), where he advocated for moderate exercise of body and mind to maintain one's health. Too much exercise would make the desire, rationality, and spirit of a person more choleric; too little, more phlegmatic. The whole concept of moderation is integrated into Galen's philosophical views about the functioning of the body.[41] But this is a development of Hellenistic times, not necessarily of earlier times. When Milo was renowned for eating a bull by himself, it was seen as heroic prowess, not as immoderation, as Galen saw it. Getting up in the middle of the night to eat is still a common practice among weightlifters

---

40. König 2005: 277.
41. Ibid., 275.

and other athletes who need to gain weight. This is perhaps not a very healthy practice, but most significantly, as König states, "The athletic regime is the furthest imaginable opposite to [Galen's] own properly rounded medical care."[42]

Galen's criticism extends to other aspects of the athletic profession. As in the epigrams about deformed boxers, Galen also makes a point that excess in training contributes to damaging the body of the retired athlete. Perhaps he even makes an allusion to depression and a lack of desire to live after retirement.

> The body of athletes is disposed in such a way, but when they retire it is much worse. Some die shortly after, others live a little longer, but never reach old age, or if they do they end up exactly like the priests of Homer: "Lame, deformed, and squint-eyed."
>
> In the same way as walls shaken to their foundations by machines of war fall easily on the next attack, athletes, their bodies enfeebled by the jolts they have received, are predisposed to become sick on the least provocation. Their eyes ordinarily sunken, readily become the seat of fluxions; their teeth, so readily injured, fall out. With muscles and tendons frequently torn, their articulations become incapable of resisting strain and readily dislocate. (*Exhortation to the Study of Medicine* 11.45–58)
>
> After this discussion of one of the bodily goods, namely, health, let us pass to the other, how athletes fare on the side of beauty. Not only do they derive none from their profession, but many who have been perfectly proportioned fall into the hands of trainers who develop them beyond measure, overload them with flesh and blood, and make them just the opposite.
>
> Pancratiasts and pugilists develop a disfigured countenance hideous to look upon. Limbs broken or dislocated and eyes gouged out of sockets show the kind of beauty produced. These are the fruits they gather. When they no longer exercise their profession, they lose sensation, their limbs become dislocated, and, as I have said, they become completely deformed. (*Exhortation to the Study of Medicine* 12.1–13)

Fear of deformation and long-term negative consequences to someone's body would certainly keep many away from professional sport. On the other hand,

---

42. Ibid., 295.

it was understood that the healthy, well-educated man was in full control of his body and mind. For him, Galen proposed a moderate exercise aimed at well-being and weight control alongside walking, of which he was a great proponent. He did so in the treatise on *Exercises with a Small Ball*. We have already commented on the trend of elite men playing ball games for their recreation. Galen could not pass up the opportunity to comment on it.

Galen starts this short essay by referring to the use of exercise for health. As in the previous treatise, health is understood as involving both body and soul. The exercise with the small ball is, according to Galen, good to work out the body as well as to delight the soul. This is an idea repeated throughout the brief treatise. Furthermore, it is the type of sport that the busy, urban man can practice without much equipment or cost. Exercise with a small ball is also varied enough to strengthen all body parts: neck, head, hand and chest, but also legs and flanks. Playing ball is even useful with regard to military strategy. This was of course one of the expected traditional advantages derived from sport. Specialized sports were no longer conceived of as bringing this advantage. Galen once more relies on the tradition to justify the practice of a new sport. He does not miss a chance to add to his loathing for professional sports, stating that they do not provide the health benefits of playing ball, neither for developing the body harmoniously, nor for weight control, nor for building character. They lack moderation, alternating between periods of overwork and of laziness. Galen's prejudice is obvious when he calls laziness what is actually recovery.

Another famous physician was Celsus (25 B.C.–50 A.D.). Celsus had very similar ideas to Galen and also opposed the lifestyle of the athlete. In his writings, he had in mind the healthy, wealthy urban man, able to escape to the countryside.

> A healthy man who is strong and his own master should not oblige himself to any rules and should need no doctor nor a rubber and anointer. It is convenient for him to have a varied life style: sometimes in the country, sometimes in the city, but more often at the farm. He should sail, hunt, rest sometimes, but more frequently exercise. For inaction weakens the body, work strengthens it. The former provides an early old age, the last longer youth.
>
> It is good also to go to the bath, sometimes to use cold water; sometimes to be anointed, sometimes to neglect it. One should not avoid any kind of food which the common folk eats, sometimes attend

a banquet, sometimes stay away from it. It is good to eat sometimes more than sufficient, sometimes no more. To take food twice a day is better than once, and always as much as one wants as long as it is digested. But while exercise and food of this sort are necessary, those of the athletes are redundant. For any intermission in the order of exercise owing to civil matters affects the body negatively, and the bodies that are full of their own customs very quickly become old and sick. (*De medicina* 1.1)

The person who has been engaged during the day, either in domestic or civic affairs, should keep some time for restoring his body. The first care is exercise, which always has to precede food. If a person has worked less and has digested well, he has to exercise more. If a person is tired and has digested less, less.

Moderate exercises are: reading aloud, training with weapons, playing ball, running, walking; but this on the flat is not more useful, since it is better to walk up and down, since this moves the body with a certain variation, unless someone is weak for whatever reason. It is better to walk in the open than under a roof, better, if the head tolerates it, under the sun than in the shade, better in the shade that the walls and the trees provide than under a roof, better straight than winding. The end of exercise should be sweat and certainly tiredness, which should be on this side of fatigue. Sometimes less, sometimes more is to be done. But in this matter the example of the athletes should not be followed, with its fixed rules and immoderate labor. Sometimes a massage should follow exercise, whether in the sun or by the fire. Sometimes a bath is to be taken, but it should be in a room as high, well lighted, and spacious as possible. (*De medicina* 1. 2)

Celsus's ideas have a long tradition in Roman thought. Romans were not as keen as Greeks to participate in excessive training and saw this as a slavish submission to the body instead of being in control of their own bodies. Seneca (4 B.C.–65 A.D.) wrote in his fifteenth epistle already a century before Galen that it is foolish and least convenient for an educated man of letters to practice sport and increase the size of his arms, neck, and flanks. The bigger one grows his body by eating, the more the mind is squeezed out. Exercising in this way is not only bad in itself, it is made worse because athletes subject themselves to slaves who alternate the flask of oil with that of wine (*Epistulae* 15.2–3). Instead, Seneca recommends some moderate runs, weight lifting and jumps, walking while dictating, and practicing voice exercises (15.5–6). The background idea as in the later writers is to substitute sport with philosophy, which became the major subject to develop one's character.

Plutarch, in *De tuenda sanitate praecepta*, also comments on the need to perform moderate exercise and is against specialized training. The treatise is conceived as a dialog between Moschion, a physician, and Zeuxippus, a philosopher. It is also dated to the first century A.D. One of the first pieces of advice for keeping healthy is to eat and drink in moderation (123e). Plutarch also mentions Hippocrates's quotation,[43] which Galen used in his *Exhortation to the Study of Medicine* 11: "Eating not unto satiety, exercising not unto exhaustion, chastity in sex are the most healthy things" (129f–30a). Right after this, the topic moves on to the exercises apt for scholars. As in Galen, there is a comparison of the body of the wrestler to the walls of a city, which shows that these were probably traditional motifs (130a) and that writers who had something to say against sport kept quoting each other. Like Seneca, Plutarch also recommends voice and breathing exercises to strengthen the lungs and the throat (130b). One ought to exercise in such a way even when alone or on a trip without being embarrassed by what others may think, just as the man who plays ball or practices shadow boxing (130e–f). This equation of voice exercises with recreational and even specialized sport indicates that there was an important shift in the education of the gentleman, and sport was no longer part of it.

I have argued for a change in the system of training from the classical period to later periods. The change was based on the introduction of an early specialization method. There is no direct evidence for it, yet the comments of the philosophers and physicians of later times and the magnificent results of completing all four periodic games within two or three years may indicate that there was such a change. According to Galen and his contemporaries, athletes ended up with a destroyed body and little education. They also ended up in poverty because they overspent while active and did not have savings or a career they could turn to afterward. Instead of blaming the athletes, who were of course the easy target, it would have been more appropriate to criticize the system that allowed these young men to destroy their bodies in search of fame. Someone other than the athletes must have been making lots of money and gaining great reputation by becoming the benefactors of sport games.

---

43. Probably based on Hippocrates, *Epidemics* 4.20.

Today, as then, sport is a great spectacle, and athletes are not always the ones who profit the most from it. Whether their minds are weak, as the ancients argued, and they are easily influenced and fascinated by fame and glory, or they are very passionate about their activity, many young athletes fall prey to powerful television chains that want to show extreme or risky sports. Sometimes it is cyclists who dope themselves in order to race two hundred kilometers each day for twenty days, sometimes it is skiers like Sarah Burke who died at twenty-nine after an accident on the halfpipe. But the spectacle seems to continue without any concern for the life or the future of the young men and women who have dedicated themselves to the sport of their liking.

On the other hand, physicians and philosophers of Roman imperial times were concerned about developing a sense of wellness. They were extremely influential, but they could not anticipate the wellness craze and body cult that we experience in our times, when children are taken away from their parents for being overweight and are not allowed to eat hamburgers at schools. One is left to wonder in our days where the part of having a healthy mind disappeared.

Final Words

The most important component of sport, any sport, is the athletes. Without athletes there would not be sport. In ancient Greece they belonged to a special group, as equally admired as envied. They were public figures and local idols. By examining the sources, and through modern parallels, I have tried to come closer to the actual athletes beyond the prejudices and anecdotal clichés of the ancient authors. Athletes trained hard, sacrificed much, and risked their health to achieve a prize, just as St. Paul observed: "Therefore, I run in such a way, not without aim; I box in such a way, not beating the air; but I discipline my body and make it my slave, so that, after I have preached to others, I myself will not be disqualified" (1 Corinthians 9.26–27). Only the expected rewards made such a life of sacrifice worthwhile. For St. Paul these were the intangible rewards of the next life; for the athletes they were material rewards in this life. Their rewards were fame and glory and, why not, money, too. The prestige of participating at the games granted athletes social advantages and political careers. For these reasons, they were willing to undergo many hardships. There were as many motivations to do sport as there were athletes.

Athletes were young men, mostly in their late teens and twenties, perhaps even in their thirties. During archaic and classical times, most of them must also have been single, since Greeks tended to marry late. They were suspended in a prolonged adolescence that was not always well understood. They trained hard starting in childhood, first perhaps just practicing general sports in the schools, but then those who showed promise could move on to specialized trainers.

Specialized training may have started at a very young age after the fourth century. The citizen athlete (especially the athlete who was also a member of the elite) had to be integrated into society, and sport served this purpose. Furthermore, specialized athletics received the criticism of poets and intellectuals not only while athletes had an active career, but also after retirement. Galen complained that retired athletes were human wrecks: without the protection of the democratic city, they had become disposable items for the entertainment of the masses, without them perhaps being fully conscious of it.

It takes certain physical and mental qualities to become an athlete. Ancient sources mention some of them. Parallels from modern sport psychologists show that the mentality of the athletes may not have been very different from our own athletes. They were committed and goal oriented; they managed to control anxiety and rise above the moment.

Athletes were heavily criticized by certain sectors of the society who saw themselves as more important in producing healthy, useful, good citizens. Their prejudices have survived to our time, most importantly the one that equates a strong body with a weak mind. I hope that this book becomes an apology to those ancient Greek athletes who can no longer speak for themselves, and most importantly, to those whom very few cared to listen to even two thousand years ago.

Appendix

List of Authors and Their Works

Aeschines (389–314 B.C.): Attic orator and politician in Athens.
> *Against Timarchus*

Antiphon (480–411 B.C.): Attic orator and politician in Athens. Condemned to death after democracy was restored in 411 because of his leading role in the oligarchic coup of The Four Hundred.
> *Prosecution for an Accidental Homicide*

Athenaeus (end of second through beginning of third century A.D.): an antiquarian who gathered many of the fragments of lyric poetry preserved until now in his work called the *Deipnosophistae* or the *Banquet of the Learned.*

Aristophanes (446–386 B.C.): the most famous writer of comedies in classical Athens, he was active as a comedian from 427 on.
> *Clouds*
> *Knights*

Aristotle (384–322 B.C.): one of the most important Greek philosophers. His influence lasted well into modern times.
> *Athenian Constitution*
> *Physiognomics*
> *Politics*
> *Rhetoric*

212 APPENDIX

Celsus (25 B.C.–50 A.D.): a Roman medical writer.
> *De medicina*

Demosthenes (384–322 B.C.): a Greek politician and orator, he opposed the Macedonian conquest of Greece.
> *Against Midias*
> *Erotic Essay*
> *Third Olynthiac*

Diodorus Siculus (90–30 B.C.): Greek historian, known for his universal history known as the *Bibliotheca historica* or *Library*.

Dionysus of Halicarnassus (60 B.C.–7 A.D.): Greek scholar contemporary to Augustus, historian, literary critic, teacher of rhetoric.
> *Ars Rhetorica*

Galen (129–201 or 216[?] A.D.): physician, philosopher, medical writer of enormous influence until the Renaissance.
> *De sanitate tuenda*
> *Exercises with a Small Ball*
> *Exhortation to the Study of Medicine* (or *Exhortation to the Study of the Arts, especially Medicine*)

Greek Lyric Anthology or *Greek Anthology*: Collection of poems, mostly epigrams, dated from the classical times to the Byzantine period.

Herodotus (484–425 B.C.): Greek historian, geographer, and ethnographer known as the "father of history." He wrote a book known as *Histories*.

Hesiod: an epic poet from Boeotia dated generally to the end of the eighth century. He is known for his didactic poem *The Works and Days* and the genealogy of the gods, *The Theogony*.
> *Works and Days*

Homer: an epic poet supposedly of the end of the eighth century, traditional author of *The Iliad* and *The Odyssey*.
> *The Iliad*
> *The Odyssey*

Isocrates (436–338 B.C.): philosopher, orator, and speech writer, he developed a theory of education in opposition to Platonic philosophy.
> *Antidosis*
> *On the Team of Horses*

Lucian (125–180 A.D.): satirist and rhetorician.
> *Anacharsis*

Mimnermus: an Ionian poet who flourished between the years 630 and 600. He composed mostly elegiac poems.
> *Elegy 1*

Paul (saint): apostle of Jesus; died 64 A.D.; writer of many books of the New Testament.
> *1 Corinthians*

Pausanias (second century A.D.): a writer most famous for his *Description of Greece*, in which he describes geographical facts, ethnological and religious practices, and archeological and artistic findings in the different regions of Greece.
> *Description of Greece*

Pindar (518–438[?] B.C.): a lyric poet known for his victory odes (epinicia) in honor of the victors of the periodic games.
> *Isthmian Odes*
> *Nemean Odes*
> *Olympic Odes*
> *Pythian Odes*

Philostratus (170–250 A.D.): a philosopher and biographer. His treatise *On Gymnastics* is dated to after 220 A.D.
> *On Gymnastics*
> *Lives of the Sophists*

Plato (428–348 A.D.): one of the most influential philosophers from classical Athens, he was a disciple of Socrates and teacher of Aristotle.
> *Euthydemus*
> *Gorgias*
> *Laches*
> *Laws*

> *Lysis*
> *Politicus*
> *Protagoras*
> *Republic*

Plutarch (46–120 A.D.): a biographer, philosopher, and essayist whose influence lasted into the Renaissance.
> *Ancient Customs of the Spartans*
> *De tuenda sanitate praecepta*
> *On the Education of Children*
> *Sayings of Spartans*
> *Sayings of Spartan Women*

Vitruvius (first century A.D.): a Roman technical writer who in his book *On Architecture* described the ideal construction of the most common public buildings, such as theatres, markets, temples, baths, and roads.
> *On Architecture*

Solon (640–558 B.C.): a lawgiver and a poet who used his poetry to explain his policies. He reformed the constitution of the Athenians setting the basis for the democratic reforms of the fifth century.
> *Elegy* fragment 27

Strabo (63 B.C.–23 A.D.): Greek geographer and historian, known for his work *Geography*.

Theognis of Megara: lyric poet of the sixth century.
> *Elegies*

Tyrtaeus: poet who composed elegies around the time of the Second Messenian War (685–668) between the Spartans and the Messenians.
> *Elegy* 10

Xenophanes: a poet and philosopher who lived between the end of the sixth and beginning of the fifth century. He is known for his social and religious criticism.
> Fragment 19

Xenophon (430–350 B.C.): a Greek historian, disciple of Socrates.
> *Constitution of the Lacedaemonians*
> *Memorabilia*
> *On Hunting*

Bibliography

Anastasiadis, V. I. 2004. "Idealized ΣΧΟΛΗ and Disdain for Work: Aspects of Philosophy and Politics in Ancient Democracy." *Classical Quarterly* 54, no. 1: 58–79.
Anderson, J. K. 1970. *Military Theory and Practice in the Age of Xenophon*. Berkeley: University of California Press.
Anshel, M. H., and R. Lidor. 2012. "Talent Detection Programs in Sport: The Questionable Use of Psychological Measures." *Journal of Sport Behavior* 35, no. 3: 239–65.
Arrigoni, G. 1985. *Le Donne in Grecia*. Rome: Laterza.
Atkinson, M., and Young, K. 2008. *Deviance and Social Control in Sport*. Champaign, Ill.: Human Kinetics.
Balme, M. 1984. "Attitudes to Work and Leisure in Ancient Greece." *Greece & Rome* 31, no. 2: 140–52.
Bannister, R. 2004. The *First Four Minutes*. Gloucestershire: Sutton Publishing.
Beaumont, L. 2012. *Childhood in Ancient Athens: Iconography and Social History*. New York: Routledge.
Beazley Archive. 2019. "Pottery Database." https://www.beazley.ox.ac.uk/index.htm.
Beck, F. 1964. *Greek Education, 450–350 B.C.* London: Methuen.
Berard, C. 1986. "L'impossible femme athlete." *AION: Annali del Seminario di Studi del Mondo Classico. Sezione Linguistica* (Archeology) 8: 195–202.
Berger, T. J. 1994. "The Greeks and the Education of Humanity." *Journal of General Education* 43, no. 1: 32–43.
Bernardini, P. A. 2016. *Il Soldato e L'Atleta. Guerra e Sport nella Grecia Antica*. Bologna: Il Mulino.
Bertman, S., ed. 1976. The *Conflict of Generations in Ancient Greece and Rome*. Amsterdam: Grüner.

Bertelli, L. 1988. "La Scholé Aristotelica tra Norma e Prassi Empirica." *Atti dell Colloquio su Poetica e Politica fra Platone e Aristotele*, 97–129. Rome: Edizione dell' Ateneo.

Bertolín Cebrián, R. 2014. "Psychological Characteristics of Ancient Greek Athletes." *Nikephoros* 27: 9–35.

———. 2013. "Change of Athlete Development Methods in Hellenistic and Roman Imperial Sport?" *Nikephoros* 26: 139–59.

———. 2008. *Comic Epic and Parodies of Epic: Literature for Youth and Children in Ancient Greece*. Hildesheim: G. Olms.

———. 2002. "Parallel Ideological Use of Literature and Sport in Ancient Greece." *Nikephoros* 15: 39–50.

Booth, A. D. 1979. "Elementary and Secondary Education in the Roman Empire." *Florilegium* 1: 10–14.

———. 1975. "Roman Attitudes to Physical Education." *Echos du Monde Classique* 19: 27–34.

Bowie, E. L. 1970. "The Greeks and Their Past in the Second Sophistic." *Past and Present* 46: 3–41.

Brelich, A. 1981 [1969]. *Paides e Parthenoi*. Roma: Edizioni dell' Ateneo.

Brown, B. 2003. "Homer, Funeral Contests and the Origins of the Greek City." In *Sport and Festival in the Ancient Greek World*, edited by D. Phillips and D. Pritchard, 123–62. Swansea: The Classical Press of Wales.

Brown, C. 1984. "The Bridegroom and the Athlete. The Proem to Pindar's Seventh Olympian." In *Greek Poetry and Philosophy: Studies in Honor of Leonard Woodbury*, edited by D. E. Gerber, 37–50. Chico, Calif.: Scholars Press.

Buxton, R. 2004. "Similes and other Likenesses." In *The Cambridge Companion to Homer*, edited by R. Fowler, 139–55. Cambridge: Cambridge University Press.

Caillois, R. 1961. *Man, Play and Games*. New York: Free Press of Glencoe.

Cambiano, G. 1993. "Hacerse Hombre." In *El Hombre Griego*, edited by J. P. Vernant, 101–38. Madrid: Alianza.

Campbell, D. A. 1977. "Three Notes on Alcman 1 P (=3 Calame)." *Quaderni Urbinati di Cultura Classica* 26: 67–72.

Canadian Sport for Life. 2019. "Long-Term Development Stages." https://sportforlife.ca/quality-sport/long-term-development/.

Chankowski, A. S. 2010. *L'éphébie hellénistique: Étude d'une institution civique dans les cités grecques des Îles de la Mer Égée et de l'Asie Mineure. Culture et Cité, 4*. Paris: Diffusion de Boccard.

Christes, J. 1998. "Jugend im antiken Rom—'Absence of Adolescence' oder 'Restless Youth'?" In *Jugend in der Vormoderne: Annährung an ein bildungshistorisches Thema*, edited by K-P. Horn, J. Christes, and M. Parmentier, 141–66. Wien: Böhlau.

Christesen, P. 2013. "Sport and Democratization in Ancient Greece (with an Excursus on Athletic Nudity)." In *A Companion to Sport and Spectacle in Greek and Roman Antiquity*, edited by P. Christesen and D. G. Kyle, 211–35. Malden, Mass.: Wiley-Blackwell.

———. 2012a. *Sport and Democratization in the Ancient and Modern Worlds.* Cambridge: Cambridge University Press.

———. 2012b. "Athletics and Social Order in Sparta in the Classical Period." *Classical Antiquity* 31: 193–255.

———. 2007. *Olympic Victor List and Ancient Greek History.* Cambridge: Cambridge University Press.

———. 2003. "Athletic Nudity at Olympia." In *Ancient Greece and the Modern World*, 561–69. Patras: University of Patras.

Clarke, M. 2004. "Manhood and Heroism." In *The Cambridge Companion to Homer*, edited by R. Fowler, 74–90. Cambridge: Cambridge University Press.

CNN. 2011. "Shaun White: A Natural Board Talent." Accessed August 26, 2019. http://edition.cnn.com/2011/SPORT/01/19/shaun.white.revealed/index.html.

Cohen, A., and J. B. Rutter, eds. 2007. *Constructions of Childhood in Ancient Greece and Italy.* Hesperia Supplement 41. Athens: The American School of Classical Studies at Athens.

Collins, P. M. 1990. "Aristotle and the Philosophy of Intellectual Education." *The Irish Journal of Education* 24, no. 2: 62–88.

Covassin T., and S. Pero. 2004. "The Relationship between Self-Confidence, Mood State, and Anxiety among Collegiate Tennis Players." *Journal of Sport Behavior* 27, no. 3 (September 1): 230–41.

Crane, G., ed. 2019. *Perseus Digital Library.* http://www.perseus.tufts.edu/hopper/.

Cribiore, R. 2001. *Gymnastics of the Mind: Greek Education in Hellenistic and Roman Egypt.* Princeton, N.J.: Princeton University Press.

Crowther, N. B. 2007. *Sport in Ancient Times.* Westport: Praeger Publishers.

———. 2004. *Athletika: Studies on the Olympic Games and Greek Athletics.* Nikephoros Beiheft 11. Hildesheim: Weidmann.

———. 1991. "Euexia, Eutaxia, Philoponia: Three Contests of the Greek Gymnasium." *Zeitschrift für Papyrologie und Epigraphik* 85: 301–4.

Csapo, E. 2006/2007. "The Cultural Poetics of the Greek Cockfight." *Australian Archaeological Institute at Athens Bulletin* 4: 20–37.

Curty, O. 2015. *Gymnasiarchika: Recueil et analyse des inscriptions de l'époque hellénistique en l'honneur des gymnasiarques.* Paris: Éditions de Boccard.

Curty, O., S. Piccand, and S. Codourey, eds. 2009. *L'huile et l'argent: Gymnasiarchie et Évergétisme dans la Grece hellénistique.* Paris: Diffusion de Boccard.

Dean-Jones, L. 2013. "The Child Patient of the Hippocratics: Early Pediatrics?" In The *Oxford Handbook of Childhood and Education in the Classical World*, edited by J. Evan Grubbs, T. Parkin, and R. Bell, 108–24. New York: Oxford University Press.

Decker, C. H. 1995. *Sport in der Griechischen Antike: Vom Minoischen Wettkampf bis zu den Olympischen Spielen.* Munich: Beck.

DeFrancesco, C., and P. Johnson. 1997. "Athlete and Parent Perception in Junior Tennis." *Journal of Sport Behavior* 20, no.1 (March 1): 20–36.

Detienne, M. 1979. *Dionysos Slain.* Baltimore: Johns Hopkins University Press.

Dmitriev, S. 2005. *City Government in Hellenistic and Roman Asia Minor.* New York: Oxford University Press.
Dougherty, C. 1993. *The Poetics of Colonization: From City to Text in Archaic Greece.* New York: Oxford University Press.
Dover, K. J. 1974. *Greek Popular Morality in the Time of Plato and Aristotle.* Berkeley: University of California Press.
Durant, M. 1996. "La gymnastique dans le Lois de Platon: Une éducation physique a visée résolument politique." *Connaissance Hellenique* 69: 42–53.
Epstein, D. 2013. *The Sports Gene: Inside the Science of Extraordinary Athletic Performance.* New York: Current (Penguin).
European Commission. 2017. "Fitness Industry in Europe." https://www.statista.com/study/38818/fitness-industry-in-europe-statista-dossier/.
Evans, E. C. 1969. *Physiognomics in the Ancient World.* Philadelphia: American Philosophical Society.
———. 1950. "Physiognomics in the Roman Empire." *Classical Journal* 45, no. 6: 277–82.
———. 1941. "The Study of Physiognomy in the Second Century A.D." *Transactions and Proceedings of the American Philological Association* 72: 96–108.
Eyben, E. 1993. *Restless Youth in Ancient Rome.* London: Routledge.
Falkner, T. M. 1990. "The Politics and the Poetics of Time in Solon's 'Ten Ages.'" *The Classical Association of the Middle West and South* 86, no. 1: 1–15.
Ferrari, G. 2008. *Alcman and the Cosmos of Sparta.* Chicago: University of Chicago Press.
Ferraro, T. 1999a. "A Psychoanalytical Perspective on Anxiety in Athletes." *Athletic Insight: The Online Journal of Sport Psychology.* https://www.athleticinsight.com/Vol1Iss2/AnalyticPDF.pdf.
———. 1999b. "Aggression among Athletes: An Asian versus American Comparison." *Athletic Insight: The Online Journal of Sport Psychology.* https://www.athleticinsight.com/Vol1Iss1/AsianPDF.pdf.
Finley, M. I., and H. W. Pleket. 1976. *The Olympic Games: The First Thousand Years.* New York: Viking Press.
Fisher, N. 2010. "Gymnasia and the Democratic Values of Leisure." In *Greek Athletics,* edited by J. König, 66–86. Edinburgh: Edinburgh University Press.
Forbes Irving, P. M. C. 1990. *Metamorphosis in Greek Myth.* Oxford: Clarendon.
Friend, J. L. 2009. "The Athenian Ephebate in the Lycurgan Period, 334/3–322/1 B.C." PhD dissertation, University of Texas, Austin.
Gauthier, P. 2010. "Notes on the Role of the Gymnasium in the Hellenistic City." In *Greek Athletics,* edited by J. König, 87–101. Edinburgh: Edinburgh University Press.
Gauthier, L. P., and M. B. Hatzopoulos. 1993. *La loi gymnasiarchique de Beroea.* Meletemata 16. Paris: Diffusion de Boccard.
Gardiner, E. N. 1930. *Athletics of the Ancient World.* Oxford: Clarendon.
———. 1910. *Greek Athletic Sports and Festivals.* London: Macmillan.

Gladwell, M. 2013. "Man and Superman." The *New Yorker*. https://www.newyorker.com/magazine/2013/09/09/man-and-superman.

Golden, M. 2013. "Hierarchies of Heroism in Greek Athletics." In *Kultur(en)- Formen des Alltäglichen in der Antike. Festschrift für Ingomar Weiler zum 75. Geburtstag*, edited by P. Mauritsch and C. Ulf, 349–56. Graz: Grazer Universitätsverlag.

———. 2010. "The Position of the Athlete in the Social Structure of Ancient Greece." *Sport Journal*. https://thesportjournal.org/article/the-position-of-the-athlete-in-the-social-structure-of-ancient-greece/.

———. 2008. *Greek Sport and Social Status*. Austin: University of Texas Press.

———. 2004. *Sport in the Ancient World from A to Z*. London: Routledge.

———. 2003. "Childhood in Ancient Greece." In *Coming of Age in Ancient Greece: Images of Childhood from the Classical Past*, edited by J. Neils and J. H Oakley, 13–29. New Haven: Yale University Press.

———. 1998. *Sport and Society in Ancient Greece*. Cambridge: Cambridge University Press.

———. 1990. *Children and Childhood in Classical Athens*. Baltimore: Johns Hopkins University Press.

Gould, D., and K. Dieffenbach. 2002. "Psychological Characteristics and Their Development in Olympic Champions." *Journal of Applied Sport Psychology* 14: 172–204.

Gregorio, F. 1999. "Comment éduquer l'homme? Isocrate contre Platon." *Chronozones* 5: 40–47.

The Guardian. 2012. "Could You Be an Athlete? Olympics 2012 by Age, Weight and Height." *The Guardian*. https://www.theguardian.com/sport/datablog/2012/aug/07/olympics-2012-athletes-age-weight-height.

Hafez, A. G. 2015. "The Social Position of Hoplites in Classical Athens: A Historical Study." *Athens Journal of History* 1, no. 2: 135–46.

Hanton S., L. Evans, and R. Neil. 2003. "Hardiness and the Competitive Trait Anxiety Response." *Anxiety, Stress, and Coping* 16, no. 2: 167–84.

Hansen, M. H. 2006. The *Shotgun Method: The Demography of Ancient Greek City-State Culture*. Columbia: University of Missouri Press.

Harlow, M, and R. Laurence. 2010. "Betrothal, Mid-Late Childhood and the Life Course." In *Ancient Marriage in Myth and Reality*, edited by L. L. Lovén and A. Strömberg, 56–77. New Castle upon Tyne: Cambridge Scholars Publishing.

Harris, H. A. 1964. *Greek Athletes and Athletics*. London: Thames and Hudson.

Harris, J. 2009. "The Revenge of the Nerds: Xenophanes, Euripides, and Socrates vs. Olympic Victors." *American Journal of Philology* 130, no. 2: 157–94.

Hauvette-Besnault A., and E. Pottier. 1880. "Inscription de Téos." *Bulletin de Correspondance Hellenique* 4, no. 4: 110–21.

Hawhee, D. 2004. *Bodily Arts: Rhetoric and Athletics in Ancient Greece*. Austin: University of Texas Press.

Heinaman R. 1990. "Aristotle and the Mind-Body Problem." *Phronesis* 35, no. 1: 83–102.

Heinimann, F. 1965. *Nomos und Physis: Herkunft und Bedeutung einer Antithese im Griechischen Denken des 5. Jahrhunderts.* Basel: Friedrich Reinhardt.

Henderson Munn, M. 2000. *The School of History: Athens in the Age of Socrates.* Berkeley: University of California Press.

Hin, S. 2007. "Class and Society in the Cities of the Greek East: Education during the Ephebate." *Ancient Society* 37: 141–66.

Hockey Canada. 2019. "Long Term Player Development." https://www.hockeycanada.ca/en-ca/hockey-programs/coaching/ltpd.aspx.

Houle, J. 2011. "An Examination of the Relationship between Athletic Identity and Career Maturity in Student-Athletes." PhD dissertation, Auburn University.

Howie, G. 2012. "The Role of the Father and the Family in an Athlete's Participation and in the Celebration of Its Victory." *Nikephoros Special Issue: Youth-Sports-Olympic Games*, edited by W. Petermandl and C. Ulf, 107–19. Hildesheim: Weidmann.

Hubbard, T. 2008. "Contemporary Sport Sociology and Ancient Greek Athletics." *Leisure Studies* 27, no. 4: 378–93.

———. 2005. "Pindar's Tenth Olympian and Athlete Trainer Pederasty." In *Same-Sex Desire and Love in Greco-Roman Antiquity and in the Classical Tradition of the West*, edited by C. Verstraete and V. Provençal, 137–71. Binghamton, N.Y.: Harrington Park.

———. 1995. "On Implied Wishes for Olympic Victory in Pindar." *Illinois Classical Studies* 20: 35–56.

Huizinga, J. 1970 [1949]. *Homo Ludens: A Study of the Play Element in Culture.* London: Paladin.

Isler-Kerenyi, C. 1969. *Nike: Der Typus der laufenden Flügelfrau in archaischer Zeit.* Stuttgart: Eugen Reutsch Verlag.

Jaeger, W. 1945. *Paideia: The Ideals of Greek Culture.* 3 vols. New York: Oxford University Press.

Jones, G. S. 1977. "Class Expression versus Social Control? A Critique of Recent Trends in the Social History of 'Leisure.'" *History Workshop* 4: 162–70.

Johnstone, S. 1994. "Virtuous Toil, Vicious Work: Xenophon on Aristocratic Style." *Classical Philology* 89, no. 3: 219–40.

Kah, D., and P. Scholz, ed. 2004. *Das Hellenistische Gymnasion.* Berlin: Akademie Verlag.

Kalimtzis, K. 2013. "Aristotle on SCHOLĒ and NOUS as a Way of Life." *Organon* 45: 35–41.

Kamen, D. 2013. *Status in Classical Athens.* Princeton, N.J.: Princeton University Press.

Kennell, N. 2013. "Age-Class Societies in Ancient Greece?" *Ancient Society* 43: 1–73.

———. 2009. "The Greek Ephebate in the Roman Period." *International Journal of the History of Sport* 26, no. 2: 323–42.

———. 1995. *Gymnasium of Virtue: Education and Culture in Sparta.* Chapel Hill: University of North Carolina Press.

Kleijwegt, M. 1991. *Ancient Youth: The Ambiguity of Youth and the Absence of Adolescence in Greco-Roman Society*. Amsterdam: Grieben.
Knab R. 1980 [1934]. *Die Periodoniken*. Chicago: Ares Publishers.
Koliadis, M. 1988. *Die Jugend in Athen der klasischen Zeit: Ansätze zu einer historischen Jugendforschung*. Frankfurt: Peter Lang.
König, J. 2017. "Athletes and Trainers." The *Oxford Handbook of the Second Sophistic*, edited by D. S. Richter and W. A. Johnson, 155–67. New York: Oxford University Press.
———, ed. 2010. *Greek Athletics*. Edinburgh: Edinburgh University Press.
———. 2009. "Training Athletes and Interpreting the Past in Philostratus' *Gymnasticus*." *Greek Culture in the Roman World*, edited by E. Bowie and J. Elsner, 251–83. Cambridge: Cambridge University Press.
———. 2005. *Athletics and Literature in the Roman Empire*. Cambridge: Cambridge University Press.
Korenjak, M. 2012. "What Does It Mean: Mens Sana in Corpore Sano? A Latin Adage and Its Curious Career." In *Nikephoros Special Issue: Youth-Sports-Olympic Games*, edited by W. Petermandl and C. Ulf, 147–53. Hildesheim: Weidmann.
Kovel, J. 1981. "Mind and State in Ancient Greece." *Dialectical Anthropology* 5, no. 4: 305–16.
Kyle, D. G. 2013. "Sport, Society, and Politics in Athens." In *A Companion to Sport and Spectacle in Greek and Roman Antiquity*, edited by P. Christesen and D. G. Kyle, 159–75. Malden, Mass.: Wiley-Blackwell.
———. 1996. "Gifts and Glory: Panathenaic and Other Greek Athletic Prizes." In *Worshipping Athena: Panathenaia & Parthenon*, edited by J. Neils, 106–36. Madison: University of Wisconsin Press.
———. 1990. "E. Norman Gardiner and the Decline of Greek Sport." In *Essays on Sport History and Sport Mythology*, edited by A. Guttmann, D. G. Kyle, and G. D. Stark, 7–44. College Station: Texas A&M University Press.
———. 1987. *Athletics in Ancient Athens*. Leiden: Brill.
Laes C., and J. Strubble. 2014. *Youth in Roman Empire: The Young and the Restless Years?* Cambridge: Cambridge University Press.
Larmer, B. 2005. *Operation Yao Ming: The Chinese Sports Empire, American Big Business and the Making of an NBA Superstar*. New York: Gotham Books.
Legras, B. 1999. *Néotēs. Recherches sur les Jeunes Grecs dans L'Égypte Ptolémaïque et Romaine*. Geneve: Droz.
———. 1998. *Éducation et culture dans le monde grec. VII–I siècle av. J.-C.* Paris: Sedes.
Levi, G., and J. C. Schmitt. 1997. *A History of Young People in the West*. Cambridge, Mass.: Belknap Press.
Loeb, J., and J. Henderson. 1999. "Loeb Classical Library." https://www.loebclassics.com.
Long, A. A. 2015. *Greek Models of Mind and Self*. Cambridge, Mass.: Harvard University Press.

———. 1982. "Soul and Body in Stoicism." *Phronesis* 27, no.1: 34–57.
Lonsdale, S. H. 1990. *Creatures of Speech: Lion, Herding and Hunting Similes in the Iliad*. Stuttgart: Teubner.
Mann, C. 2001. *Athlet und Polis im archaischen und frühklassischen Griechenland*. Göttingen: Vandenhoeck & Ruprecht.
Mann, C., S. Remijsen, and S. Scharff, eds. 2016. *Athletics in the Hellenistic World*. Stuttgart: Frank Steiner.
Marrou, H. I. 1950. *Histoire de l'éducation dans l'antiquité*. Paris: Éditions du Seuil.
Marthinus, J. M. 2007. "Psychological Effects of Retirement of Elite Athletes." PhD dissertation, Stellenbosch University, South Africa.
McLean, B. H. 2002. *An Introduction to Greek Epigraphy to the Hellenistic and Roman Periods from Alexander the Great down to the Reign of Constantine (323 B.C–A.D. 337)*. Ann Arbor: University of Michigan Press.
McLean, D. D., and A. R. Hurd. 2012. *Kraus' Recreation and Leisure in Modern Society*. 9th ed. Las Vegas: Jones & Barlett Learning.
McDonnell, M. 1991. "The Introduction of Athletic Nudity: Thucydides, Plato, and the Vases." *Journal of Hellenic Studies* 111: 182–93.
Micalella, D. 2008. "Organizzazione degli Spazi Urbani e Politica: Il Posto della Scholé nella Citta Ideale di Aristotele." *Ancient Society* 38: 23–38.
Miller, S. 2004a. *Ancient Greek Athletics*. New Haven: Yale University Press.
———. 2004b. *Aretē: Greek Sport from Ancient Sources*. 3rd ed. Berkeley: University of California Press.
Moretti, L. 1957. *Olympionikai: I vincitori negli antici agoni olimpici*. Rome: Academia Nazionale dei Lincei.
Müller, S. 1996. "Herrlicher Ruhm im Sport oder im Krieg? Der Apobatēs und die Funktion des Sports in der griechischen Polis." *Nikephoros* 9: 41–69.
———. 1995. *Das Volk der Athleten: Untersuchungen zur Ideologie und Kritik in der Griechisch-Römischen Antike*. Trier: Wissenschaftlicher Verlag.
Nagy, G. 1994. *Pindar's Homer: The Lyric Possession of an Epic Past*. Baltimore, Md.: Johns Hopkins University Press.
Neer, R. 2001. "Framing the Gift: The Politics of the Siphnian Treasury at Delphi." *Classical Antiquity* 20: 273–336.
Neyer, M. 1994. "Identity Development and Career Maturity Patterns of Elite Resident Athletes at the United States Olympic Training Centre." PhD dissertation, University of Florida, Gainesville.
Newby, Z. 2005. *Greek Athletics in the Roman World: Victory and Virtue*. New York: Oxford University Press.
Nicholson, N. 2006. *Aristocracy and Athletics in Archaic and Classical Greece*. Cambridge: Cambridge University Press.
———. 2003. "Aristocratic Victory Memorials and the Absent Charioteer." In *The Cultures within Ancient Greek Culture: Contact, Conflict, Collaboration*, edited by C. Dougherty and L. Kurke, 101–28. Cambridge: Cambridge University Press.
———. 2000. "Polysemy and Ideology in Pindar 'Pythian' 4.229–30." *Phoenix* 54, no. 3–4: 191–202.

Nimas. T. 2000. "The Athletic Games as Criterion for the Choice of Husband in Greece: Myth and Reality." *Nikephoros* 13: 221–40.
Nilsson, M. P. 1955. *Die Hellenistische Schule*. Munich: Beck.
NPR. 2012. "Michael Phelps Exits the Olympics, and Enters Retirement at 27." https://www.npr.org/sections/thetorch/2012/08/08/158422864/michael-phelps-exits-the-olympics-and-enters-retirement-at-27.
Olivová. V. 1984. *Sports and Games in the Ancient World*. London: Orbis.
Osborne, R. 1997. "Men without Clothes: Heroic Nakedness and Greek Art." *Gender & History* 9, no. 3: 504–28.
O'Sullivan, L. 2012. "Playing Ball in Greek Antiquity." *Greece & Rome* 59, no. 1: 17–33.
Packard Humanities Institute. 2007. "Searchable Greek Inscriptions." https://inscriptions.packhum.org.
Papakonstantinou, Z. 2012. "Youth Sport Participation and Victory in Archaic Greece." In *Nikephoros Special Issue: Youth-Sports-Olympic Games*, edited by W. Petermandl and C. Ulf, 121–30. Hildesheim: Weidmann.
Patrucco, R. 1971. "La Psicologia dell'Atleta." *Maia* 23: 245–53.
Peponi, A. 2004. "Initiating the Viewer: Deixis and Visual Perception in Alcman's Lyric Drama." *Arethusa* 37, no 2: 295–316.
Pettersson M. 1992. *Cults of Apollo at Sparta:* The *Hyakinthia*, the *Gymnopaidiai* and the *Karneia*. Stockholm: Svenska Institutet I Athen.
Pleket, H. W. 2012. "The Social Status of Greek Athletes." In *Nikephoros Special Issue: Youth-Sports-Olympic Games*, edited by W. Petermandl and C. Ulf, 103–5. Hildesheim: Weidmann.
———. 2005. "Athleten im Altertum: Soziale Herkunft und Ideologie." *Nikephoros* 18: 151–63.
———. 2004. "Einige Betrachtungen zum Thema 'Geld und Sport.'" *Nikephoros* 17: 77–89.
———. 2001. "Zur Soziologie des antiken Sports." *Nikephoros* 14: 157–212.
———. 1979. "Licht vit Leuven over de Romeinse Jeugd?" *Lampas* 12: 173–92.
———. 1976: "Games, Prizes, Athletes and Ideology." *Arena* (= *Stadium*) 1: 49–89.
———. 1974. "Zur Soziologie des Antiken Sports." *Mededelingen van het Nederlands Instituut te Rome* 36: 57–87.
Poliakoff, M. 1987. *Combat Sports in the Ancient World: Competition, Violence and Culture*. New Haven: Yale University Press.
Pomeroy, S. 1997. *Families in the Classical and Hellenistic Greece: Representations and Realities*. Oxford: Clarendon.
Poulakis T., and D. Depew, eds. 2004. *Isocrates and Civic Education*. Austin: University of Texas Press.
Pratt, L. 2007. "The Parental Ethos of the *Iliad*." In *Constructions of Childhood in Ancient Greece and Italy*, edited by A. Cohen and J. B. Rutter, 25–40. Hesperia Supplement 41. Athens: The American School of Classical Studies at Athens.
Pritchard D. 2020. "Athletic Participation, Training, and Adolescent Education." In The *Oxford Handbook of Sport and Spectacle in the Ancient World*, edited by T. Scanlon and A. Futrell. Oxford: Oxford University Press.

———. 2012. *Sport, Democracy, and War in Classical Athens*, Cambridge: Cambridge University Press.

———. 2003. "Athletic, Education, and Participation in Classical Athens." In *Sport and Festival in the Ancient Greek World*, edited by D. Phillips and D. Pritchard, 293–349. Swansea: The Classical Press of Wales.

Rankinen T., M. S. Bray, J. M. Hagberg, et al. 2006. "The Human Gene Map for Performance and Health Fitness Phenotypes: The 2005 Update." *Medicine and Science in Sport and Exercise* 38, no 11: 1863–88.

Raschke, W. J. 2013. "Contest, Unity and Marriage in the Sanctuary of Zeus at Olympia." In *Kutur(en)-Formen des Alltäglichen in der Antike: Festschrift für Ingomar Weiler zum 75. Geburtstag*, edited by P. Mauritsch and C. Ulf, 101–20. Graz: Grazer Universität Verlag.

Red Bull. 2010. "Shaun White's Full Run—Red Bull Project X." https://www.youtube.com/watch?v=xk4p9uo2BS0.

———. 2009. "Shaun White's Private Pipe." https://www.youtube.com/watch?v=e1Zoh2JC_XA.

Reed, N. 1998. *More Than Just a Game: The Military Nature of Greek Athletic Contests*. Chicago: Ares Publishers.

Reid, H. L. 2011. *Athletics and Philosophy in the Ancient World: Contests of Virtue. Ethics and Sport*. New York: Routledge.

Reinhold, M. 1976. "The Generation Gap in Antiquity." In *The Conflict of Generations in Ancient Greece and Rome*, edited by S. Bertman, 15–54. Amsterdam: Grüner.

Reinmuth, O. W. 1971. *The Ephebic Inscriptions of the Fourth Century B.C.* Leiden: Brill.

Remijsen, S. 2013. "Greek Sport in Egypt: Status Symbol and Lifestyle." In *A Companion to Sport and Spectacle in Greek and Roman Antiquity*, edited by P. Christesen and D. G. Kyle, 349–63. Malden, Mass.: Wiley-Blackwell.

Richter, D. S., and W.A. Johnson, eds. 2017. *The Oxford Handbook to the Second Sophistic*. New York: Oxford University Press.

Riordan, J. 1993. "The Rise and Fall of Soviet Olympic Champions." *OLYMPIKA: The International Journal of Olympic Studies* 2: 25–44.

Rodrigue, L. 2017. "L'enfance selon Aristote." *Revue des Études Grecques* 130: 375–97.

Roy, J. 1998. "Thucydides 5.49.1.–50.4: The Quarrel between Elis and Sparta in 420 B.C. and Elis' Exploitation of Olympia." *Klio* 80, no. 2: 360–68.

Samaras, T. 2012. "Leisured Aristocrats or Warrior-Farmers? Leisure in Plato's *Laws*." *Classical Philology* 107, no. 1: 1–20.

Sansone, D. 1992. *Greek Athletics and the Genesis of Sport*. Berkeley: University of California Press.

Scanlon, T. F. 2005. "The Dispersion of Pederasty and the Athlete Revolution in Sixth-Century B.C. Greece." In *Same-Sex Desire and Love in Greco-Roman Antiquity and in the Classical Tradition of the West*, edited by C. Verstraete and V. Provençal, 63–85. Binghamton, N.Y.: Harrington Park.

———. 2002. *Eros and Greek Athletics*. Oxford: Oxford University Press.
Sergent, B. 1984. *Homosexuality in Greek Myth*. Boston: Beacon Press.
Serwint, N. 1993. "The Female Athletic Costume at the Heraia and Prenuptial Initiation Rites." *American Journal of Archeology* 93, no. 3: 403–22.
Sienkewicz, T. J. 2007. *Ancient Greece: Education and Training*. Hackensack, N.J.: Salem Press.
Skaltsa, S. 2009. "Hellenistic Gymnasia: The Built Space and the Social Dynamics of a Polis Institution." PhD dissertation, Oxford University, Oxford, UK.
Sorabji, R. 1974. "Body and Soul in Aristotle." *Philosophy* 49, no. 1: 63–89.
Steinrück, M. 2000. *Iambos: Studien zum Publikum einer Gattung in der frühgriechischen Literatur*. Hildesheim: Georg Olms.
Strang, J. R. 2007. "The City of Dionysos: A Social and Historical Study of the Ionian City of Teos." PhD dissertation, State University of New York, Buffalo.
Strauss, B. S. 1993. *Fathers and Sons in Athens: Ideology and Society in the Era of the Peloponnesian War*. Princeton, N.J.: Princeton University Press.
Tarrant, H. 2003. "Athletics, Competition and the Intellectual." In *Sport and Festival in the Ancient Greek World*, edited by D. Phillips and D. Pritchard, 351–63. Swansea: The Classical Press of Wales.
Too, Y. L., ed. 2001. *Education in Greek and Roman Antiquity*. Leiden: Brill.
Torre, P. S. 2009. "How (and Why) Athletes Go Broke." *Sports Illustrated*. https://www.si.com/vault/2009/03/23/105789480/how-and-why-athletes-go-broke.
Tremel, J. 2004. *Magica Agonistica: Fluchtafeln im antiken Sport*. Nikephoros Beihefte 10. Hildesheim: Weidmann.
Weinberg, R., and D. Gould. 2011. *Foundations of Sport and Exercise Psychology*. 5th ed. Champaign, Ill.: Human Kinetics.
Wheeler, E. L. 1982. "Hoplomachia and Greek Dances in Arms." *Greek Roman and Byzantine Studies* 23, no. 3: 223–33.
Whitehead, D. 1983. "Competitive Outlay and Community Profit: Philotimia in Democratic Athens." *Classica et Mediaevalia* 34: 55–74.
Willets, R. F. 1955. *Aristocratic Society in Ancient Crete*. New York: Routledge.
Wilson, P. 2003. "The Politics of Dance: Dithyrambic Contest and Social Order in Ancient Greece." In *Sport and Festival in the Ancient Greek World*, edited by D. Phillips and D. Pritchard, 163–96. Swansea: The Classical Press of Wales.
Wisse, J. 1989. *Ethos and Pathos from Aristotle to Cicero*. Amsterdam: Hakkert.
Wöhrle, G. 1990. *Studien zur Theorie der Antiken Gesundheitslehre*. Hermes Einzelschriften 56. Stuttgart: Franz Steiner.
Woodbury, L. 1982. "Cyrene and the TELEUTA of Marriage in Pindar's Ninth Pythian Ode." *Transactions of the American Philological Association* 112: 245–58.
Wylleman, P., D. Lavellee, and D. Alfermann. 1999. *Career Transitions in Competitive Sports*. Monograph 1. Biel, Switzerland: Fédération Européenne de Psychologie des Sports et des Activités Corporelles.
Xu, J. 2007. "China's Disposable Athletes." *Time Magazine*. http://content.time.com/time/world/article/0,8599,1644120,00.html.

Yegül, F. 1992. *Baths and Bathing in Classical Antiquity*. Boston: MIT Press.
Yi, J. 2004. "MCMAP and the Marine Warrior Ethos." *Military Review*, November–December: 17–24.
Young, D. C. 1996. "First with the Most: Greek Athletic Record and 'Specialisation.'" *Nikephoros* 9: 175–97.
———. 1985. The *Olympic Myth of Greek Amateur Athletics*. Chicago: Ares Publishers.

Index

References to illustrations appear in italic type.

Abascantus, 53, 152–53
Achilles, 85–86, 109, 124
Acusilaus, 14–15
Aelius Nepos, 53
Aeschines, 144, 211
Aeschylus, 79, 191n8
Against Midias (Demosthenes), 25
Against Timarchus (Aeschines), 144
Agamemnon, 86
age-class system, 16n13, 29–31. *See also* structural age of athletes
age divisions, 17–19. *See also* biological age of athletes
ageneioi, 13n4
Alcibiades, 193n12, 194–95
Alcimidas, 116
Alexidamus, 183–84
Amphictyony, 157n56
Anacharsis (Lucian), 50n27, 103, 108, 156, 161–63
Anastasiadis, 191
Ancient Customs of the Spartans (Plutarch), 165–66
Antidosis (Isocrates), 91, 127, 130
Antilochus, 84, 85

Antiphon, 141, 211
anxiety, 111–12
Aphous, 111–12
apobatēs, 5n8, 167
apodromos, 184
Apollo, 154, 183
Apollo Lycaeus, 72
Apollonius, 39
Archibius, Titus Flavius, 43
Archippus of Mytilene, 39
architecture, 134–39
Aristides, 158n58
Aristophanes, 7, 24–25, 29n54, 38n9, 128–29, 211
Aristotle: on age divisions, 18, 20n21, 181; on development of body and mind, 131; on leisure, 191–92; list of works by, 211; perception of youth by, 22–23, 25n38, 97, 108; on sport specialization, 51, 52, 56. *See also specific titles of works by*
arousal, 105n17
Ars Rhetorica (Dionysus of Halicarnassus), 196
Artemidorus, 93, 94, 115, 168n15

227

Artemidorus, Mark Anthony, 194n16
Artemis Orthia festival, 178, 179n12
Asclepiades, Marcus Aurelius, 35–38, 43, 55, 59, 99–100, 171, 193
Asclepiodotus, 172n22
aspis, 170–71
Astyanax, 44, 45
Atalanta, 182, 183
Athenaeus, 8, 101–2, 112–13, 163, 211
Athenian Constitution (Aristotle), 21n28, 25
athletes: biological age of, 11–16, 123, 170; burnout of, 51n29, 58n38; classes of, 2n2; coaching of, 112, 114–15, 130, 141n30, 143, 146–55; diet of, 5, 85–86, 99, 133, 182–84, 194; external influences of, 114–19; as freaks of nature, 68–80; genetics and success of, 61–64, 71n21; Greeks in Roman Empire, 92–95; as influential groups, 30–31; involvement from families of, 115–18; negative emotions of, 108–14; physiognomy of, 64–68; positive characteristics of, 102–8; professionalization of, 34–35, 57, 187–88; psychological characteristics of, 96–97; recreational, 188–96; retirement of, 60, 112–14, 194; specialization of, 35n2, 49–60, 188, 196; statistics on, 31–33; structural age of, 16–22. *See also* competitions; *names of specific athletes*; sport; sport and war
Aurelius, Marcus, 37
Autolycus (Euripides), 112–13, 163

ball playing, 196–99. *See also* sport
bankruptcy, 113n33
Bannister, Roger, 94n12, 94n14, 95n15, 98n6
baths and bathing, 36, 37, 39, 60, 135n14, 194

biological age of athletes, 11–16, 123, 170. *See also* athletes
body and mind, 124–35, 155–56
Bolt, Usain, 16n11
burnout, 51n29, 58n38

Callias, 44
Callicrates, 103–5
Callistratus Philothaleus, 48
Canada, 51n28, 187
Canadian Sport for Life model, 51n28
Celsus, 7, 204–5, 212
charioteers, 5, 82, 109n27
child-rearing age, 18, 182n32. *See also* marriage; structural age of athletes
China, 49
Chresimus, Marcus Aurelius, 193n13
class. *See* age-class system; social class and sport
Cleinus, 117
Cleomedes of Astypalaea, 113–14
Cleoxenus of Alexandria, 44, 56
Clouds (Aristophanes), 29n54, 128–29, 211
coaching and coaches, 112, 114–15, 130, 141n30, 143, 146–55. *See also gymnastēs*; *paidotribēs*
competitions: cooperation and, 97–102; defined, 97, 144; *hoplomachia*, 170, 171; Isolympic games, 148n47; Isthmian games, 5, 8, 157; Nemean games, 5, 8, 157; Olympic games, 5, 8, 11, 157, 160, 166; Panathenaea games, 5, 36, 100, 144, 167; Panhellenic games, 5, 36; prizes for, 5, 85–86, 99, 133, 182–84, 194; Pythian games, 5, 8, 157; torch races, 5n8, 100–101, 144, 171; types of, 5, 144n35. *See also* athletes; sport
competitiveness, 97–98, 109–10
Constitution of the Lacedaemonians (Xenophon), 169
1 *Corinthians* (Paul), 208, 213

Cratinus, 115
crown games, 5, 144. *See also* competitions
curse tablets, 109–11
Cylon, 193n12
Cyrene, 183

Damagetus, 14–15, 116
Damarchus of Parrhasia, 71
Damiscus of Messene, 13, 170n19
dancing, 189
Dandis, 15
Deinolochus, 118
De medicina (Celsus), 204–5
Demetrius, Marcus Aurelius, 36, 53n32, 55
Demosthenes, 25, 167, 212
De sanitate tuenda (Galen), 20n20, 202
Description of Greece (Pausanias), 213
De tuenda sanitate praecepta (Plutarch), 206
Diagoras, 14, 15, 116
diaulos, 5n8, 167
diet, 18–19, 58–59, 146, 164, 176, 178n5, 196
Diodorus Siculus, 194, 212
Dionysus of Halicarnassus, 196
Domesticus, Marcus Ulpius, 39, 43, 193n13
Domesticus, Ulpius Firmus, 39, 43
Dorieus, 14, 15, 43–46, 48
Dromeus (athlete), 15
dromeus (term), 184

early specialization sports, 4, 35, 49n19, 51, 53–59, 206. *See also* specialization of athletes
education: of girls, 173–75; in music, 131–32, 146, 172, 175, 201; physical education, 123–35; school sport, 123, 139–46; teachers' salaries, 175. *See also* gymnasia; military service and training; *paideia*
emmeleia, 189–90

endorphins, 107
envy, 109nn25–26
Epeius, 85, 168
ephebeia (ephebate), 3, 4, 16n13, 21n28, 119, 139–40
Epistratus, 100–101
Epstein, David, 61
equestrian sports, 5, 60n40
Ergoteles, 15
Eris, 78
Eros, 180
Erotic Essay (Demosthenes), 167
euandria, 171
Eubotas, 107
Eudemus Thallonius, 153–54
eugenics, 62–64, 116
Eumelus, 85
euoplia, 171
Euripides, 112–13, 163
Euthydemus (Plato), 169
Euthymus of Locroi Epizephyrioi, 71–72
Eutychianus, 109–10, 111, 153
Exercises with a Small Ball (Galen), 204
Exhortation to the Study of Medicine (Galen), 75, 203, 212

family involvement of athletes, 115–18
female athletes, 11
food. *See* diet
freak of nature, athlete as, 68–80

Galen, 212; on age divisions, 20n20; on benefits of sport, 107–8; on physiognomy, 66, 68; on sport, 102. *See also specific titles of works by*
generational conflict, 181–82
genetics, 61–64, 71n21, 116
girls' education, 173–75
Glaucus, 14, 55–56, 57, 71, 117
Gorgias (Plato), 143, 146
Greek historical periods, 4n7

230 INDEX

Greek Lyric Anthology, 8, 72, 87–88, 117, 199–200, 212
The Guardian (publication), 11
gymnasia, 134–39. *See also* education
gymnastēs, 50n27, 146–55. *See also* coaching and coaches

Hadrian, 37n6, 103–4
Halikarnassos, 137
Harding, Tonya, 109n26
Heracles, 69–70, 79, 93, 101, 102, 103, 105, 108
Hermaeus, 53
Hermes, 154
Hermocrates, 148–49
Herodotus, 142, 162–63, 164, 182, 212
Hesiod, 6, 7, 17, 181, 212
Hetoimocles, 51
Hierocles, 195
Hippocleides, 182
Hippocles, 116
Hippodameia, 182
Hipposthenes, 51
Histiodorus, 138
hockey, 187n2
Homer, 6, 7, 68–69, 74, 124–25, 168, 212. See also *specific titles of works by*
homosexuality, 179–80
hoplitodromoi, 5n8, 78–80, 167–68, 183
hoplomachia, 170, 171
horse events, 5, 60n40
Huizinga, 188
hunting. See *On Hunting* (Xenophon)
hydrotherapy. *See* baths and bathing
hypo-paidotribēs, 150–51. *See also* coaching and coaches

Iccus, 112
The Iliad (Homer), 27–28, 69, 81, 84–87, 97–98
infibulation, 179–80
initiation rituals, 177–80
Inventus, Gaius Licinius, 193n13

Isocrates, 7, 91, 127, 129–31, 141, 194–95, 213
Isolympic games, 148n47
Isthmian Games, 5, 8, 157. *See also* competitions

Johnson, Ben, 16n11
Jordan, Michael, 64n5

Kerrigan, Nancy, 109n26
Kleijwegt, M., 22n32, 27–29
Knights (Aristophanes), 25, 211
koinē, 53n32, 132

Laches (Plato), 145, 168–69
Laetus, Marcus Betilenus, 106
Laodamas, 124
late specialization sports, 4, 35, 49n19, 50–52, 56. *See also* specialization of athletes
Laws (Plato), 21n29, 127–28, 180n19, 189–91
leisure, defined, 188–89, 191–92
Leon, 46–47
Lewis, Carl, 15n11
life expectancy, 21
lions, 74–75, 79
Lives of the Sophists (Philostratus), 66
Long Term Athlete Development (LTAD), 51n28, 187
Long Term Player Development (LTPD), 187n2
Lucian, 7, 50n27, 103, 108, 156, 161–63
Lysis (Plato), 180, 196n24

Marcus Aurelius Demostratus, Damas, 93, 94
marriage, 17–18, 20nn21–22, 21n26, 21n29, 181–84. *See also* child-rearing age
martial arts, 163n7, 200
massage, 50n27, 59, 146, 205
medical writers, 199–206
meirakion, 141, 169

Memorabilia (Xenophon), 25
Metrobius, Titus Flavius, 39
Miletus, 137, 154
military service and training, 58, 140, 156, 164, 168–75, 194n16. *See also* sport and war; warfare
Milo of Croton, 13, 16n12, 58, 69–70, 75, 161, 194
Mimnermus, 7, 24, 213
mind and body, 124–35, 155–56
monsters, 68–80
Moschus, 44–45
music education, 131–32, 146, 172, 175, 201
mythical creatures, athletes as, 68–80

natural talent versus training, 81–84, 92–95
neanikōs, 24–25
neaniskos, 136n22, 169
negative emotions of athletes, 108–14. *See also* athletes
Nemean Games, 5, 8, 157. *See also* competitions
Nemean Odes (Pindar), 82–83, 116
Nicasylus of Rhodes, 13n6
Nicias, 168–69
Nicostratus Hilarius, 153
nudity, 179n11

Odysseus, 83, 86, 124
The Odyssey (Homer), 69, 85, 124, 196
Oenomaus (king), 182n29
Olympic Games, 5, 8, 11, 157, 160, 166. *See also* competitions
Olympic Odes (Pindar), 18n16, 82, 116, 182–83
On Architecture (Vitruvius), 134–35
O'Neal, Shaquille, 64n5
On Gymnastics (Philostratus): on athletes as mythical creatures, 72; on coaches, 97, 114; on food, 58–59; on genetics of athletes, 62–63; on *gymnastēs*, 146; on negative characteristics of athletes, 196; on origin of sport, 160, 167; on physiognomy, 65, 66–67, 68; on sport and war, 164, 168n16; on training system, 50n27, 56–58, 91–92
On Hunting (Xenophon), 28, 102–3, 108, 129
On the Education of Children (Plutarch), 133–34
On the Team of Horses (Isocrates), 194–95
Optatus, 114
Owens, Jessie, 15n11

paideia: of new aristocratic system, 139–43, 159, 178; of old aristocratic system, 28, 103, 124, 127–28, 158, 165, 184; *paidia* and, 189. *See also* education
Paides e Parthenoi (Brelich), 178
paidetikē. *See* palestra
paidia, 189
paidotribēs, 50n27, 135n16, 141–42, 144, 146–55. *See also* coaching and coaches
palama, 105
palestra, 135–37. *See also* gymnasia
Panathenaea games, 5, 36, 100, 144, 167
pancratium, 5, 27, 163n7
Panhellenic games, 5, 36
paradoxos, 93–94
paramilitary sports, 167–68. *See also* sport and war
Paul (saint), 7, 208, 213
Pausanias, 8, 213; on coaches, 147; on Eubotas, 107; on Polydamas, 70; on Stomius, 161; on training, 55; on victors of *periodos*, 14, 15, 39, 105
pederasty, 179nn10–11, 180n20
Peisidorus, 117
Peloponnesian War, 181n25
pentathlon, 5n9, 161

performance-enhancing drugs, 49n22, 50
periodic games. *See* competitions
periodonikēs, 13–14, 48, 93
periodos, 60; victors of, 14, 15, 38–39, 40–42, 52
phalanx, 166, 169, 171
Phayllus, 164
Phelps, Michael, 71n21, 94n13
Pherenike, 117
Pherias of Aegina, 13
Philippus, 72
Philo of Alexandria, 108
philoponia, 108
philosophy, 130–31
Philostratus, 7, 213. *See also specific titles of works by*
physical education, 123–35. *See also* sport
Physiognomics (Aristotle), 65
physiognomy, 64–68
Pindar, 18n16, 82–83, 98, 116, 182–83, 213
piracy, 175–76
Plato, 7, 213–14; on body and soul, 126–27; definition of sport by, 190–91; on joy, 190; on marriage and child-rearing age, 17, 21n29, 181; on *paideia*, 127–28, 142–43; on play, 189; on training systems, 89–91. *See also specific titles of works by*
play, defined, 188, 189
Plutarch, 8, 109, 133–34, 144n35, 214. *See also specific titles of works by*
Polemo of Ionia, 66
Politics (Aristotle): on age of athletes, 18, 20n21, 25, 140; on early spectators, 141; on education, 131–32, 165; on leisure, 191–92; on role of sport, 18–19, 49, 199
Politicus (Plato), 142–43, 145, 152
Polydamas, 57, 70, 75, 194

Polyneices, 92
Polypoites, 85
Polythrous, 175
ponos, term, 83
population statistics, 31–33
presbyteros, 150
prizes, 5, 85–86, 99, 133, 182–84, 194
professionalization of athletes, 34–35, 57, 187–88. *See also* athletes
Prometheus Bound (Aeschylus), 191n8
Prosecution for an Accidental Homicide (Antiphon), 141
Protagoras (Plato), 128, 145–46
psychological characteristics of athletes, 96–97. *See also* athletes
Publius Aelius Tertius, 155
pyrrhichē, 189
Pythian Games, 5, 8, 157. *See also* competitions
Pythian Ode (Pindar), 54–55, 83, 98, 183

race in armor, 5n8, 78–80, 167–68, 183
recreation, defined, 189. *See also* recreational sport
recreational sport, 188–96
Republic (Plato), 17–18, 71, 89–90, 201n38
research methodology, 6–8
retirement from sport, 60, 112–14, 194
Rhetoric (Aristotle), 22–23, 97
rooster, 72–73
running, 5n8, 162, 164

salaries, 49n20, 153, 154, 155, 174, 175
Sayings of Spartans (Plutarch), 87, 165–66
Sayings of Spartan Women (Plutarch), 89, 165
scholē, 191, 192n11
school sport, 123, 139–46. *See also* physical education

Second Messenian War, 88, 165, 214
Seven against Thebes (Aeschylus), 79
sexuality, 179–80, 184n38
Shield Games of Hera, 36
shields, 78–79, 167–68, 170–73
Siculus, Diodorus, 194
soccer, 188n3
social class and sport, 16n13, 29–31, 56n35. *See also* age-class system
Socrates, 25, 89, 128, 142–44, 169
Solon, 7, 214; on age divisions, 19–20, 23, 181; palestra law by, 144; on pleasure of sport, 108; on purpose of sport, 156, 161–63
soul and body, 126–27
Soviet Union, 49
specialization of athletes, 35n2, 49–60, 188, 196. *See also* athletes
sport: Aristotle on, 19; extrinsic purpose of, 155–58; historical overview of, 1–5; initiation aspects of, 177–80; negative emotions and, 108–14; as occupation, 193–96; origin of, 160; physical education, 123–35; positive benefits of, 102–8; professionalization of, 34–35, 57, 187–88; recreational, 188–96; as ritual sacrifice, 179n13; at schools, 123, 139–46; social class and, 16n13, 29–31, 56n35. *See also* athletes; competitions; sport and war
Sport, Democracy, and War in Classical Athens (Pritchard), 159
sport and war, 156, 159–61; military service and training, 58, 140, 156, 164, 168–75, 194n16; paramilitary sports, 167–68; usefulness of, 161–66. *See also* warfare
Sport Canada, 51n28, 187
steroids, 49n22, 50
Stomius, 161
Strabo, 136, 214

stress, 111–12
structural age of athletes, 16–22. *See also* athletes
Suetonius, 66
suicide, 112, 113, 113n34

talent selection versus identification, 63
Telesicrates, 183–84
telos, 184
Theagenes, 14, 37–38, 108–9, 144n35
Themistocles, 158
Theognetus of Aegina, 88
Theognis of Megara, 7, 81–82, 214
The Theogony (Hesiod), 181
Theseia festival, 171–73
Third Olynthiac (Demosthenes), 25
thyreos, 170–71
Timanthes of Cleonae, 113
torch races, 5n8, 100–101, 144, 171
training systems, 49–50; versus natural talent, 81–84, 92–95; Plato on, 89–91
Trajan, Marcus Ulpius, 43
Tsuburaya Kokichi, 113
Tyrtaeus, 7, 25–26, 164–65, 214

U.S. Marine Corps, 163n7
USSR, 49n21

vases, 72–80
Vitruvius, 7, 134–35, 214

warfare: Peloponnesian War, 181n25; Second Messenian War, 88, 165, 214. *See also* military service and training; sport and war
Wasps (Aristophanes), 24–25, 38n9
wellness, 187
werewolves, 71–72
White, Shaun, 94n11, 111n29
White Men Can't Jump (film), 62
wine, 59
wolves, 71

Works and Days (Hesiod), 17
wrestling, 5n9, 32n75, 162, 163n7, 189

Xenophanes, 7, 125–26, 200, 214
Xenophon, 7, 108, 129, 214. See also *specific titles of works*

Yao Ming, 64
Young, David, 31

youth: ancient perceptions of, 22–26; modern perceptions of ancient, 26–29; structural age of athletes, 16–22
Youth Olympic Games, 188

Zenon, 195
Zeus Lycaeus, 71, 72, 104–5, 125, 200